Qualitative Research Methods for Media Studies

Qualitative Research Methods for Media Studies provides students and researchers with the tools they need to perform critically engaged, theoretically informed research using methods that include interviewing, focus groups, historical research, oral histories, ethnography and participant observation, textual analysis and online research. Each chapter features step-by-step instructions that integrate theory with practice, as well as a case study drawn from published research demonstrating best practices for media scholars. Readers will also find in-depth discussions of the challenges and ethical issues that may confront researchers using a qualitative approach. Qualitative research does not offer easy answers, simple truths or precise measurements, but this book provides a comprehensive and accessible guide for those hoping to explore this rich vein of research methodology.

With new case studies throughout, this new edition includes updated material on digital technologies, including discussion of doing online research and using data to give students the tools they need to work in today's convergent media environment.

Bonnie S. Brennen is the Nieman Professor of Journalism in the Diederich College of Communication at Marquette University. Her research focuses on the intersection between labor and journalism history as well as on relationships between media, culture and society. She is the author of *For the Record: An Oral History of Rochester, New York Newsworkers*, and a novel, *Contradictions*. She is editor of *Assessing Evidence in a Postmodern World* and co-editor, with Hanno Hardt, of the *American Journalism History Reader*, *Picturing the Past: Media, History & Photography* and *Newsworkers: Toward a History of the Rank and File*. In October 2015 she was inducted into the Hall of Fame at the University of Iowa School of Journalism and Mass Communication.

Qualitative Research Methods for Media Studies

Second Edition

Bonnie S. Brennen

Routledge
Taylor & Francis Group

NEW YORK AND LONDON

Second edition published 2017
by Routledge
711 Third Avenue, New York, NY 10017

and by Routledge
2 Park Square, Milton Park, Abingdon, Oxon OX14 4RN

Routledge is an imprint of the Taylor & Francis Group, an informa business

First edition published by Routledge 2013

Library of Congress Cataloging-in-Publication Data
Names: Brennen, Bonnie author.
Title: Qualitative research methods for media studies / Bonnie S. Brennen.
Description: Second edition. | New York : Routledge, 2017. | Includes
    bibliographical references and index.
Identifiers: LCCN 2017002793 | ISBN 9781138219212 (hardback) |
    ISBN 9781138219229 (pbk.)
Subjects: LCSH: Mass media—Research—Methodology.
Classification: LCC P91.3 .B74 2017 | DDC 302.23/072—dc23
LC record available at https://lccn.loc.gov/2017002793

ISBN: 978-1-138-21921-2 (hbk)
ISBN: 978-1-138-21922-9 (pbk)
ISBN: 978-1-315-43597-8 (ebk)

Typeset in Minion
by Apex CoVantage, LLC

MIX
Paper from
responsible sources
FSC   FSC™ C013985

Printed in the United Kingdom
by Henry Ling Limited

Contents

CHAPTER **1**

Getting Started

Value things not because of their worth but because of their meaning.
—Gabriel Garcia Marquez

You may have heard it described as "research-lite," an approach for the math-phobic, "less rigorous" or even "easier" than quantitative research, but, truth be told, qualitative research is actually a messy endeavor that is challenging, time-consuming and difficult to get right. Qualitative research does not provide us with easy answers, simple truths or precise measurements. It can be controversial, contradictory and ambiguous. However, it can also be insightful, enlightening, emancipatory and fascinating.

The second edition of *Qualitative Research Methods for Media Studies* provides you with specific instruction on how to undertake research using a variety of different qualitative methods. The methods addressed in this book are common qualitative methods that are particularly relevant to answering media-related communication research questions. The methods chapters include updated examples of and discussion about published scholarly research using the methods being addressed. In addition, you will find activities and research exercises for each method to help you learn how to conduct research using qualitative methods. The second edition also addresses recent technological changes and advancements that offer new strategies for conducting and evaluating qualitative research.

Each method addressed in *Qualitative Research Methods for Media Studies, Second Edition* is grounded theoretically, culturally and historically. This text offers guidance on framing qualitative research questions, instruction on the interpretation of research findings and discussion on how to integrate theory with practice. It also discusses the implications of qualitative research in the field of media studies and considers ethical issues and challenges researchers confront related to specific qualitative methods.

As you will soon discover, full disclosure is always appropriate in the realm of qualitative research. This book is based on my personal experiences teaching qualitative research methods to graduate students at Marquette University, Temple University and the University of Missouri, Columbia. My approach to qualitative research is influenced by my own research activity using a variety of qualitative methods as well as by discussions and debates I have had over the years with graduate students and research colleagues. My own research is based on the theoretical framework of British Cultural Studies. In my work I specifically draw on Raymond Williams's definition of theory as the systematic explanations of real-world everyday practices, and it is this understanding of theory that guides this second edition of *Qualitative Research Methods for Media Studies*.

I agree with Williams's cultural materialist understanding of culture as a way of life, as well as his description of history as "a continuous and connected process" (Williams, 1983, p. 146). As a cultural materialist, I find that all documents of material culture, including newspapers, books, films, popular music, television programs, comic strips and current fashions, along with posts on newer media such as Facebook, Twitter, Instagram and LinkedIn, are produced under specific political and economic conditions, and that any or all of these cultural products can provide us with insights about our society at a particular historical place and time.

The cultural approach to communication that I take in *Qualitative Research Methods for Media Studies, Second Edition* understands the communication process as a means of production that is based on the discourse of individuals and groups and is produced within a specific cultural, historical and political context. It is through our use of language that we make meaning and construct our own social realities. Because language is a fundamental part of all qualitative analysis, I believe that it is important to use the correct words to describe aspects of the qualitative research process. Throughout this book I provide you with appropriate words and concepts that are particularly relevant to qualitative research.

I must be honest with you and tell you that I disagree with the belief that researchers can do qualitative research without using an explicit theoretical framework or that it is easy to mix qualitative and quantitative methods seamlessly. Instead, I agree with Cliff Christians and James Carey (1989) that there are important differences between qualitative and quantitative methods that are related to philosophical orientation, cultural traditions, research values and priorities as well as specific worldviews or ideological positions. For me, while it is possible to combine qualitative and quantitative methodologies, the use of mixed methods should be driven by the research questions you ask, and it must be theoretically and philosophically grounded.

In order for you to understand the theoretical orientation that guides *Qualitative Research Methods for Media Studies, Second Edition*, I feel it is important for you to get a sense of my views on key issues relevant to the field of qualitative research. Although the theoretical perspective that I incorporate into my work frames the content of this book, it is useful to understand that in a fundamental sense, all research is a collaborative effort. Throughout the process of writing this book I have bounced ideas off fellow researchers, graduate students, friends and family members. Through my discussions with others I have worked through a variety of conceptual issues, methodological puzzles and research concerns related to the process of qualitative research. I would like to thank my colleagues at Marquette University for their support of my research and give a special shout-out to John Pauly for writing the invaluable *Beginner's Guide to Doing Qualitative Research in Mass Communication* and serving as a wonderful sounding board for this project. I have been fortunate to have an excellent research assistant, Sandra Videmsky, and I thank her for her thoughtful assistance on this project. In addition, I appreciate the insightful questions and thought-provoking comments from my children Andrea and Scott, and, once again, the second edition of this book is dedicated to Hanno Hardt, who was a wonderful mentor and friend. I continue to miss his unfailing encouragement and guidance.

While I appreciate all of the help I have received throughout this project, clearly the buck stops here, and I take full responsibility for any errors or omissions that you may find in this text.

Quantitative vs. Qualitative Research

When we think about quantitative social science research, we see that it strives to be systematic, precise and accurate as it tries to determine validity, reliability, objectivity and truth. Quantitative research attempts to isolate specific elements, and it uses numbers and numerical correlations within value-free environments to measure and analyze the "causal relationships between variables" (Denzin and Lincoln, 1998a, p. 8). Because it uses numbers to quantify data, quantitative research is often considered more authentic, important and scientific. For some, numbers are seen as more reliable than thoughts. As one statistician suggested, some people "worship the statistician as someone who, with the aid of his magical computing machine, can make almost any study 'scientific'" (Blalock in McKee, 2003, p. 123).

In contrast, qualitative research is interdisciplinary, interpretive, political and theoretical in nature. Using language to understand concepts based on people's experiences, it attempts to create a sense of the larger realm of human relationships. As Steinar Kvale (1996) explained, the subject matter of qualitative research is not "objective data to be quantified, but meaningful relations to be interpreted" (p. 11). Qualitative researchers consider alternative notions of knowledge and they understand that reality is socially constructed. They showcase a variety of meanings and truths, and draw on a belief in and support of a researcher's active role in the research process.

At this point you may be wondering how socially constructed realities are actually created through language. About twenty years ago I came across an *Utne Reader* article, "Stop Lights and Phone Sex" (Proctor, 1995), that provides us with a useful example of the construction of a language-based symbolic reality. The essay contrasted the socially constructed reality of a man named Charlie with the lived reality of Fido the dog. In the article, Charlie used symbols to experience different cultures, learn about his environment and pass on the knowledge he attained to future generations. Fido lived in the present, experiencing only what he saw, tasted and smelled. While initially it might seem that Charlie's socially constructed reality was superior to Fido's, the essay maintained that in addition to the knowledge gained from symbolic reality, symbols can also alter our perceptions, and manipulate our feelings, our moods and our tastes. Offering examples from a misplaced zero in a banking transaction that made Charlie happy because he thought he had more money than he had, to a phone sex hotline where Charlie paid money to be told lies about his sexual prowess, to an unusual art museum exhibit made out of garbage that Charlie loved because critics called the artist a visionary, the article explains that while "[s]ymbols can lead Charlie to do things he wouldn't normally do, buy things he wouldn't normally buy, and think things he wouldn't normally think; Fido is blissfully unaffected" (Proctor, 1995, p. 50). As this example illustrates, researchers should be aware that as we use symbols to construct our own social realities, sometimes those symbols are also using us.

As we consider connections between a socially constructed reality and the qualitative research process, it is important to consider the notion of transparency. When researchers openly describe their theoretical foundations and research strategies, along with the basis for their decisions, intentions and motivations, readers become aware of the potential uses and implications of the research (Rakow, 2011).

Qualitative researchers tend to use a variety of different methodologies in their work. For example, in my own research I have used several types of textual analyses, including discourse analysis and ideological critique, as well as historical analysis, case studies and open-ended in-depth interviews. No matter what qualitative method researchers use, their choice of method is based on the questions they wish to ask, the specific historical context that relates to their research questions as well as the theoretical framework they plan to use for their research. In an effort to clarify the research process, each methods chapter in *Qualitative Research Methods for Media Studies, Second Edition* discusses research using a single qualitative method. However, as you begin your own research efforts you will sometimes come across qualitative research that combines two or more methods. This is because qualitative researchers often incorporate the notion of triangulation, which is the use of multiple methods to increase the rigor of their analyses and to develop in-depth understandings of social experience.

In the realm of media studies, by which I mean research that looks at aspects of news, information and/or entertainment in mass communication, journalism, broadcasting, advertising, public relations, visual communication and new media, quantitative researchers tend to see communication as a behavioral science. They draw on scientific models of communication and use a variety of methodological strategies to measure the effects of different types of communication on various groups in society. For example, quantitative researchers consider topics such as the effects of television violence on children, the effects of race and ethnic identity on the evaluation of public service announcements and the effects of political advertising on voters.

In contrast, qualitative researchers consider the diversity of meanings and values created in media. Rather than focusing on media effects or influences, they attempt to understand the many relationships that exist within media and society. For example, qualitative researchers who study media might look at how people understand advertising messages about cancer, how children are represented in online communities or how breaking news is framed in daily news photos. As John Pauly (1991) noted, the goal of qualitative research "is simply to render plausible the terms by which groups explain themselves to the world and to clarify the role that mass communication plays in such explanations" (p. 7).

The Development of Qualitative Research

The use of qualitative methods in media studies research emerged as a viable alternative to challenge the research status quo. When we look at the rise of qualitative research during the second half of the twentieth century, we see that it begins with a rejection of social science quantitative research ideas, procedures and protocols.

Although much of the early journalism and mass communication research was influenced by Pragmatism and framed from a cultural and historical understanding of communication, by the 1940s political scientists, sociologists and social psychologists were making important contributions to media research using quantitative social-scientific methodologies. As the field of mass communication research developed in post-World War II American society, communication researchers, who often saw science as a liberating force, embraced a scientific definition of mass communication and developed methodological techniques to measure the social effects of communication.

Preoccupied with the functional aspects of mass communication, researchers constructed scientific models that defined the field, illustrated its scientific nature and legitimated mass communication research as a social science endeavor. Critical cultural theorist Hanno Hardt (1992) found that the conceptualization of the field of communication as a behavioral science encouraged an emphasis on methodological concerns such as sampling, measurement, research design and instrumentation, which tended to overshadow considerations of theoretical issues regarding the role of media and communication within society.

While quantitative social science research remained the dominant approach to mass communication research throughout much of the twentieth century, some researchers did not see the need for social science to "imitate the natural sciences in form or method" (Christians and Carey, 1989, p. 354). Scholars like Neil Postman maintained that attempts to understand human feelings and behavior should not be considered science because it was difficult to show cause-and-effect relationships within human behavior. Although researchers were unable to prove or disprove interpretations of human experience, Postman (1988) suggested that the more insightful research in media studies drew its relevance and strength "from the power of its language, the depth of its explanations, the relevance of its examples and the credibility of its theme" (p. 13).

Researchers who questioned the dominant social science perspective of mass communication often envisioned communication as a cultural practice, through which issues of power, class and social identity could be negotiated. Like Postman, other researchers found that quantitative methods could not help them to answer central questions regarding the role of "communication as the social production of meaning" (Jensen, 1991, p. 18), and researchers began to turn to alternative theoretical perspectives and qualitative methods to understand communication as a social and cultural practice. Media studies scholars began drawing on the theoretical perspectives of British Cultural Studies, Critical Theory, Political Economy, Feminism and Postmodernism among other interdisciplinary perspectives to frame their qualitative research studies.

The Qualitative Studies Division of the Association for Education in Journalism and Mass Communication (AEJMC) and the Philosophy of Communication Division of the International Communication Association (ICA) were formed in the late 1970s to provide qualitative researchers with academic homes where they could present theoretically informed media-related research. While mainstream mass communication research journals tended to reject qualitative research that did not use an historical method, scholarly journals such as the *Journal of Communication Inquiry*, *Critical Studies in Mass Communication*, the *Journal of Communication* and *Media, Culture and Society* consistently published qualitative research. By the end of the twentieth century, qualitative methodologies had been fully integrated into the realm of communication and media studies; academic conferences regularly showcased theoretically informed qualitative research; and most of the scholarly journals in our field published qualitative research.

In the twenty-first century, qualitative research is an integral part of the field of media studies. However, you may be surprised to learn that there are still some social science researchers who remain hostile to the use of qualitative research methods in media and communication research. Some of these researchers see qualitative research "as an attack on reason and truth" (Denzin and Lincoln, 1998a, p. 7), while others maintain that their resistance not only reflects a desire to separate knowledge from opinion and to differentiate between "hard" science and "soft" research but also is framed by a belief that truth can be independent of politics (Carey, 1989, p. 99).

In our current digital age, students and media researchers often have a fascination with data, which they see as facts, statistics and/or information that can be collected together to calculate, analyze and plan things. They envision data as neutral, objective, authentic and/or truthful and maintain that it exists independent of observation and outside of human interpretation. Perhaps this is why I routinely hear students and researchers say: "the data shows . . ." or "the data tells me . . ." However, the use of data is just like the use of all other evidence and as such it requires human intervention to be understood. Researchers are integral to the research process. They offer insights, observations and evaluations, which is why at the most fundamental level, all research methods may be seen as qualitative. As Vidich and Lyman (1998) explained, "[W]e judge for ourselves on the standard of whether the work communicates or 'says' something to us—that is, does it connect with our reality? Does it provide us with insights that help to organize our own observations? Does it resonate with our images of the world?" (p. 44).

Conceptual Orientations

Although *Qualitative Research Methods for Media Studies, Second Edition* is not a book about theory, it is helpful for you to understand that researchers use theory to make sense of their findings and to orient their work within a larger conceptual orientation. Both qualitative and quantitative researchers like to draw on intellectual maps and models to help them represent their philosophical worldviews. These intellectual maps are often referred to as paradigms, and these paradigms provide a set of views and beliefs that researchers use to guide their work. An understanding of paradigms is of particular importance to qualitative researchers because they often find methodological questions of secondary importance to the larger philosophical issues and questions.

When we think about different research paradigms, there are three conceptual elements that quickly come to mind: epistemology, ontology and methodology. Denzin and Lincoln (1998b) clearly explained each of these concepts: "Epistemology asks: How do we know the world? What is the relationship between the inquirer and the known? Ontology raises basic questions about the nature of reality. Methodology focuses on how we gain knowledge about the world" (p. 185). For qualitative researchers, each of these elements influences the methods that they choose to use in distinct and significant ways.

And yet, since qualitative researchers pick and choose their theoretical positions from a variety of perspectives, some scholars find it difficult to create a single qualitative paradigm or intellectual map that represents a specific worldview and trajectory for qualitative research perspectives and traditions. These researchers prefer to see qualitative research not as a paradigm but instead as an interdisciplinary theoretical response to, and a reaction against, quantitative social science research. As David Hamilton (1998) suggested, the tradition of qualitative research is "a messy social movement, one that is structured as much by recombination of different activities as by their differentiation, divergence and continuity" (p. 113).

Guba and Lincoln (1998) maintained that qualitative research is not a unique paradigm but rather is influenced by several distinct paradigms, including Positivism, Post-Positivism, Critical Theories and Constructivism. Each of these paradigms is thought to provide specific values and principles that guide all of our research strategies and activities.

In contemporary society, Positivism remains the dominant paradigm of the physical and social sciences. Positivists consider reality to exist and scientific truth to be knowable and findable through rigorous testing that is free from human bias. The aim of inquiry of Positivism focuses on explanation, prediction and control while knowledge accumulates as factual building blocks in the form of "generalizations or cause-effect linkages" (Guba and Lincoln, 1998, p. 212). Within a Positivist paradigm, the value of research is determined through internal validity, which is how findings correspond to the issue being studied, and external validity, which is the extent to which the findings can be generalized and related to similar studies. In addition, the reliability, or the extent to which the findings can be reproduced or replicated by another researcher, as well as the objectivity, or lack of bias, are also central considerations in evaluating the value of research. Researchers use experimental methods to verify hypotheses, and, as you may have already figured out, these methods are primarily quantitative in nature.

The Post-Positivist paradigm is quite similar to Positivism. However, it responds to recent criticisms of Positivism in a few key areas. While reality is thought to exist, Post-Positivists consider that because people are flawed, they may not be able actually to understand it. Findings that can be replicated are thought to be probably true. While Positivists seek to verify their hypotheses, Post-Positivists use a variety of experimental methods, including some qualitative methods, in an effort to falsify their hypotheses. This is because Post-Positivists also draw upon the concepts of internal and external validity, reliability and objectivity to evaluate the quality of their research.

The other paradigms that influence qualitative research are Constructivism and Critical Theories. Both paradigms incorporate various non-Positivist alternative worldviews that blend research issues and theoretical positions, blur disciplinary boundaries and draw upon all types of qualitative methodologies. They include a variety of theoretical positions, including (but not limited to) Neo-Marxism, Feminism, Cultural Materialism, Critical Race Theory, Post-Structuralism and Postmodernism. Critical theorists consider reality and truth to be shaped by specific historical, cultural, racial, gender, political and economic conditions, values and structures. In their research they critique racism, sexism, oppression and inequality, and they press for fundamental and transformative social change.

Constructivism represents a theoretical shift regarding the concept of reality from realism to relativism. Constructivists lean towards an anti-foundational understanding of truth, rejecting any permanent "standards by which truth can be universally known" (Guba and Lincoln, 2003, p. 273). They work to build consensus and they favor negotiated agreements that are made by community members. Constructivists replace Positivist concepts of external and internal validity with notions of authenticity and trustworthiness.

Guba and Lincoln (2003) add an additional paradigm, Participatory/Cooperative Inquiry, to their list of paradigms influencing qualitative research. Participatory/Cooperative Inquiry is a transformative perspective that emphasizes the subjectivity of practical knowledge and the collaborative nature of research. While new paradigms are always interesting to consider, at this point it is not necessary for us to get bogged down debating the number of paradigms, if any, that influence qualitative research. What I would like you to remember from this discussion is that researchers who come from Positivist and Post-Positivist perspectives maintain a belief in a singular, big-"T" understanding of truth as well as a notion of a unified reality. Positivists and Post-Positivists try to exclude the influence of values from their work and they see ethics as being separate from their research concerns. Positivists and Post-Positivists see researchers as neutral observers who primarily rely on quantitative methods to test, verify, falsify or reject their research hypotheses.

In contrast, the alternative worldviews of Critical Theories, Constructivism and Participatory/Cooperative Inquiry, among others, all believe in multiple interpretations of a little-"t" understanding of truth and envision many constructed and competing notions of reality. All of these alternative paradigms consider values to shape their research and find ethical considerations essential to their work. They see researchers' subjectivity as integral to the research process and they draw primarily upon qualitative methods to answer their research questions.

There seems to be no clear consensus among researchers on whether qualitative methods actually constitute a paradigm in themselves or whether the field, instead, is influenced by a variety of other paradigms. Yet I think it is important to remember that it is the worldview, philosophy or theoretical framework that guides the questions qualitative researchers ask as well as the method or methods they choose to use in their research. Qualitative researchers do not pick a method they wish to use and then frame their research questions around their chosen method. For qualitative researchers, the choice of method comes from the questions they wish to ask.

You may wonder how you might go about selecting an appropriate theoretical framework, worldview or research paradigm to guide your work. I often tell my students that while researchers may try out a variety of perspectives, a theoretical framework usually picks you. What I mean by this is that each of you will develop a specific view of the world that makes sense to you. After some trial and error, each of you will discover a paradigm and/or conceptual perspective that fits with the specific way that you see the world.

What follow are some questions for you to consider to help you get started with your search for your own theoretical framework. Considering these questions will provide you with guidance in order to begin your media studies research.

- What does objectivity mean to you?
- What is neutrality?
- Do you believe it is possible for a researcher to be completely objective? Why, or why not?
- Do you see the field of media studies as a social science or as part of the tradition of humanities?
- What is your view of the role of science in contemporary society?
- Is human reality pre-set or is it shaped by specific historical, cultural and/or economic conditions?
- What is the goal of media studies research?
- Do you believe that truth is relative?
- What is a researcher's role in the research process?
- Do you think that researchers should try to bring about social change? Why, or why not?
- Do you think that we can measure people's opinions, feelings and/or concerns? Why, or why not?
- Are there cause-and-effect relationships that can be determined in people's behavior?
- Is there a single notion of truth that we can find out and/or know?
- Do you think that reality is socially constructed? Why, or why not?

While there are no right or wrong answers to these questions, your responses will help you to determine the type of research that is best suited to your own worldview and the particular qualitative methods that may best fit with your perspective. You may also wish to compare your answers with the earlier discussion of Positivism, Post-Positivism, Critical Theories, Constructivism and Participatory/Cooperative Inquiry. For those of you who embrace the relativity and fluidity of Critical Theories, Constructivism and/or Participatory/Cooperative Inquiry, you will find the multiple perspectives of qualitative research methods comforting and understandable. However, for those of you who reside comfortably within a Positivist paradigm, seeking precise answers, objectivity, neutrality and a knowable and findable Truth, the messiness of qualitative methods may test your worldview, common sense and patience.

References

Carey, James W. (1989). *Communication as culture: Essays on media and society.* Boston, MA: Unwin Hyman.

Christians, Clifford G., and Carey, James W. (1989). The logic and aims of qualitative research. In Guido H. Stempel and Bruce H. Westley (Eds.), *Research methods in mass communication* (pp. 342–362). Englewood Cliffs, NJ: Prentice Hall.

Denzin, Norman K., and Lincoln, Yvonna S. (1998a). Introduction: Entering the field of qualitative research. In Norman K. Denzin and Yvonna S. Lincoln (Eds.), *The landscape of qualitative research: Theories and issues* (pp. 1–34). Thousand Oaks, CA: Sage.

Denzin, Norman K., and Lincoln, Yvonna S. (1998b). Major paradigms and perspectives. In Norman K. Denzin and Yvonna S. Lincoln (Eds.), *The landscape of qualitative research: Theories and issues* (pp. 185–193). Thousand Oaks, CA: Sage.

Guba, Egon G., and Lincoln, Yvonna S. (1998) Competing paradigms in qualitative research. In Norman K. Denzin and Yvonna S. Lincoln (Eds.), *The landscape of qualitative research: Theories and issues* (pp. 195–220). Thousand Oaks, CA: Sage.

Guba, Egon G., and Lincoln, Yvonna S. (2003). Paradigmatic controversies, contradictions, and emerging confluences. In Norman K. Denzin and Yvonna S. Lincoln (Eds.), *The landscape of qualitative research: Theories and issues* (2nd ed., pp. 253–291). Thousand Oaks, CA: Sage.

Hamilton, David. (1998). Traditions, preferences, and postures in applied qualitative research. In Norman K. Denzin and Yvonna S. Lincoln (Eds.), *The landscape of qualitative research: Theories and issues* (pp. 111–129). Thousand Oaks, CA: Sage.

Hardt, Hanno. (1992). *Critical communication studies: Communication, history and theory in America.* London: Routledge.

Jensen, Klaus Bruhn. (1991). Introduction: The qualitative turn. In Klaus Bruhn Jensen and Nicholas W. Jankowski (Eds.), *A handbook of qualitative methodologies for mass communication research* (pp. 1–11). London: Routledge.

Kvale, Steinar. (1996). *InterViews: An introduction to qualitative research interviewing.* Thousand Oaks, CA: Sage.

McKee, Alan. (2003). *Textual analysis: A beginner's guide.* London: Sage.

Pauly, John J. (1991). *A beginner's guide to doing qualitative research in mass communication.* Columbia, SC: Association for Education in Journalism and Mass Communication.

Postman, Neil. (1988). Social science as moral theology. In *Conscientious objections: Stirring up trouble about language, technology, and education* (pp. 3–19). New York: Alfred A. Knopf.

Proctor, Russell F. (1995, May–June). Stop lights and phone sex. *Utne Reader,* pp. 48, 50.

Rakow, Lana F. (2011). Commentary: Interviews and focus groups as critical and cultural methods. *Journalism and Mass Communication Quarterly, 88* (2): 416–428.

Vidich, Arthur J., and Lyman, Stanford M. (1998). Qualitative methods: Their history in sociology and anthropology. In Norman K. Denzin and Yvonna S. Lincoln (Eds.), *The landscape of qualitative research: Theories and issues* (pp. 41–110). Thousand Oaks, CA: Sage.

Williams, Raymond. (1983). *Keywords: A vocabulary of culture and society.* London: Fontana Press.

CHAPTER **2**

Doing Qualitative Research

Believing, with Max Weber, that man is an animal suspended in webs of significance he himself has spun, I take culture to be those webs, and the analysis of it to be therefore not an experimental science in search of law but an interpretive one in search of meaning.

—Clifford Geertz (1973, p. 5)

Two very different understandings of the communication process emerged in Western cultures during the nineteenth century. Cultural theorist James Carey referred to these two perspectives as the transmission view and the ritual view of communication. The transmission view envisions communication as a process of sending, transmitting or delivering information in order to control others. Drawing on a transportation metaphor, and favoring technological advances within the communication process, the transmission view focuses on sending messages over distances in order to distribute common knowledge and ideas. In contrast, the ritual view associates the communication process with the ancient notion of communion. From the perspective of a ritual view of communication, people share customs, beliefs, ideas and experiences, a process that reinforces and maintains a common culture. As we compare the transmission view and the ritual view of communication, we can see that these perspectives also serve as metaphors that illustrate fundamental differences between qualitative and quantitative research.

Carey (1989a) illustrated differences between the transmission and the ritual views of communication through his analysis of a newspaper. From a transmission perspective a newspaper disseminates news and information, and "questions arise as to the effects of this on audiences: news as enlightening or obscuring reality, as changing or hardening attitudes, as breeding credibility or doubt" (p. 20). The transmission view questions that Carey raised are the same types of questions quantitative social scientists ask in their media-related research. Assessing a newspaper from a ritual view focuses less on news as information than on news as a dramatic ritual act that invites audience participation. Newspaper readers are thought to join in with the dramatic action to help make sense of their historically based cultural experiences and to socially construct their realities. As with qualitative scholars, from a ritual view readers do not focus on media effects, structures or functions; instead, the use of language in a newspaper provides readers with dramatic and engaging presentations of the world.

Language is a fundamental aspect of all qualitative research. It is through our discourse—or, in other words, our writing and speaking—that we communicate ideas and information, create communities and construct our social realities. At a basic level, qualitative research strives to understand the traditions, contexts, usages and meanings of words, concepts and ideas. As Neil Postman (1988) suggested, the purpose of research is "to rediscover the truths of social life; to comment on and criticize the moral behavior of people; and finally to put forward metaphors, images, and ideas that can help people live with some measure of understanding and dignity" (p. 18).

However, you may find that some of the qualitative research you come across is extremely complex, difficult to decipher and full of theoretical terms and discipline-specific jargon. Over the years, many of my students have expressed their frustration at trying to comprehend some of the qualitative research they encountered, and they have wondered why it was presented in such a manner. Just as Andy Dufresne in *The Shawshank Redemption* asked Warden Samuel Norton, "How can you be so obtuse?" I too wonder why all qualitative scholars do not insist on crafting clearly presented, understandable research. Since the goal of qualitative research is understanding, I would encourage all researchers to write so that their work is accessible, allowing everyone who is interested to join in the conversation.

Given the crucial role of language in qualitative research, I believe it is important to use the most appropriate words to help us to explain our work clearly, precisely, carefully and correctly. When we look at social science research, we see that quantitative researchers draw on the denotative or explicit meanings of words in order to operationalize their research terms and create a precise coding system. In contrast, qualitative researchers understand that our everyday language "is lushly metaphorical, wildly contradictory, willfully connotative, and cynically strategic" (Pauly, 1991, p. 6), and in their work they focus on the denotative as well as the connotative meanings and implications of the words that they use. If we think, for example, of the denotative definition of the word *mother*, we know that "mother" is defined as a female parent. This is the definition that quantitative researchers would use in studies involving mothers. However, the connotative meaning of a mother often signifies care, tenderness, compassion and love. Qualitative researchers understand that while words and concepts have important denotative meanings, they also have connotative interpretations that are important to consider. In their research they not only incorporate the denotative meanings of words but also embrace the variety of connotative meanings found within language.

Qualitative researchers do not identify variables, operationalize research terms, construct hypotheses, conduct experiments, measure data or replicate findings. Instead, they ask research questions, search for meaning, look for useful ways to talk about experiences within a specific historical, cultural, economic and/or political context, and consider the research process within relevant social practices. What follows is a list of commonly used terms in both qualitative and quantitative research. When possible, try to use the terms that best describe the type of work that you are doing.

Common Qualitative and Quantitative Terms

Qualitative research	*Quantitative research*
Research question	Hypothesis
Subjective	Objective
Engaged researcher	Neutral observer
Transformative intellectual	Disinterested scientist
Research process	Operationalization
Critique	Predict
Experience	Experiment
Information	Data
Analysis	Measurement
Interpretation	Bias
Understanding	Explanation, prediction and control
Imbued with values	Value-free
Reconstructions	Cause and effect

Qualitative research	Quantitative research
Occurrence	Replication
Authenticity	Validity
Trustworthiness	Reliability
Contexts	Variables
Insights	Generalizations

The Ethics of Qualitative Research

Because of the active role of the researcher and an understanding that all inquiry is fundamentally subjective, qualitative researchers use a variety of strategies to develop ethical ways of dealing with the people they encounter during the research process. Of fundamental concern is the principle that all individuals who participate in qualitative research projects must voluntarily agree to participate in the studies without any psychological or physical pressure, manipulation or coercion. Qualitative researchers must provide potential participants with accurate information on the intention of their studies, and there can be no deception regarding the motives of the research. Individuals' agreement to participate in qualitative research must be an informed consent based on complete, accurate and open information. Participants must be told that they are part of a research project and should be explicitly informed about all aspects of the research. In addition, participants must be informed that they are able to withdraw from a research project at any time they wish. When appropriate, participants' privacy and confidentiality should be protected and secured, and all qualitative research should be based on authentic and accurate research. "Fabrications, fraudulent materials, omissions, and contrivances" (Christians, 2003, p. 219) are unethical and inappropriate for qualitative researchers.

Maurice Punch (1998) found that researchers are still trying to recover from the consequences of Stanley Milgram's 1960s-era obedience experiments in which participants were manipulated and lied to, without consent, to encourage them to administer what they thought were painful electric shocks to individuals who did not learn quickly enough. Milgram's "controversial research methods in laboratory experiments, allied to the negative reactions to revelations about medical tests on captive, vulnerable, and non-consenting populations, led to the construction of various restrictions on social research" (Punch, 1998, p. 168).

When researchers convince themselves that the use of deception is for a greater good and they maintain that deception ultimately results in little harm to the participants, they rely on manipulation, secrecy and lies to gather evidence. Ethicist Sissela Bok (1989) explained that lying easily becomes a way of life, and she suggested that researchers seek alternatives to lying, deceiving and/or manipulating their research participants. Bok insisted that researchers can use other, less invasive methods to gather evidence. She suggested that researchers fully disclose the actual intentions of all of their research projects, or that if they are unable to gather information without producing harm, they should pick another research topic.

Most contemporary researchers understand the collaborative nature of qualitative methods and they strive to make sure that the concept of informed consent is taken seriously and fully realized. Given the collaborative nature of qualitative research, some ethicists have questioned whether any social research can ultimately be ethically correct (Ryen, 2011). Theorists have recently suggested that both quantitative and qualitative research may be seen "as a metaphor for colonial knowledge, for power, and for truth" (Denzin and Lincoln, 2008, p. 1). From this perspective, researchers offer representations of the Other that may be culturally, economically or politically motivated. At worst, these representations perpetuate stereotypical views of different cultures, which may result in additional ways to control others. Yet, Michelle Fine (1998, p. 139) reminded us that

> [w]hen we look, get involved, demur, analyze, interpret, probe, speak, remain silent, walk away, organize for outrage, or sanitize our stories, and when we construct our texts in or on their words, we decide how to nuance our relations with/for/despite those who have been deemed Others.

Fine maintained that, while there is no easy solution to "othering," researchers willing to "work the hyphen" can collaborate with research participants to construct interpretations that privilege their experiences and stories. Other researchers have suggested that the concept of protecting subjects from harm is based on a positivist assumption of true knowledge existing in an untainted external reality. While Ryen (2011) acknowledged that qualitative researchers must accept their moral responsibilities, she maintained that "the stories we get are produced *with* rather than *by* someone: they are contextually produced, designed for a particular audience, serve locally produced purposes and are embedded in wider cultural contexts" (p. 421). Ultimately, qualitative researchers should balance understanding the ethical challenges involved in protecting participants while supporting the freedom to do their own scholarship. Overall, a primary goal of contemporary qualitative researchers is to emphasize the collaboration and cooperation with research participants, as they work to build trust and empathy, while they strive to limit the exploitation of at-risk individuals, groups and cultures.

The Qualitative Research Process

While each of the methods chapters provides guidance on how to conduct research using a specific qualitative method, this chapter now focuses on general aspects of the qualitative research process. Given the interdisciplinary nature of qualitative research, there are a variety of ways in which scholars present their work. Yet, the qualitative research process often consists of five distinct phases: (1) choosing a topic of study; (2) constructing a research question and picking a method of analysis based on an interpretive paradigm or theoretical framework; (3) gathering evidence; (4) analyzing and interpreting evidence; and (5) crafting a research report.

Choosing a Research Topic

In the field of media studies, John Pauly (1991) noted that qualitative researchers often study mass communication as a product, as a practice or as a commentary. Researchers who consider aspects of mass communication as a product look at elements of media as texts that represent "integrated strategies of symbolic action" (p. 4). Unlike quantitative researchers who code distinct parts of messages found in advertisements, public relations campaigns, news stories or in other media artifacts, qualitative researchers look at media products in their entirety in an attempt to understand common practices, issues and concerns. Qualitative researchers also study elements of media studies as cultural practices through which people make meaning out of their lives, as well as considering media practices as a commentary on relationships between media and society. In some cases, researchers may combine two or more of these strategies to analyze media-related practices.

For example, perhaps you are interested in studying the roots of the Internet and you know that the technology we use for the Web began with the development of the telegraph. If you wanted to study the telegraph as a product, you might want to research the history of Western Union as a media company. Or, given that Western Union was the first communication empire, you could study the telegraph as a cultural practice, one that created, in Carey's (1989b) words, different production, organizational and administrative techniques

> that demanded a new body of law, economic theory, political arrangements, management techniques, organizational structures, and scientific rationales with which to justify and make effective the development of a privately owned and controlled monopolistic corporation.
>
> (p. 205)

However, the development of the telegraph not only allowed information to travel quickly over long distances but also changed news into a commodity that "could be transported, measured, reduced and timed" (Carey, 1989b, p. 211). The telegraph sped up the process of news; because each word sent across its wires was expensive, it also increased the costs of publishing a newspaper.

You could also study the telegraph as a commentary. From this perspective you might focus on changes in the nature of news that began with the development of the telegraph and evaluate the impact those changes have had on contemporary society.

Understanding that as a researcher you will be an active participant in the qualitative research process, it is important for each of you to consider what potential research topics, issues and/or concerns are of particular interest to you. Think about research studies you have read about, heard about or seen presented. Which ones did you find particularly relevant, interesting or important? Are there certain commonalities among these studies? Perhaps the research that resonated most with your interests all focused on aspects of sports coverage, or addressed different types of public relations campaigns or highlighted new media pioneers. Thinking about past research that caught your interest will give you ideas for potential research topics that are well suited to your interests.

Once you have a research topic in mind, it is time to do some background research to see what has already been written on the topic. You can begin your background research by checking online search engines, research guides and databases, and looking through relevant academic journals and books. By the way, checking the references of a research study that you like will often lead you to similar published research in that area. Qualitative researchers routinely draw on existing research about topics of interest to gather relevant research for their literature reviews and to help them craft research questions.

The theoretical framework you choose for your study will also help you to frame the topic area and the method that you use, as well as your strategies of analysis. For example, perhaps you were a fan of the critically acclaimed television show *Mad Men*, and watching its historically authentic portrayal of advertising piqued your interest in learning what it was actually like to work in an advertising agency during the 1960s and 1970s. If you decided to use a liberal feminist approach for your research, one key area you would focus on in your study would be gender relations. In addition to learning about work responsibilities, types of clients and the creative process, you would want to consider the role of women working in advertising agencies during the 1960s and 1970s. You could research the positions they held, their work routines and their salaries, as well as gender-related career challenges that they may have faced working in advertising agencies. Remember that a theoretical framework is not intended to limit your research but rather to help focus and guide your inquiry toward specific topics, issues and/or concerns.

Crafting Research Questions

All qualitative research questions should be clearly stated, specific and researchable. When you are crafting a research question, the first step is to make sure that the question you want to research can be answered. While a question such as "What does God think about new communication technologies?" may be interesting to consider in a philosophical sense, there is no way such a question can be answered through qualitative research. Or perhaps you are interested in understanding the role of technology in contemporary culture. While this is an important area of media studies research, as a research topic it is too large for a single study and you would need to focus your interests more narrowly on one aspect of the topic. You might choose to research a specific communication technology such as Twitter, Facebook or Snapchat. It is also helpful to narrow your research topic to a particular group of people, geographic region or time period.

Qualitative research questions should be open-ended in nature, encouraging you to understand a variety of potential responses, experiences and connections. They should also allow you to discover aspects of the topic that you may not have previously considered. Qualitative research questions should not yield a simple yes-or-no answer, because meaning is made and understanding is constructed from the reasons why people engage or do not engage with media. In addition, if you frame a question that results in a negative answer, your research project is usually over before it has started. For example, a research question such as "Has social media altered the way people get their news?" is an overly broad yes-or-no question that will provide you with minimal information about how people actually access news through social media. A more open question such as "How do Millennials interact with news presented on Twitter?" is a focused and researchable question, and one that can help you to understand how a specific group of people interacts with Twitter.

I recommend considering the following questions to help you get started crafting your research questions and choosing a conceptual framework for your qualitative research:

- What topic, issue or concern is of particular interest to you?
- What has been written on this topic before?
- What theoretical perspectives were previously used in research on this topic?
- What types of research methods have been used in other research on this topic?
- Are there any gaps in the literature that you would like to explore? If so, how might you fill in those gaps?
- What is the goal of your research?
- What types of methods do you think will help you to answer the types of questions you wish to ask?
- What types of insights can a theoretical framework give you with this research project?
- What conceptual frameworks provide you with guidance in crafting your research question?
- Which of these theoretical perspectives are you most comfortable using for your research project?

Gathering and Analyzing Evidence

Once you have crafted a research question and chosen a theoretical framework and methodology to use, it is time to begin the evaluative process. While strategies for gathering, analyzing and interpreting evidence are often method-specific and are addressed more fully in each of the methods chapters in this book, in general the goal of qualitative analysis is "to contribute to a process of understanding, and to provoke other, probably contradictory, contributions" (Fiske, 1998, p. 370). Qualitative researchers try to gather all the evidence that they can find and they like to immerse themselves in all relevant materials related to their research. Unlike quantitative researchers, who rely on sampling techniques to generate statistical relevance, qualitative researchers generally consider that more is more.

However, they also understand that evidence may be significant even if it is not statistically relevant. Sometimes it is the outliers, the aberrations, the unusual findings that provide researchers with the most meaningful and significant insights. For example, Hanno Hardt's (2000) critical analysis of a bayoneted photograph album discussed the power and potential of photographs to disrupt and restructure cultural media history. Immersed in the conditions of war, the pierced images of a solitary photo album served as a reminder of the destruction of lives and memories by an enemy as well as the role of images in constructing a social and cultural reality. Ultimately, the goal of interpretation, whether it is based on an advertisement, news report, photograph, website, press release or television show, is to help us to understand the essence of that media practice.

Qualitative research aims to understand the myriad meanings that people make. However, it is not enough for qualitative researchers to describe their observations, experiences and/or textual readings. Context is a central part of the interpretive process, and researchers must place their interpretations within the relevant historical, cultural, political and/or economic contexts. For example, if a person swings a club during a golf game, the meaning is much different than if that same person swings a club against an intruder.

Social practices and cultural traditions provide important context that qualitative researchers draw on throughout the process of analysis. As Clifford Christians and James Carey (1989) explained, "the interpretive process is not mysterious flashes of lightning as much as intimate submersion into actual traditions, beliefs, languages, and practices" (p. 363). Within the interpretive process, qualitative researchers do not take people's behaviors at face value but instead draw on the relevant contexts to help consider potential motives for their actions.

Qualitative researchers also attempt to reflect critically on their role as researchers, a process known as reflexivity. Reflexivity helps researchers understand how their interpretations of evidence are influenced not only by historical context, personal experiences and language but also by their race and ethnicity, class and gender. Reflexivity is discussed more fully in Chapter 7.

Using Big Data

In contemporary digital society, researchers have access to a variety of big data sets that offer them a wealth of information on media-related topics. While qualitative researchers should contextualize their findings and critically reflect on all of their interpretations, these days they also need to address myriad issues associated with the use of big data. Boyd and Crawford (2012) envisioned big data as a technological and cultural "phenomenon" involving technology, analysis and mythology. When using big data researchers incorporate computational technologies to evaluate and analyze huge data sets. Many individuals who search, aggregate and cross reference big data believe that these gigantic data sets offer "a higher form of intelligence and knowledge" (p. 663) that can provide us with more truthful, accurate and/or objective insights than other types of research. However, although big data provides researchers with more information, for qualitative researchers the additional data does not necessarily make it any more accurate or objective. Without analysis and interpretation, big data is just raw data.

Using big data sets may certainly provide researchers with valuable information on economic, political and/or social issues. However, its use also raises important ethical concerns regarding informed consent, privacy, corporate and/or governmental control and restrictions on basic freedoms and liberties. Qualitative researchers also worry about businesses exploiting social media data for commercial gains, and they are concerned about conducting research projects based solely on the accessibility of big data (Bone et al., 2016). For example, Twitter regularly makes sample big data sets available to advertisers and researchers. While the materials it provides are a sampling of the Twitter feeds, which do not include tweets from protected accounts and may not be representative of a complete feed, considerable research on Twitter is being done solely because the information is available, accessible and free.

Understanding that huge data sets are often filtered, synthesized and reduced to mathematical models and that big data gathered from online sources may be unreliable, qualitative researchers continue to emphasize contextualizing and interpreting all data sets, and they remind us that "bigger data are not always better data" (Boyd and Crawford, 2012, p. 668).

Crafting a Research Report

In the field of media studies, qualitative researchers seek to understand aspects of the relationship between media and society and to interpret the multiplicity of meanings constructed in media. Qualitative researchers want to join in the ongoing scholarly conversation, and they strive to provide thoughtful and insightful interpretations that will enlarge our understandings of important communication issues. While some qualitative research reports are primarily descriptive in nature, many are analytical, drawing on concepts and theories to analyze and interpret key findings.

Still other qualitative reports are theoretical and philosophical discussions about important media studies issues and concerns. The individual methods chapters include examples of published studies that illustrate a variety of strategies for presenting qualitative research.

Pauly (1991) found that scholars often present research based on one of three main strategies: "the realist tale, the confessional tale, and the impressionist tale" (p. 22). Researchers who opt for a realist tale write in the third person, a strategy that conveys a sense of neutrality, impartiality and objectivity. Researchers drawing on a confessional tale describe their own experiences, often in the first person, to help understand their personal cultural journeys in conducting the studies. In contrast, researchers who craft an impressionist tale attempt to challenge readers' assumptions and expectations, and often focus on the text's role in our interpretations. No matter which presentation style a researcher chooses, ultimately it is important to remember that the stories qualitative researchers tell are shaped by their writing styles, personal histories and the theoretical perspectives they use, as well as considerations of race, ethnicity, class, gender and the specific contexts surrounding their work (Denzin and Lincoln, 1998).

While there are a variety of ways in which qualitative research may be presented, the majority of research reports include the following elements:

- Introduction
- Research Question(s)
- Theoretical Framework
- Literature Review
- Methodology
- Analysis, Interpretations and Commentary
- Conclusion
- References

Although the above is a popular order for elements in qualitative research reports, it is important to remember that the order of the elements may vary. Some researchers interact with previously published literature throughout their reports, forming an extended conversation with other researchers. Other qualitative researchers begin with a discussion of their theoretical framework and literature review before they develop their research questions.

Qualitative research reports usually begin with an introduction, which provides relevant context and background for the study. The author may include a statement of why she or he chose to do this research. The introduction will also describe the research question or questions for the study.

Following the introduction is a section that addresses the theoretical framework used to guide the research project. This section defines the theoretical foundations for the study, and it also explains the usefulness of key concepts that are drawn from the theory that the researcher uses in his or her research.

A literature review of all relevant scholarly research generally follows the theoretical framework discussion. Research that has been published on the same or a similar topic should be included. The literature review should not only give readers an understanding of what research has been done in this area but also describe how the new research project fits into the broader field of study and why it is important to pursue the study.

The methodology section begins with a general description of the methodology used in the research study and a rationale for the choice of method. The methodology section also includes a detailed description of the specific research plan that will be used in the study.

While the introduction, research question, literature review and methodology offer important context for the study, the analysis section provides the concrete evidence of the research that is used to answer the research question. The author includes an analysis of the evidence he or she has collected, as well as commentary and interpretations of the evidence. This section is the most in-depth portion of the research, and the analysis should interact with conceptual issues and respond to previous studies addressed in the literature review.

The conclusion provides the author with an opportunity to summarize the findings, situate the research within a larger theoretical and/or philosophical context and suggest areas of future research.

Finally, all research consulted and quoted in the study should be listed in a reference section.

In the following chapters you will find examples of a variety of approaches for crafting research reports. While the writing styles may differ, each of the elements that are described in this chapter should be found in the studies.

References

Bok, Sissela. (1989). *Lying: Moral choice in public and private life*. New York: Vintage Books.
Bone, John, Emele, Chukwuemeka David, Abdul, Adeniyi, Coghill, Goerge, and Pang, Wei. (2016). The social sciences and the web: From 'lurking' to interdisciplinary 'big data' research. *Methodological Innovations*, 9: 1–14.
Boyd, Danah, and Crawford, Kate. (2012). Critical questions for big data: Provocations for a cultural, technological, and scholarly phenomenon. *Information, Communication & Society*, 15 (5): 662–679.
Carey, James W. (1989a). A cultural approach to communication. In *Communication as culture: Essays on media and society* (pp. 13–36). Boston, MA: Unwin Hyman.
Carey, James W. (1989b). Technology and ideology: The case of the telegraph. In *Communication as culture: Essays on media and society* (pp. 201–230). Boston, MA: Unwin Hyman.

Christians, Clifford G. (2003). Ethics and politics in qualitative research. In Norman K. Denzin and
Yvonna S. Lincoln (Eds.), *The landscape of qualitative research: Theories and issues* (2nd ed.,
pp. 208–243). Thousand Oaks, CA: Sage.
Christians, Clifford G., and Carey, James W. (1989). The logic and aims of qualitative research. In
Guido H. Stempel and Bruce H. Westley (Eds.), *Research methods in mass communication*
(pp. 342–362). Englewood Cliffs, NJ: Prentice Hall.
Denzin, Norman K., and Lincoln, Yvonna S. (1998). Introduction: Entering the field of qualitative
research. In Norman K. Denzin and Yvonna S. Lincoln (Eds.), *The landscape of qualitative
research: Theories and issues* (pp. 1–34). Thousand Oaks, CA: Sage.
Denzin, Norman K., and Lincoln, Yvonna S. (2008). Introduction: The discipline and practice
of qualitative research. In Norman K. Denzin and Yvonna S. Lincoln (Eds.), *Collecting and
interpreting qualitative materials* (pp. 1–43). Thousand Oaks, CA: Sage.
Fine, Michelle. (1998). Working the hyphens: Reinventing self and other in qualitative research.
In Norman K. Denzin and Yvonna S. Lincoln (Eds.), *The landscape of qualitative research:
Theories and issues* (pp. 130–155). Thousand Oaks, CA: Sage.
Fiske, John. (1998). Audiencing: Cultural practice and cultural studies. In Norman K. Denzin and
Yvonna S. Lincoln (Eds.), *The landscape of qualitative research: Theories and issues* (pp. 359–
378). Thousand Oaks, CA: Sage.
Geertz, Clifford. (1973). *The interpretation of cultures: Selected essays.* New York: Basic Books.
Hardt, Hanno. (2000). Pierced memories: On the rhetoric of a bayoneted photograph. In *In the
company of media: Cultural constructions of communication, 1920s–1930s* (pp. 151–162, 177–
178). Boulder, CO: Westview Press.
Pauly, John J. (1991). *A beginner's guide to doing qualitative research in mass communication.*
Columbia, SC: Association for Education in Journalism and Mass Communication.
Postman, Neil. (1988). Social science as moral theology. In *Conscientious objections: Stirring up
trouble about language, technology, and education* (pp. 3–19). New York: Alfred A. Knopf.
Punch, Maurice. (1998). Politics and ethics in qualitative research. In Norman K. Denzin and
Yvonna S. Lincoln (Eds.), *The landscape of qualitative research: Theories and issues* (pp. 156–
184). Thousand Oaks, CA: Sage.
Ryen, Anne. (2011). Ethics and qualitative research. In David Silverman (Ed.), *Qualitative research:
Issues of theory, method and practice* (3rd ed., pp. 416–438). London: Sage.

CHAPTER 3

Interviewing

Interviewing is rather like a marriage: everybody knows what it is, an awful lot of people do it, and yet behind each closed front door there is a world of secrets.

—Ann Oakley (1981, p. 41)

What can be more natural than asking questions? Questions are a central part of the communication process, integral to our everyday conversations. We ask questions to gather information, evaluate opinions and establish common views and to understand key aspects of our lives. Interviewing has been used as a research method for thousands of years. The Egyptians surveyed people to determine their social and economic status. Romans used interviews with participants in the Peloponnesian Wars to gather source material in order to construct a history of the wars, and Socrates used dialogue to gather key philosophical insights (Kvale, 1996).

For many years, journalists, sociologists, political scientists, psychologists and clergy have drawn on interviews for their academic research, clinical counseling and diagnosis, and to try to understand people's social, economic and cultural conditions, as well as their political and religious views. These days, many researchers agree that because people speak from a variety of different backgrounds and perspectives, interviewing is a valuable method that may be used to gather a large amount of useful, interesting, relevant and/or important information. Some of the information accessed through interviews helps to broaden our knowledge base while other information may also help us to understand alternative points of view. In contemporary society, a variety of different types of interviews are routinely used in marketing surveys, legal interrogations, public opinion polls, job interviews, advertising surveys, medical interviews, therapeutic conversations and research questionnaires.

Recently, in just one week I was interviewed by a reporter about media labor issues, I participated in two research institute telephone interviews about my online news preferences, and I completed numerous online surveys regarding various horse products, my grocery shopping habits and my perceptions of the US presidential candidates, political issues and concerns. As Gubrium and Holstein (2002b) suggested, in contemporary society interviews are widely used to obtain personal information and have become "an integral, constitutive feature of our everyday lives" (p. 11).

Simply stated, an interview is a focused, purposeful conversation between two or more people. Some interviews are only a few minutes long, while others last days, weeks or even months. Most research interviews are face-to-face conversations between one interviewer and one interviewee (also known as a respondent), with an interviewer asking questions and an interviewee answering them. However, interviews are also conducted online, in social networking sites, over the telephone and through mail-in surveys and telephone questionnaires. While this chapter focuses primarily on qualitative interviews, two additional types of interviews are also addressed in this book. Group interviews, known as focus groups, provide extensive information in a less costly format and are discussed more fully in Chapter 4. Oral history uses in-depth unstructured interviews to gather individuals' life histories and is the focus of Chapter 6.

In general, researchers use three basic types of interviews: structured, semi-structured and unstructured open-ended conversations. Structured interviews use a specific and standardized procedure, which includes pre-established questions that encourage a limited range of response and are open to a minimum of interpretation. For all participants in a given structured interview study, the same questions are asked in a predetermined order, using a consistent approach, format and words; interruptions, improvisations and/or deviations are not allowed with this type of interview. Structured interviewing is most often used for survey research; it focuses on gaining factual information from respondents with the goal of obtaining accurate and precise data that can be coded and may help "to explain behavior within pre-established categories" (Fontana and Frey, 1994,

p. 366). Structured interviews are administered online through Facebook, Twitter and other social networking sites as well as through telephone surveys, email questionnaires, mail-in surveys and face-to-face questionnaires.

Semi-structured interviews are also usually based on a pre-established set of questions that are asked to all respondents. However, there is much greater flexibility with semi-structured interviews. Interviewers may vary the order of the questions and may also ask follow-up questions to delve more deeply into some of the topics or issues addressed, or to clarify answers given by the respondent.

Unstructured interviews focus on the complex voices, emotions and feelings of interviewees, as well as the meanings within the words that are spoken. Unstructured interviews are in-depth purposeful conversations that seek complex information about complicated issues, emotions and/or concerns in an attempt to understand the historical, social, economic and cultural experiences of individuals and/or groups. They strive to go beyond commonsense explanations to explore and reflect upon the "contextual boundaries of that experience and perception" (Johnson, 2002, p. 106). Unstructured interviews usually begin with a general list of topic areas, themes and/or open-ended questions that an interviewer draws upon, and they encourage the conversations to develop organically.

Qualitative Interviews

Surveys, questionnaires and other types of structured interviews emphasize the collection of quantifiable facts that can be used to generalize about elements of human behavior. In contrast, qualitative interviewing is less concerned with data collection and instead strives to understand the context and meanings of the information, opinions and interests mentioned by each interviewee. Through face-to-face, in-depth guided conversations using semi-structured or unstructured interview questions, qualitative interviewing explores respondents' feelings, emotions, experiences and values within their "deeply nuanced inner worlds" (Gubrium and Holstein, 2002a, p. 57). Qualitative interviewing is heavily influenced by a constructivist theoretical orientation, which considers reality to be socially constructed; from this perspective, respondents are seen as important meaning-makers rather than "passive conduits for retrieving information" (Warren, 2002, p. 83). In recent years, with issues of representation becoming a central concern, we often see traditional research boundaries becoming blurred as qualitative interviewers and respondents collaborate to construct empowering narratives that allow diverse perspectives and multiple voices to emerge (Fontana, 2002).

Most qualitative interviews are face-to-face in-depth conversations that consider both verbal and non-verbal responses. For that reason, using Twitter, Facebook, text messages or even email to conduct qualitative interviews is not advised. It is impossible to get enough depth in 140 characters, and the openness and public access of Facebook often restricts the level and depth of conversations. While email and text messages are immediately transcribed, without the benefit of non-verbal gestures to augment the written responses it is difficult to determine what an interviewee actually feels about an issue or topic. Emoticons and acronyms aside, humor and sarcasm are particularly challenging to interpret without the additional input of non-verbal communication. In addition, both email and texting encourage brief and succinct responses rather than lengthy and complex interactions.

When researchers are unable to conduct face-to-face qualitative interviews, they opt for telephone interviews and frequently use FaceTime, video chat or Skype to facilitate their interviews. Smart phones make it easy to videotape face-to-face interviews, and they also make it convenient to record telephone interviews and save the files electronically. For example, Google Voice records incoming calls in MP3 formatted files, which can be downloaded or listened to online, and programs such as TapeACall record incoming and outgoing telephone interviews that can be saved in a variety of sharable formats.

Qualitative researchers also use telephone interviews to identify and understand people who have gone through traumatic experiences. Although it is more challenging to develop rapport and maintain a consistent focus with telephone interviews, researchers are finding them an effective alternative tool to address sensitive and personal topics, particularly among marginalized individuals and groups (Drabble et al., 2016).

Listening is central to qualitative interviewing. Researchers often start each interview with one introductory question and base their follow-up questions on the respondents' answers as well as on their own background research and other interviews they have conducted. Because qualitative interviews follow respondents' knowledge and interests, the interview process can take unexpected turns and detours. Interviewers must listen carefully to the conversation and remain open and flexible throughout each interview. In his conversations with people from all walks of life, Pulitzer Prize-winning oral historian Studs Terkel (1992) sought to present a "feeling tone" that combined intelligence with emotion in an attempt to explore the many possibilities in people that existed but had not yet been expressed. It is that feeling tone that helps to give qualitative interviewers access to, in Clifford Geertz's (1973) words, the "thick description" of our lives.

Ethical Considerations

Because interviewers frame each research project, introduce issues and topics into the conversation, and influence the direction each interview will take, it is important to remember that imbalances may exist in the power relations between respondents and interviewers. Researchers using qualitative interviewing as a methodology should be sensitive to potential ethical dilemmas arising from the use of personal information. Qualitative interviewers should use their knowledge and experience to act with integrity, honesty and fairness (Kvale, 1996). All qualitative interviewers have a moral responsibility to protect their respondents from physical and emotional harm. There should be absolutely no deception about the scope, intention, goals or any other aspect of a qualitative research study. It is imperative to disclose whether there might be any potential harm to respondents who are participating in qualitative interviews.

As a researcher, you should make sure when each respondent agrees to be interviewed that the consent he or she gives is an informed consent. It is crucial that each respondent knows exactly what your research study is about and how you plan for his or her interview material to be used. Be sure to explain how your research study will shed light on the relationship between media and society or how it will enhance some aspect of the human condition. Each respondent has a right to privacy and it is important to protect each person's identity when he or she requests it. Remember to ask each interviewee whether he or she is comfortable with his or her real name being used in the research project. If not, ask the person to choose a pseudonym in place of his or her real name. Once your research project is complete, you may wish to share your research findings with your respondents; they will be interested in your interpretations as well as what other respondents had to say.

Using Qualitative Interviews

If you plan to use qualitative interviews as a methodology for your research study, there are several key research strategies that will help to guide your project. Kvale (1996) outlined seven research steps to be taken when using qualitative interviews, and this chapter now focuses on each of these steps: (1) conceptualizing a research question and outlining the theoretical framework guiding the research; (2) designing the research study; (3) conducting the interviews; (4) transcribing the interviews; (5) analyzing the information obtained from the interviews; (6) verifying the information from the interviews; and (7) writing up the findings of the study.

Conceptualizing a Study

As with other qualitative methods, it is important to begin each research project by conceptualizing your study. Chapter 2 provides you with guidance that will help you to conceptualize your qualitative research study. However, I think it is important to remember to choose a topic that is based on your own interests, concerns or experiences. There is nothing worse than trying to complete a research project that you no longer find interesting.

Designing a Study

When designing a qualitative interview study, you will want to consider the backgrounds of people you would like to interview, and how you will identify and gain access to them. You will need to craft a list of potential questions and/or topic areas to focus on, and you should also consider the time frame necessary to complete your research. You may be wondering how many interviews you will have to undertake to complete a qualitative interview research project. Unfortunately, there is no magic number of interviews that must be done. The right number of interviews will vary, depending on the length and depth of the conversations, the information obtained, the topic area and the focus of your research project. Ultimately, it is important to interview as many people as necessary in order to gather insights and understanding about your topic or issue. During the course of the interviews, when you hear the same information repeatedly and you feel that you are learning less and less from each new interview, you may feel that you have covered the topic thoroughly and it may be a good time to end the interview process.

It is also important to complete background research on each of your respondents so that you are knowledgeable about basic aspects of their lives, interests and activities. While social networking sites such as LinkedIn, Twitter and Facebook are not appropriate places to conduct qualitative interviews, they are great resources for identifying potential interviewees and obtaining background information on the people you plan to interview.

Gaining an interviewee's trust is an essential part of each qualitative interview. Fontana and Frey (1994) suggested that one way of establishing rapport is for an interviewer to see a situation from a respondent's perspective. It is also important for interviewers to understand the language, customs and culture of each person that they talk with. Background research provides you with key information about each interviewee and it will help you to ask informed and interesting questions and build rapport. These days researchers tweet requests for interview information about their studies and they ask individuals who might be interested in their research to follow them. Researchers also use LinkedIn, Facebook and other social networking sites to help them find potential interviewees. Learning as much as you can about the issues and topics will also help you to gain access to key interview sources. Newcomb (1999) found that because media professionals do not have the opportunity or time to teach researchers about important aspects of their fields, access and rapport can be greatly enhanced when researchers have done extensive background research before the interviews and already have "specific knowledge of professional, organizational, and technical matters" (p. 100).

Once you have identified potential interviewees, you will need to persuade each person to participate in your study. In your initial email, phone call or letter to each potential respondent, outline the purpose of your study, mention your ideal research time frame and explain your rationale for interviewing the person. Be sure to follow up your initial contacts; it may take several attempts before some individuals will agree to be interviewed. Once an individual has agreed to be interviewed it is certainly appropriate to send them a LinkedIn or Facebook friend request or to follow them on Instagram or Twitter. When scheduling interviews, plan to meet in a quiet place that is comfortable and convenient for the respondent. Researchers must be flexible throughout the interview process and should understand that conflicts may arise with an individual that necessitate the rescheduling of an interview. It is also important to leave plenty of time for each interview so that you will not have to rush. It is embarrassing to be in the middle of an interesting conversation and realize that you have to cut the conversation short because you are late for your next appointment.

Conducting Interviews

Once you have scheduled a few of your interviews, it is time to begin interviewing respondents. Barbara Walters, whose casual yet probing interview style has come to define the field of personality journalism, has excellent advice to keep in mind at the beginning of each interview. She noted:

> A conversation, even a brief one, should have all the best features of any functioning human relationship, and that means genuine interest on both sides, opportunity and respect for both to express themselves, and some dashes of tact and perception.
>
> (1970, p. xiv)

For both semi-structured and unstructured qualitative interviews, plan to bring a list of potential questions or topic areas as well as the background information you have collected on each interviewee and your notes about the topic. I recommend recording all interviews. You may also wish to take notes during your interviews; it is helpful to jot down key concepts and topic areas to help keep the conversation flowing and to prompt follow-up questions. Some researchers recommend bringing photographs, magazine articles and other cultural artifacts to the interviews. They find that discussing the materials is a great way to spark in-depth discussion about an issue or topic and they suggest that sharing elements of popular culture can be particularly helpful in situating noteworthy events.

At the beginning of each interview it is important to explain the purpose of your research study in order to help the respondent to see the relevance of the project and to express your genuine interest in her or his views and experiences. Be sure to refer to each interviewee by name and to pronounce each person's name correctly. The initial small talk and icebreaking questions that are used at the beginning of qualitative interviews help the interviewer get to know the interviewee, as well as to gain trust, build rapport and to establish the tone of the conversation.

While many different types of questions are used in interviews, qualitative interviewers begin primarily with icebreaker questions and then proceed with probing and follow-up questions.

Icebreakers

Icebreaker questions are used to engage respondents in a conversation about key aspects of their personal lives, and they should begin to establish an environment where questions can be asked and answered in a non-judgmental manner. Social networking sites are a great place to gather information about your interviewee's heroes, favorite sports teams, hobbies, favorite vacations or family activities. Feel free to comment on mutual interests, current events, the interviewee's fashion sense, musical tastes or even the weather. Walters (1970) suggested asking creative icebreaker questions based on a person's interests or career. Over the years she has asked artists what is the most intriguing or beautiful thing that they have ever seen, queried musicians on how they would inspire a child to play an instrument and questioned news makers about recent experiences that have given them pleasure.

The background information you have gathered on each interviewee is especially helpful in framing icebreaker questions to get the conversation going. *New Yorker* writer A. J. Liebling recommended trying to understand enough about your interviewees' background to let them know that you appreciate their interests and want them to tell you more. Liebling (1963) explained that the icebreaker question he used to begin his well-known interview with jockey Eddie Arcaro was "How many holes longer do you keep your left stirrup than your right?" (p. 157). Arcaro responded that he could tell that Liebling had been around jockeys a lot, and in response to his question Arcaro spoke enthusiastically about his career and provided Liebling with great insights about his life as a jockey. Liebling wrote that although he had only been around jockeys a week before the interview, he had learned from his research that on US racing tracks, jockeys rode with their stirrups longer on their left side.

Probing Questions

Once trust has been established through your icebreaker questions, it is time to focus your questions more directly on the research topic. The questions you ask should be simple, sincere, direct and open-ended, encouraging respondents to explain and elaborate about their experiences. Open-ended questions offer respondents the freedom to respond with little influence from the interviewer. Try to ask questions that encourage personal opinions and commentary. Questions such as "How did you first get started in public relations?" or "Tell me about your first advertising position?" will encourage a respondent to talk more openly about her or his career. Whenever possible, try to limit the number of specific factual questions and yes/no questions that you ask. While sometimes you will need to corroborate specific information, questions like "What year did you begin to work at JWT?" or "Did you major in digital journalism in college?" will do little to keep a conversation going. Thoughtful, well-crafted, open-ended questions will encourage your interviewees to give interesting, authentic, in-depth answers. Unfortunately, as Metzler (1977) noted, the reverse is also true. When crafting interview questions, it is important to remember that "a superficial, insincere question will get you an equally shallow answer" (p. 132).

As you probe each topic, be sure to ask follow-up questions for clarification and to delve deeply into the experiences, emotions and feelings of each respondent. Questions such as "Can you tell me more about your first broadcast interview?" or "Can you give me an example of the types of stories you covered while you were on the science beat?" should help you to get in-depth information about your research topic.

Asking Difficult Questions

During the course of an interview, you may need to ask a respondent a difficult question about a sensitive aspect of his or her life. Sensitive questions should be addressed carefully and respectfully, and should only be raised after you have established trust with an interviewee. One strategy is to depersonalize difficult questions by putting them in the third person and beginning the line of questioning by addressing the topic indirectly. For example, rather than asking an interviewee, "Did you ever hire any minorities for your news organization?" you might begin to explore the topic by asking, "What were the general hiring practices when you started in broadcast news?" You might then mention that during other interviews, some respondents discussed racism in network broadcasting and, depending on the respondent's comments, you could follow up by asking a question such as "Have you observed or experienced any racism as a journalist?"

Perhaps you have reason to believe that one of your interviewees is sexist. Rather than putting the individual on the spot by asking whether he or she thinks his or her views or actions are sexist, you might begin a discussion of this issue by saying something such as "During the course of my other research interviews, some respondents referred to you as sexist." On the basis of the respondent's response, you may be able to probe the sensitive topic more deeply. Walters (1970) found that when addressing sensitive issues, it was helpful to ask respondents to comment on a well-known quotation, which may provide insight into the issue. For example, she suggested that instead of asking an individual to answer a sensitive question about how he or she feels about getting old in the media business, a better strategy is to ask the person to comment on a remark like the one credited to Brigitte Bardot: "The best years of my life were when I was 17."

Interviewing Techniques

In qualitative interviewing, the interviewer's role is to encourage authentic, useful and in-depth responses from each respondent. Interviewers must learn how to assist respondents to freely share their stories, experiences and opinions. It is sometimes challenging to get access to the right respondents who are willing to speak openly and express their personal feelings about issues, topics and concerns. Not all respondents are able to provide meaningful, interesting responses to your questions. Some respondents will speak freely about the specifics of what they did, but they remain uncomfortable explaining why they acted the way they did.

To become a skilled qualitative interviewer you should continually practice your interviewing skills. The best interviewers are creative, flexible and open to trying a variety of different strategies. It is helpful to adopt a neutral stance during your interviews and to refrain from influencing a respondent's commentary. Whenever possible, use non-threatening language and make sure that your non-verbal gestures, looks and body postures reinforce your interest in and support for the interviewee. Some journalists and law enforcement officers have adopted strategies that are intended to gain a psychological advantage over their interviewees. While they may position themselves so that the sun is in the eyes of a respondent, or they may stand while a respondent is sitting (Sontheimer, 1941), these strategies are inappropriate for qualitative interviewers, who should make sure their respondents are comfortable throughout their interviews.

I recommend that you consider the non-verbal cues that you give during the interview process. Make sure that you do not shake your head negatively, frown or gaze away during your interviews. Use silences in the conversation to help respondents gather their thoughts rather than to push them into speaking. Refrain from asking leading questions because they may influence a respondent's responses and can derail the conversation. It is important to avoid sexist, racist and/or demeaning questions as well as questions that illustrate your personal opinions, biases and/or prejudices.

For example, during the 2011 Miss Universe contest one of the finalists, Leila Lopes, was asked what has been called "the dumbest question in the universe" (Ravitz, 2011). Lopes was asked, "If you could change one of your physical characteristics, which one would it be and why?" Of course, the question asked Lopes to consider whether she measured up to the demeaning stereotypical standards of female beauty. Lopes, who responded that she was happy with her appearance and encouraged people to respect others, became the first Miss Universe from Angola. It is also important not to be over-solicitous, trying to ingratiate yourself with an interviewee. A statement such as "Some of my best friends are Muslim" is actually "patronizing—and bigoted" (Walters, 1970, p. 18).

Berger (1998) found that during the course of each interview, research interviewers interact with respondents in at least one of four different ways: they primarily incorporate understanding responses, probing responses, evaluative responses and/or phatic responses. An understanding response is used to clarify information. The interviewer will repeat a statement made by the respondent and say something like "Correct me if I heard you wrong. Did you just say that crisis communication is the most important aspect of public relations?" Probing responses take the form of follow-up questions such as "Tell me more about your role in the development of Pokémon GO." Probing responses are used to delve more deeply into a person's commentary, access how an interviewee feels about an issue or understand an individual's actions. Evaluative responses make value judgments about what an interviewee has said and are generally avoided in qualitative interviewing. Statements such as "I disagree with your opinion of the role of women in advertising" shouldn't be used because they can alienate a respondent and derail the conversation. Interviewers frequently use phatic responses to let respondents know that they understand what has been said and want respondents to keep talking. Comments such as "uh huh," "OK" or "Yes, I understand" are comforting phatic responses that let the interviewee know you are listening, and may also encourage a reticent respondent to speak more freely.

While qualitative interviewers focus on respondents' emotions and experiences, they must also maintain control of each interview; therefore, it is important for interviewers to avoid becoming the focus of the conversation. This can be challenging, because once trust has been established, it is only natural for a respondent to begin asking an interviewer questions. Fontana and Frey (1994) suggested diffusing the relevance of an interviewer's opinions by explaining that an interviewer's feelings, opinions and experiences are not relevant to the research project. In my own experience, a comment such as "I appreciate your interest in my views, but what's important is your opinion and not mine" will help to refocus the conversation and remind a respondent of the purpose of the interview. One final interview strategy: be sure to ask all respondents at the end of their interviews whether they have anything else to add to the conversation. After many years of interviewing, I am still surprised at how much people will share with you when they feel comfortable and supported and know that you are truly interested in what they have to say.

The idealized interviewee is well-spoken, cooperative, knowledgeable, truthful, precise, motivated, coherent and focused, providing the interviewer with great stories, lively descriptions and wonderful examples (Kvale, 1996). Of course, no such a person exists. Many respondents have some of these characteristics, and it is a qualitative interviewer's challenge to motivate and draw out the best stories from each interviewee. There are times when no matter how much background information has been acquired and how many skillful interviewing strategies are used, an interviewer is unable to establish trust with one of his or her respondents. The respondent does not open up, and replies with monosyllabic answers to all of the interviewer's creative questions. While the strategies discussed in this chapter as well as the chapters on Oral History and Focus Groups (Chapters 6 and 4 respectively) will help you to learn the craft of qualitative interviewing, it is important to realize that ultimately not everyone will be a good interviewee.

Transcribing Interviews

It is much easier to work with a transcript of each interview rather than continually referring back to the recordings. Therefore, you will want to transcribe each interview while the conversation is fresh in your mind. Transcribing interviews is a time-consuming process, and sometimes interviewers can become frustrated by the time it takes to complete a research project based on qualitative interviews. It generally takes between two and four hours to transcribe a one-hour interview. For example, during the qualitative interviewing research project "Good Journalism: On the Evaluation Criteria of Some Interested and Experienced Actors," Risto Kunelius (2006) interviewed seventy-nine individuals. Each interview lasted approximately ninety minutes and yielded approximately 1,300 single-spaced pages of transcription. Clearly, Kunelius's time commitment was extensive for his qualitative research project. See Chapter 6, on Oral History, for additional information and strategies on recording, transcribing and editing interviews.

In general, qualitative researchers prefer not to edit interview transcripts apart from correcting the spelling errors of voice recognition software and removing false starts from the conversation. Most researchers caution against editing transcripts to improve upon a respondent's language or grammar because doing so can change the tone and meaning of the interview. For example, Rebecca Skloot (2010) wrote about how she learned the importance of understanding the meaning of a person's language while she was doing interviews for her book *The Immortal Life of Henrietta Lacks*. Combining scientific and historical research with interviews, Skloot's award-winning non-fiction book traced the development of the "HeLa" cell line that originally came from Lacks' cancer cells. While Skloot noted that she was initially tempted to edit some quotations so that the respondents might sound better, Skloot was warned by a family member of Lacks that she should not change the quotations of people she interviewed to make them grammatically correct. Skloot was told, "If you pretty up how people spoke and change the things they said, that's dishonest. It's taking away their lives, their experiences, and their selves" (p. ix). After the conversation, Skloot wrote that she realized that the way people spoke provided important insights into their backgrounds, customs and culture, and she decided not to alter any of the respondents' quotations for her book.

Analyzing the Information

It is through a researcher's analysis and interpretation that issues, concerns and contradictions are brought into the open, discussed and sometimes even resolved. If relevant, it is useful to consider ways to evaluate each interview in order to enrich an aspect of our understandings of the relationship between media and society. The interpretation of interview information actually begins during the interview. It is helpful to attempt to verify each respondent's answers and clarify any initial interpretations that you might begin to have during the course of each interview. Comments such as "Are you saying that citizen journalism can coexist with mainstream journalism?" or "Do you mean that the television show *The X-Factor* has altered the popular music business?" are examples of questions that may help you to situate information shared with you by each respondent.

After an interview has been transcribed, you can work with the transcript to identify important insights and information, outline key concepts, opinions, patterns and themes, and make a note of interesting stories and experiences. The theoretical framework you use will provide you with contextual guidance that will help you to conceptualize the material you gather from your interviews. As Gubrium and Holstein (2002a) explained, "Each theoretical perspective implicates a set of procedures or ways of organizing, categorizing, and interpreting data. There is no single approach to qualitative analysis" (p. 673).

Verifying Information

While Chapter 1 addresses basic differences between qualitative and quantitative research as it relates to the assessment of evidence, one potential issue with using qualitative interviews as a research method relates to the reliability of the information provided by respondents. Some researchers continue to worry that respondents' answers may be self-serving and that they may attempt to intentionally deceive the researcher. Some respondents' memories are faulty; others will lie or tell interviewers anything they can think of to end their interviews; and yet other respondents are a little too eager to please and will attempt to tell interviewers what they think the researchers want to know (Berger, 2000). Newcomb (1999) suggested that researchers should examine all interviews for accuracy in detail as well as for basic truthfulness. While personal opinions and perceptions may be considered authentic responses from each respondent, specific factual information gathered from each interview should be verified from other research sources as well as corroborated by other respondents during subsequent interviews.

Writing a Research Report

Researchers using qualitative interviews as a methodology will want to provide a contextual frame of reference from which the interview quotations are interpreted. Quoted material should be analyzed and interpreted, and researchers should keep a balance between the use of quotes and analysis of the insights. It's best to use shorter quotes or to use one or two quotes to illustrate a point rather than bombarding the reader with pages and pages of quotes.

The following research article, by Folker Hanusch, illustrates one way in which interviews are used in qualitative research. "Cultural Forces in Journalism: The Impact of Cultural Values on Māori Journalists' Professional Views," first published in *Journalism Studies* in 2016, drew on twenty in-depth qualitative interviews with Māori journalists to explore the role that cultural values played among indigenous journalists in New Zealand. In his introduction Hanusch made a case for addressing cultural values and practices in order to provide a more nuanced analysis of journalism.

"Cultural Forces in Journalism: The Impact of Cultural Values on Māori Journalists' Professional Views," by Folker Hanusch

From *Journalism Studies*, 2016

Introduction

The study of the various influences on journalists' professional views and practices has a long and rich history, spanning more than 60 years. Scholars have theorised about and examined a number of different levels, ranging from influences on the individual level to those on the structural level. In relation to the structural or systems-level influences, studies have tended to focus in particular on political and economic aspects of social systems (see e.g. Hallin and Mancini, 2004; Siebert, Peterson, and Schramm, 1956; Weaver, 1998). In addition, cultural studies approaches have focussed on aspects of ideology and hegemony, interested in the power relations that shape the news (e.g. Entman and Rojecki, 2000; Hall, 1989).

While political and economic determinants are of unquestionable importance in understanding journalism and news culture, this paper argues that additional variables are crucial to consider. One such variable relates to a nation's or community's cultural environment and how this impacts on journalistic practice and news content. The relative lack of research in this area is somewhat surprising, because it is often acknowledged in existing research that cultural differences can account for variation in journalists' professional views as well as news content. Yet, such acknowledgments are often tacit, broad and somewhat murky, as the role of culture is very rarely examined in detail.

In order to shed more light on the ways in which culture—and cultural values more specifically—impact on journalism, this paper reports on a study of Māori journalism culture in Aotearoa New Zealand. Based on 20 in-depth interviews with Indigenous journalists, it focuses on the role that various well-documented cultural values and practices play in Māori journalism today. In so doing, the study demonstrates the opportunities, which the consideration of cultural values can present for studying journalism culture more broadly.

Notice how the literature review offered a working definition of the concept of cultural values and how it addressed previous research linking journalistic practices with cultural values. Research on indigenous news media was also showcased to illustrate how research on cultural influences may provide a more nuanced understanding of journalism culture.

Journalism and Cultural Values

Culture is a very flexible term that is often used in a wide variety of contexts. It can, for example, mean anything between broad (culture is everything) and narrow (cultural institutions such as the opera) understandings. Further, there are national cultures, organisational cultures, sub-cultures and cultures of shared social practices such as the cultures of consumption or beauty makeovers (Shoemaker and Vos, 2009, p. 104). At the social systems level, culture is often defined as relating to shared social practices on a national level. One example is Schwartz's (2004, p. 43) definition of culture as the "rich complex of meanings, beliefs, practices, symbols, norms and values prevalent among people in a society". The study of culture and cultural values has a rich tradition particularly in the fields of anthropology and cross-cultural psychology, and includes such work as conceptualisations of instrumental and terminal values (Rokeach, 1973), traditional versus secular and survival versus self-expression values (Inglehart, 1997), as well as Hofstede's (2001) five cultural value dimensions (masculinity, individualism, uncertainty avoidance, power distance and long-term orientation) and Schwartz's (2004) seven cultural value orientations (intellectual autonomy, affective autonomy, embeddedness, egalitarianism, hierarchy, harmony and mastery).

Despite this wealth of knowledge, only a limited number of studies have attempted to explicitly link cultural values with journalistic practice. The work that does exist has mostly applied Hofstede's (2001) work, such as a comparison of German and Australian newspaper's reporting of foreign death, which linked differences in visual treatment, language conventions and ethical codes to differences in the two countries' scores on two of Hofstede's cultural value dimensions (Hanusch, 2009). An analysis of the framing of news stories about the internet in China which appeared in the Hong Kong, Singapore, US and UK press argued that Hofstede's (2001) long- versus short-term dimension was a significant factor in determining most types of news frames, and often more than one cultural value dimension was influential (Zhou, 2008). Ravi's (2005) cross-cultural study of newspaper reporting in the lead-up to the Iraq War found that Pakistani and Indian newspapers were more focussed on aggregates of fatal events, while British and US newspapers focussed more on individual events. Ravi argued that the reason for this difference may lie in societal values, as the Asian countries placed a higher value on the community, while the Western countries were more individualist.

Cultural value research in journalism also extends to photojournalistic coverage, with a study of news and feature photographs in 10 elite American and Korean newspapers finding significant differences in photographic style (Kim and Kelly, 2008). American photojournalists displayed more individualist tendencies, while their Korean counterparts worked more strictly in line with their societal obligations, acting "according to the group's interest rather than according to their own interpretations" (Kim and Kelly, 2008, p. 171). Similarly, an analysis of the newspaper coverage of the 2010 Haiti earthquake in 15 countries has argued that the degree of graphic photographs could be traced to sociocultural differences, such as individual countries' religious traditions and levels of societal violence (Hanusch, 2012).

A survey of Taiwanese and US journalist's work motivations also showed significant variations in job satisfaction along Hofstede's (2001) individualism dimensions (Chang and Massey, 2010), and Winfield, Mizuno, and Beaudoin (2000) have argued that collectivist values play an important role in Chinese and Japanese press systems. Despite the political and economic differences that exist between the two systems on the surface, the authors argued that "the concepts of group harmony, collectivism and the place of the individual within the group explain similar aspects of both press systems at the beginning of the twenty-first century" (Winfield Mizuno, and Beaudoin, 2000, p. 347). Kanayama and Cooper-Chen's (2005) study of Japanese and international newspaper coverage of the pregnancy of Princess Masako argued that countries with a higher Masculinity score on Hofstede's (2001) scale tended to portray her in a more traditional frame and with a stronger focus on pregnancy than countries with a low Masculinity score. Hanitzsch's (2007) much-cited theoretical discussion of journalism culture also accounts for cultural values by linking Hofstede's power distance dimension to journalist's attitudes towards power.

While empirical analyses of cultural values in news have been limited, proponents of normative media models have regularly cited culture and cultural values as crucial, such as during the debate over Asian values in journalism (Xu, 2005). During the 1980s and 1990s, the political leadership of Singapore and

Malaysia argued for Asian nations to draw on their traditional beliefs and values in building modern and economically strong societies (Massey and Chang, 2002, p. 992). In line with such an approach, journalism should also be based in Asian values, such as respect for authority, group dynamics and an emphasis on communalism (collectivism) rather than a focus on individualist values (Xu, 2005). Subsequent studies did find evidence that key values such as harmony and supportiveness were present in news reporting of Brunei, Malaysia and Singapore (Massey and Chang, 2002, p. 999). On the African continent, proponents of an Afro-centric approach to journalism have similarly argued that what they see as individualism and divisionism in Western journalism does not accord with local contexts and is unhealthy (Kasoma, 1996). Lately, attention has been paid to an Indigenous African approach to journalism, based on the tradition of *ubuntuism* (e.g. Blankenberg, 1999; Fourie, 2008), which can be understood as a community-focussed approach that expresses "compassion, reciprocity, dignity, harmony and humanity in the interest of building and maintaining a community with justice and mutual caring" (Fourie, 2008, p. 62). Objectivity may not be a necessary component of *ubuntu* journalism because it is impossible for journalists to be spectators, as they are always defined through group relations and their membership of the community. Thus, "active involvement and dialogue with the community rather than detachment in the name of objectivity and neutrality may be required" (Fourie, 2008, p. 65). At the same time, such normative models have been criticised for failing to take account of the distinct cultural variations among Asian and African nations, and the fact they can be (and often are) easily misused to prevent criticism of those in political power (Tomaselli, 2003; Xu, 2005).

Indigenous News Media

A further area where culture has been identified as influential in shaping journalism is the Indigenous media sector. Improvements in and better access to information technology over recent decades have contributed to a significant growth of Indigenous media outlets, leading to an "explosion" of such media around the world (Alia, 2010, p. 7). The rapid development of Indigenous media had been aided by technological advances in the latter part of the twentieth century, as well as trans-national efforts by Indigenous peoples for recognition in the 1970s and 1980s. While the term "Indigenous" is itself problematic, as it may "collectivize many distinct populations whose experiences under imperialism have been vastly different" (Smith, 1999, p. 6), it is often employed at the global level, especially by Indigenous movements and organisations themselves. The World Indigenous Television Broadcasters Network, for example, has been one highly visible trans-national effort by Indigenous journalists to raise their profile.

Indigenous journalism tends to occur in two broad varieties: the first relates to Indigenous-owned and operated news media organisations, while the second includes Indigenous-focussed news within mainstream news organisations, in particular public broadcasters. In both cases, however, Indigenous journalism can be defined as the "production and dissemination of information about contemporary affairs of general public interest and importance, by Indigenous peoples for the benefit of Indigenous but also non-Indigenous communities" (Hanusch, 2013b).

While such media are not new—Indigenous newspapers, for example, have existed in a number of countries since the 1800s (Curnow, 2002; Littlefied and Parins, 1984; Meadows and Molnar, 2002)—little attention had been given to this sector until the late 1990s (Meadows and Molnar, 2002, p. 9). The twenty-first century has, however, seen a burgeoning amount of studies concerned with Indigenous media (see e.g. Alia, 2010; Molnar and Meadows, 2001; Wilson and Stewart, 2008). Much attention has been paid to the political aspects of Indigenous journalism and its role in wanting to provide a counternarrative to mainstream news reporting, which frequently stereotypes Indigenous people (Alia, 2009, p. 41). Another focus has been the role that journalists can play in empowering Indigenous societies and acting as means for politically mobilising their communities (Pietikäinen, 2008; Salazar, 2003). A further prominent aspect, however, has been the role that cultural values play in Indigenous media practices. Indigenous news media therefore provide a unique opportunity to shed more light on the various ways in which culture and cultural values affect, enhance and challenge journalists' professional views and their practices.

For example, in northern Europe Pietikäinen (2008) identified a "Sámi Way" of doing journalism. This, she argued, was deeply entrenched in local cultural values and worldviews, in particular as indigenous news media made it "possible to practise culturally typical ways of communication, to recognize experiences, perspectives and topics often disregarded by other media" (Pietikäinen, 2008, p. 177). Such an approach resonates strongly with research in developing societies around the globe which have advocated culturespecific ways of doing journalism. In this sense, Indigenous journalists appear to consider as their primary goal the provision of information that is relevant to their audiences, their culture and the overarching goal of contributing to the survival of Indigenous identities (see also Hanusch, 2013a; Santo, 2004). Grixti (2011), in examining Indigenous approaches to journalism, highlighted the fact that in societies that hold predominantly individualist values—such as Australia, Canada, New Zealand and the United States—Indigenous societies tend to hold collectivist values, which results in journalism that is focussed more on the community, rather than individual success. This aspect is reminiscent of the previously discussed studies which have found significant differences in the journalism of individualist and collectivist national societies. Indigenous journalists also often have a different relationship with the land, an aspect highlighted in a study of Native American newspapers, which were found to have invoked traditional cultural values when reporting on the environment (Loew and Mella, 2005).

In Aotearoa New Zealand, a country that has—compared to many other countries—a relatively burgeoning Indigenous news sector, a number of analyses have found similar aspects that contribute to this discussion. Māori journalists have for some considerable time employed culturally-specific ways to news-making. For example, early newspapers took names of local birds, because they represented qualities that were similar to those of traditional orators and singers, who were colloquially known as "talking birds" (*manu korero* in Māori) (McRae, 2002, 44–46). In a further sign of the continuation of *tikanga* Māori (Māori cultural values) through nineteenth-century journalism, Ka'ai-Mahuta (2010) points out that *waiata* (traditional songs) and *haka* (traditional posture dances) often served as forms of political critiques, demonstrating the way in which culture is also employed strategically for political purposes.

When Māori journalism began appearing on television in the 1980s, the producers of the news programme *Te Karere* made a point of practising a culturally-specific journalism which reported from a Māori perspective. For example, interviewees' tribal affiliations were regularly mentioned: "These things are important, because Māori people need to know someone's tribal affiliation in order to properly consider what they are saying in public" (Fox, 1993, 129). This practice still continues today (Rankine et al., 2007). *Te Karere* also incorporated a wider range of news values and gave a wider variety of people a voice, in line with the Māori belief that everyone deserves their say (Fox, 1992). Te Awa's (1996) study of the radio programme *Mana News* also showed sources were given more airtime than on mainstream news media, and stories focussed less on news values like conflict, but rather offered solutions in so-called bad news stories (see also McGregor and Comrie, 1995). Interviews on television are often introduced with more or less short *mihi* (greetings), subjects are treated with much respect, and journalists frequently use *whakatauk* and *pepeha* (which can be described as proverbs, although their meaning is broader in Māori) (Adds et al., 2005). Stuart (2002) has noted that some journalists only report final decisions of *hui* (meetings), so as not to contravene the idea that discussions held at *marae* (traditional meeting grounds) should remain there once resolved. In addition, Māori journalist Wena Harawira (2008) has argued that there are cultural concepts which are important for journalists to adhere to, such as when interviewing elders, where certain cultural protocols are applied.

The examples discussed here show that paying more attention to cultural influences on journalism practices can contribute to a more comprehensive understanding of journalism culture. Yet, cultural aspects have often been incidental to such studies, rather than their focus. Further, the vast majority of studies, especially in the context of Māori journalism, have been concerned with analyses of published news content and linking it to cultural values. In order to arrive at a more complete picture, however, it is also necessary to study the producers of such content and to inquire into their professional views.

In the following methodology section, Hanusch described Māori journalism, the demographics of the interviewees and how the twenty Māori journalists were chosen to participate in the study. Eighteen of the interviews were conducted in person while two interviews were done on Skype.

Methodology

Assuming that culture and cultural values affect the way journalists think about and practise their work, this study's main purpose was to identify in more detail how and to what extent these factors play a role. To do so, this paper focusses on Māori journalists in Aotearoa New Zealand. Māori journalism has a long history and advances in recent decades—both in terms of technological improvements as well as improved access and funding—have resulted in an increase in Māori news and current affairs.

Māori journalism is present in a variety of formats in Aotearoa New Zealand. Its development over the past 30 years or so has been partly due to the country's government showing a willingness to—belatedly—honour agreements made in the Treaty of Waitangi, which had been signed by the English Crown and Māori chiefs in 1840. When the Waitangi Tribunal—a permanent commission of inquiry that makes recommendations on claims brought by Māori relating to actions or omissions of the Crown that breach the promises made in the Treaty of Waitangi (Waitangi Tribunal, 2013)—ruled in 1986 that the Māori language was a *taonga* (a treasured possession) that needed to be protected and nurtured (Walker, 2004, p. 268), it led to renewed government funding for the broadcasting sector, which was seen as crucial to the revitalisation of the language. In 2004, it led to the establishment of Māori Television, a wholly Indigenous-operated station with the aim of revitalising Māori language and culture (Middleton, 2010). Five years into its existence, the channel was reaching half of the 100,000 Māori living in the country, and one-third of New Zealanders overall (Maori Television, 2009).

Māori Television produces more than 250 hours of local programming, including a daily news programme in the Māori language (*Te Kaea*), as well as current affairs shows in English (*Native Affairs*) and in Māori (*Te Tepu*). The state broadcaster Television New Zealand (TVNZ) is home to the nation's longest-running Māori-language news programme *Te Karere*, which began in 1983, as well as the English-language current affairs programme *Marae Investigates*. News and current affairs in Māori is also broadcast on radio around the nation, provided by Radio Waatea and distributed through the 21-station *iwi* network, a collective of tribal stations. While Māori print media are far from being as prominent as they were during the nineteenth century, magazines such as *Mana*, *Te Karaka* and *Tū Mai* provide some level of current affairs from a Māori perspective. These news outlets typically aim for Māori audiences, yet in the recent past, some have become increasingly popular with non-Māori. The programme *Native Affairs* has proved especially successful, winning numerous awards, including Best Current Affairs Series at the 2011 Aotearoa Film and Television Awards.

In order to examine the way in which journalists experience cultural influences in their work, in-depth interviews were conducted with 20 Māori journalists working across the Māori media spectrum. Respondents were drawn from Māori Television (eight journalists involved in the production of *Te Kaea* and *Native Affairs*), Television New Zealand (eight journalists reporting and producing for *Te Karere* and *Marae Investigates*), Radio Waatea (three journalists) and *Mana* magazine (one journalist). All but two respondents were interviewed in person at their news organisations in Auckland between August 29 and September 2, 2011. Two additional interviews were conducted via Skype, one in late September 2011 and another in February 2012. The study purposively selected respondents from a wide variety of editorial roles, and included reporters, directors, producers, news editors and general managers. The interviewed journalists further represented a wide variety of *iwi* (tribes), an important consideration due to persistent differences in individual tribal values and worldviews.

Attention was also paid to having a mix of demographics and backgrounds represented in the study. In terms of age, one-quarter of the sample was over 50, while half were aged in their thirties. The youngest respondent was 24 years old, the oldest was 64. Six journalists had more than 20 years of experience, while another six had worked in the industry for less than 10 years. Nine of the respondents were women and 11 were men. Men had generally been in journalism for longer. Interviewees were highly educated, with 13 journalists holding at least a Bachelor's degree from a New Zealand university, while five others had a diploma or certificate from a polytechnic. Only two journalists did not have a degree, but had studied at university for a few years. Typically, journalists had studied courses in Māori language and development as well as journalism/media studies. At least half had studied journalism or media studies.

The analysis sections addressed the intent of Māori journalists to revitalize the Māori language and showcased the ways in which their cultural heritage and its emphasis on dignity and integrity impacts their relationships with sources and their journalistic reportage. Please note how the examples from the interviews were used to reinforce key points. The quotes were not left to stand by themselves; instead, Hanusch evaluated and analyzed the information and placed it into its proper cultural context.

Results and Discussion

Māori culture can perhaps best be described through the prism of *tikanga* Māori, which is on a very basic legal level defined as "Māori customary values and practices" (Mead, 2003, p. 11). At the same time, Mead (2003, p. 12) argues that the concept of *tikanga* is more than that and defines it as "the set of beliefs associated with practices and procedures to be followed in conducting the affairs of a group or an individual". *Tikanga*, which can vary widely in terms of scale, governing large ceremonies to small individual actions, can help organise social behaviour and guide people on how to act in certain circumstances. "They provide templates and frameworks to guide our actions and help steer us through some huge gatherings of people and some tense moments in our ceremonial life. They help us differentiate between right and wrong in everything we do and in all of the activities that we engage in" (Mead, 2003, p. 12). While many aspects of *tikanga* are the same throughout the country, there is also a significant degree of variation between the different *iwi* which reside in the country, making it necessary in most cases to refer to the *tikanga* of the local people (Mead, 2003, p. 8).

Tikanga still play an extremely important role in Māori society today, and it was very quickly clear that, for the vast majority of journalists interviewed for this study, they were a crucial consideration in their personal as well as professional behaviour. All were committed to their role in revitalising the Māori language and culture more broadly, and many of the younger journalists had been educated at the total immersion schools which have existed in Aotearoa New Zealand since the early 1980s. Many of the older journalists were sending their children to these schools. Almost every journalist noted that they lived by *tikanga* and while this was often not a conscious process, it was nevertheless ingrained in them through their upbringing, giving them a strong connection to their culture. As one Māori TV journalist said: "I am a Māori, I cannot have *tikanga* not be a part of my life." She cited examples such as not wearing shoes in the house, not sitting on tables or playing with food, and not putting a hairbrush on the table as expressions of her living by *tikanga* Māori in a very practical sense.

When asked about cultural influences in general, all journalists acknowledged that their particular cultural values shaped what they did in their job. In fact, it was extremely difficult, if not impossible, for them to separate their values from their work. A Māori TV journalist thought that journalists, particularly at a station like Māori TV, even had a responsibility to show these values in action, and more broadly assist in the maintenance of culture. "It is important for us to be seen to be—as much as we can be—applying *tikanga* in what we do. Because television being a platform that engages so many people and that has the ability to bring in so many people to watch it—if we're not doing it, why would anyone else bother?" Examples of adherence to *tikanga* included going through incantations or traditional welcoming ceremonies before interviewing sources. One Radio Waatea journalist also noted the importance of humility for Māori. He said while most people answered the question of what was most important with "*he tangata, he tangata, he tangata*" ("it is people, it is people, it is people"), an elderly lady had told him she thought it was actually "*me tū whakaiti*" ("make yourself small"). "That's a metaphor for humility. If you got humility, you, your descendants, your family will never get hurt. You'll go through life and you'll never get hurt . . . so those sort of things can permeate down to the year 2011 and actually in some small way be seen in the way you write your stories."

Journalists' responses thus show a close link between personal and professional values, which demonstrates the way in which culture and cultural values can be important influences on journalistic culture more broadly.

Journalism and *Manaakitanga*

A much-noted principle for both personal and professional behaviour was *manaakitanga*, which can be defined as "nurturing relationships, looking after people, and being very careful about how others are treated" (Mead, 2003, p. 29)—an important characteristic of a collectivist culture. All journalists also expressed a strong commitment to passing these values on to their children. *Manaakitanga* is a particularly important value in dealing with other people, as it applies even in cases of conflict. As Mead (2003, p. 29) points out, "it cannot be stressed enough that *manaakitanga* is always important no matter what the circumstances might be". The interviewed journalists repeatedly highlighted that it was important to respect their sources and, in a way, care for them so they would be represented accurately in their stories. They did not see a need to be particularly confrontational in their approach to get stories.

Journalists said they felt it was their responsibility to provide their sources with a certain level of protection when reporting controversial stories, and it was important to treat stories and sources with dignity and integrity. A TVNZ journalist explicitly said she cared for her sources: "I think my approach to story-telling is Māori, so it's *kaupapa* Māori [a philosophical doctrine, incorporating the knowledge, skills, attitudes and values of Māori society]. I treat my talent—and the way I treat the story, is in a *kaupapa* Māori context. So it's about caring about the subject, about our talent, about the end result." A colleague at the same programme pointed out that he thought sources felt safe with them. "I think we get more access to our people, because they feel safe with us. And they feel comfortable with us that we will tell their story from their perspective and how they want to tell it."

The respect that journalists generally accord their sources also allows them to gain better access to sources. A young Māori TV journalist thought that sources were more open to them because "we haven't hounded them, or not listened to them". This respect also extends to people who journalists might have a personal dislike for. As one Māori TV journalist pointed out:

> We have a view that everyone's got a brother, everyone's got a sister, everyone's got a daughter, everyone's got a mother, and everyone therefore has mana [a supernatural force in a person, place or object, which can equate somewhat to prestige, power, charisma or authority]. You can't disrespect someone's mana. I mean, Don Brash [a controversial politician known for conservative views and who has been very critical of Māori], personally, I might have an issue with. But you can't go out there and "have him". You've got to bring him in, you got to treat him like you treat everyone else, and I think, people, Māori generally, don't like the idea of . . . going at them just for the sake of going at them, because that's not how we do it.

Such comments resonate with the earlier discussed evidence from studies that pointed to the importance of collectivist values in the journalism of a number of Asian and African countries. Māori culture places a high degree of importance on collectivist values, aligning it with other collectivist cultures identified by Hofstede (2001) as well as cultures characterised by values such as embeddedness and hierarchy (Schwartz, 2004).

Reporting on *Marae* and *Hui*

Existing studies have focused on the way in which Māori journalists report on events at *marae* (traditional meeting grounds) and *hui* (meetings) in showing differences in journalistic practice. Even after more than 200 years of European settlement in Aotearoa New Zealand, *marae* form the cultural centre of Māori life (Mead, 2003, p. 216). Here, elaborate *hui* are held, in accordance with various rules that govern their procedure. As sites of public deliberation among Māori, they also form important news sources for journalists, for whom it is extremely important to be fluent in protocol to avoid upsetting those who are gathered. As such, *hui* have been sources of much frustration for mainstream journalists who have failed to follow the rules, either out of ignorance or wilful disobedience.

Yet, for Māori journalists, it is much easier to adhere to the rules that are set on *marae*. Journalists interviewed for this study spoke at length about the importance of first going through the appropriate protocols when entering *marae*, such as participating in *pōhiri* (welcome ceremonies). While this can be a tedious process, it is considered crucial. Said one Māori TV journalist with more than 20 years of experience:

> As journalists we need to go through that process as well. We started to skirt them because it takes so bloody long, so that by the time you got your story, you almost missed your deadline. But I think there is a way to be able to do it with respect, with dignity; and not be too much of a journalist where you ignore all those things.

Most journalists said they would adhere to the rules, because at the end of the day, conduct on *marae* was just like at parliament, as one experienced journalist pointed out: "They have *tikanga* down there, which sometimes restricts you as a journalist. Where you can film, where you can't film; who you can access, who you can't access; but you as a journalist have to make good decisions and find the best way to get the story done. And that's what you have to do on a *marae* as well." Nevertheless, as a number of journalists pointed out, this did not necessarily prevent them from getting a story, and the fact they were Māori meant they could often get better access or move more freely on *marae*, due to their better understanding of the rules. At the same time, different *iwi* have varying *tikanga* at *hui*, and journalists noted it was important to adhere to the local *tikanga* wherever they went. This is an important aspect which also demonstrates that Māori culture is not monolithic and varies between different *iwi*, as well as social groupings, further complicating cultural influences.

The Influence of Language

Māori media play a crucial role in revitalising the Māori language, a function ascribed to broadcast media through government funding. A large number of the respondents said they entered journalism because of the opportunity this gave them to contribute to increased use of the language. Language and culture are intertwined inextricably, and many journalists noted the way in which using their own language allowed them to express themselves in a culture-specific way. As discussed previously, early newspapers adopted and adapted Māori language to the new circumstances, and this has continued into the modern day (Adds et al., 2005; Harawira, 2008; McRae, 2002). Most respondents argued that the ability to use the Māori language provided them with poetic licence, which conveyed more emotion and beauty. A TVNZ journalist said she particularly liked using it in "feel good" stories, "because there are so many proverbial sayings that you could use. Māori is so metaphoric and it's a waste if you don't use it." A Māori TV journalist also thought using the language allowed journalists to make reference to the way in which their ancestors used to think and operate.

In this regard, one experienced journalist related a story he had produced 25 years ago, which here serves to express the essence of the way in which journalists can tell stories differently in Māori and use cultural context. The journalist had travelled to the anniversary of the 1886 eruption of Mt Tarawera, during which more than 400 people had been killed. He travelled there by plane with a mainstream journalist, sharing a camera crew. When they arrived at the lake, the mountain was shrouded in mist and the journalists were stranded because the plane could not take off again in the conditions. The mainstream journalist was upset at the weather, arguing he was not able to report the story because one could not see anything. But for the Māori journalist, this was a unique opportunity:

> You see, to us, fog or mist is a very sacred thing. And there were lots of stories you could tell around mist. When mist covers the mountain, there are stories around that. So when he [the mainstream journalist] went away, I said to the cameraman: "No, no, we're going to tell the story, this is a great story". We call it *tohu*—I don't know what it is in English; a sign, I suppose. And it was like it was being cloaked in grief. That mist cloaked the whole mountain, that one day 100 years ago when we lost over 400 people. So my story was focussed like that . . . Those are just some of the things that you can do, because it's not just the language, but what the language does is—it allows you to bring the whole cultural perspective.

Culture as a Limiting Factor

The fact that culture and cultural values play such an important role in affecting journalists' practices also means that culture is a limiting influence on journalism. Because Māori society is relatively small, and journalists are often closely connected to their *iwi*, they are confronted with an ethical dilemma when covering controversial stories about their own community. Māori journalists are well-embedded in their communities and often need to take account of their obligations to family members in this collectivist culture. This can clash with journalistic declarations of wanting to be a watchdog on Māori leaders. In Māori culture, elders command utmost respect from those who are younger, which creates difficulties especially for junior journalists. A number of respondents pointed out that their job was made more difficult because they were part of their communities, which meant they needed to be able to go back to their *iwi* even after having covered controversial stories about them. Here, attitudes were somewhat divided, in that some journalists argued they would always be able to cover controversial stories about their own *iwi*, while others deemed it a conflict of interest and it was better to have someone else do a particular story. This demonstrates how culture is also a limitation in journalism, and points to the cultural coercion Cohen (1974, p. 85) notes when he argues that "the constraints that culture exerts on the individual come ultimately not from the culture itself, but from the collectivity of the group".

A number of journalists noted there was often pressure from elders or Māori politicians on Māori journalists, expecting positive treatment. A Māori TV journalist said politicians often felt a sense of entitlement about their work. "So if you're a Māori journalist, you are expected to only do nice stories about Māori politicians. You're not allowed to ask them hard questions or scrutinise them or hold them to account, because you're Māori." Another colleague mentioned the fact that she was a woman also sometimes made her work harder, noting it was "a man's world in Māori". However, a fellow Māori TV journalist said elders sometimes simply avoided the question rather than telling journalists they could not ask certain questions, or that they were not allowed to interview them because they were female. In addition, a number of the younger journalists interviewed for this study saw their primary purpose as aiding the revitalisation of the Māori language, rather than being a watchdog. For those journalists, it could be argued that playing an oppositional role towards those in power would be even more difficult.

A senior TVNZ journalist said one problem for younger journalists was the hierarchy in Māori society. "It goes back to Māori belief that the older you are, the more right you have to speak. So obviously the younger you are the less right you have to speak, let alone ask me questions." Thus, older journalists found it certainly easier to criticise others, with a Radio Waatea journalist mentioning the fact that older journalists had been criticizing those in power probably all their lives because they were of the same generation. On the other hand, he knew to expect mainly propaganda pieces from some of the junior reporters because they were so close to their tribe and may not want to offend their uncle. He said some journalists did not want to compromise their families and tribes, and that was fine. "We understand that because we know how the Māori world works."

The conclusion below took the analysis to an interpretive level, addressing insights regarding how Māori culture influences journalism as well as assessing restrictions Māori journalists face due to the social structure and values of Māori society. Hanusch suggested that his findings resonated with other research that has addressed the differences between individualist and collectivist cultures and maintained that cultural values should be evaluated along with economic, political and structural issues within journalism.

Conclusion

While often acknowledged implicitly, the role culture and cultural values play in shaping journalists' professional views and practices has still only rarely gained detailed consideration. Yet, as this study of Māori journalists has shown, paying close attention to these social systems-level influences on news work can provide us with rich insight into the ways in which culture shapes journalistic work. The journalists interviewed for this study displayed an acute awareness of their own culture, and the need for them to be both true to that culture as well as the professional demands of journalism. As a result, a kind of journalism is practised that is unique to the cultural context of Māori, with particular emphasis on aspects such as showing respect to others, following cultural protocols, and making use of culturally-specific language. At the same time, journalists are restricted by these very same values and the social structure of Māori society.

There is of course a political motivation for some of this, as demonstrated by Māori Television's stated aim of contributing to the revitalisation of Māori language and culture. But it is arguably also a more natural way of practising journalism for Māori journalists, and in many ways a subconscious influence. Many of the findings here resonate with the previously discussed literature on cultural values in journalism, in particular as it relates to differences between individualist and collectivist cultures. In identifying and focusing on those cultural values that play a crucial role in Māori journalism, this analysis also identifies strategies for conducting similar analyses in other contexts, be their focus Indigenous, alternative or mainstream in nature. Culture—and cultural values more specifically—provide a key prism through which to analyse journalism. The way these values operate is often difficult to ascertain, and a comparative view is crucial to establish some of the different approaches. In the case discussed in this paper, the difference was in Indigenous values *vis-à-vis* mainstream (Western news) values within one country. This, in addition to the experience of having their own culture colonised, may have made Māori journalists more aware of their own culture and arguably more likely to use their own culture strategically to differentiate their journalism from mainstream. This is less likely to be the case in cross-national comparisons, where culture may be a much less visible and especially less articulated influence, making it harder to ascertain these influences.

It may be argued that the focus of this paper has been culture-centric, and political and economic influences are ignored or underestimated. This is far from the author's intention, and in fact it is important to point out here that political and economic considerations play a crucial role also in Māori journalism, as the respondents in this study indicated. These have been outlined elsewhere (Hanusch, 2013a). Māori journalists operate very much with political goals—such as the view to balancing negative coverage in mainstream media and contributing to a sense of empowerment for their people. Economic considerations, such as limited state funding, also influence Māori journalism to a great extent. Indeed, it has been argued that there are various dimensions in Indigenous journalism that interplay with each other, such as language advocacy, cultural identity and political activism (Grixti, 2011). Culture and cultural values which guide journalists' behaviour come naturally into this mix, and it is important to see them as such—as one part of a larger, more complex mix of influences.

Further, this paper does not propose to argue that one approach—Māori or Western—is the better approach to journalism. The aim is merely to show how different cultures may have different values that influence the way they practise their journalism, rather than passing judgement about the relative value of any one approach. Cultures and cultural values change over time (Inglehart, 1997) and the relatively long history of the coexistence of Indigenous and Western journalism approaches in Aotearoa New Zealand would suggest there have been influences in both directions. The modern-day success of Māori Television's Native Affairs programme, for example, demonstrates that the Māori approach to current affairs is successful with non-Indigenous audiences, and may well be influencing broader New Zealand journalism culture. For instance, there has been a trend for some years now for mainstream journalism to properly pronounce Māori place names and to improve behaviour at *hui*. Such developments demonstrate the complexity in researching the influence of culture and cultural values on journalism.

There are some limitations to this study, of course. Firstly, the relatively small sample only allowed for the exploration of general themes as they relate to cultural influences. Other aspects, such as social or age group membership may additionally influence journalistic practice, yet analysis of these was beyond the scope of this paper. Further, as with any interviews-based study, what journalists say they do may not always actually be what they do. At the same time, much of the evidence provided by the journalists interviewed here aligns with the existing literature on Māori journalism. It would nevertheless appear important to examine the news produced by these journalists in further detail to triangulate some of the evidence discussed here. This also applies to further generalisations and studies of national values and their influence on news-making. Meanwhile, it is hoped that this study can help inspire similar studies which focus on the influence of culture and cultural values on journalism. One particularly fruitful area may lie in comparative journalism and communication studies. As discussed early in this paper, most of the evidence in this area has come from comparative studies in showing potential cultural factors in differences in journalistic practice. Taking cultural value systems into account may thus help expand journalism studies, opening up added complexity for the study of journalistic culture.

Interviewing Exercises

1. Interview someone you know, face to face, for thirty minutes on a topic of your choice. Before the interview, construct a list of questions that you plan to ask. During the interview, be sure to ask all of the questions on your list. You may also ask follow-up questions based on your respondent's commentary. After the interview, discuss the interview process. Be sure to comment on your comfort level during the interview as well as what you learned from the conversation. Were there questions you wanted to ask but didn't? Did you find the list of questions helpful or hindering?
2. Repeat the interview outlined in the first exercise but this time choose someone you are not familiar with. After the interview, please comment on the challenges of interviewing someone you don't know. How would background information have helped you prepare for the interview? Compare your experiences during this interview with those during the previous interview.
3. Interview someone about his or her work history. The interview should last between thirty and sixty minutes. In advance of the interview, outline a series of topic areas or open-ended questions to ask during your interview. Be sure to do some background research to help you frame your interview questions. After the interview is complete, comment on your comfort level during the interview as well as what you learned from the conversation. Compare this interview with one of your previous interviews. Did you find it more comfortable to conduct an interview with a set of predetermined questions or did you prefer the more open-ended approach?

References

Adds, Peter, Bennett, Maia, Hall, Meegan, Kernot, Bernard, Russell, Marie, and Walker, Tai. (2005). *The portrayal of Maori and te Ao Maori in broadcasting. The foreshore and seabed issue.* Wellington: New Zealand Broadcasting Standards Authority.
Alia, Valerie. (2009). Outlaws and citizens: Indigenous people and the 'New Media Nation.'" *International Journal of Media and Cultural Politics*, 5 (1&2): 39–54. doi:10.1386/macp.5.1-2.39_1

Alia, Valerie. (2010). *The new media nation: Indigenous peoples and global communication*. New York: Berghahn Books.

Berger, Arthur Asa. (1998). Depth interviews: Favorite singers and recordings. In *Media research techniques* (2nd ed., pp. 55–62). Thousand Oaks, CA: Sage.

Berger, Arthur Asa. (2000). *Media and communication methods: An introduction to qualitative and quantitative approaches*. Thousand Oaks, CA: Sage.

Blankenberg, Ngaire. (1999). In search of real freedom: Ubuntu and the media. *Critical Arts, 13* (2): 42–65. doi:10.1080/02560049985310121

Chang, Li-jing Arthur, and Massey, Brian L. (2010). Work motivation and journalists in Taiwan and the US: An integration of theory and culture. *Asian Journal of Communication, 20* (1): 51–68. doi:10.1080/01292980903440814

Cohen, Abner. (1974). *Two-dimensional man: An essay on the anthropology of power and symbolism in complex society*. Berkeley: University of California Press.

Curnow, Jenifer. (2002). A brief history of Maori-language newspapers. In *Rere atu, taku manu*, edited by Jenifer Curnow, Ngapare K. Hopa, and Jane McRae (pp. 17–41). Auckland: Auckland University Press.

Drabble, Laurie, Trocki, Karen, Salcedo, Brenda, Walker, Patricia, and Korcha, Rachael. (2016). Conducting qualitative interviews by telephone: Lessons learned from a study of alcohol use among sexual minority and heterosexual women. *Qualitative Social Work, 15* (1): 118–133.

Entman, Robert, and Andrew Rojecki. (2000). *The Black image in the White mind: Media and race in America*. Chicago: University of Chicago Press.

Fontana, Andrea. (2002). Postmodern trends in interviewing. In Jaber F. Gubrium and James A. Holstein (Eds.), *Handbook of interview research: Context and method* (pp. 161–180). Thousand Oaks, CA: Sage.

Fontana, Andrea, and Frey, James H. (1994). Interviewing: The art of science. In Norman K. Denzin and Yvonna S. Lincoln (Eds.), *Handbook of qualitative research* (pp. 361–376). Thousand Oaks, CA: Sage.

Fourie, Pieter J. (2008). Ubuntuism as a framework for South African media practice and performance: Can it work? *Communicatio: South African Journal for Communication Theory and Research, 34* (1): 53–79.

Fox, Derek. (1992). The Maori perspective of the news. In M. Comrie and J. McGregor (Eds.), *Whose News?* (pp. 170–180). Palmerston North: Dunmore Press.

Fox, Derek. (1993). Honouring the treaty: Indigenous television in Aotearoa. In T. Dowmut (Ed.), *Channels of resistance: Global television and local empowerment* (pp. 126–137). London: BFI.

Geertz, Clifford. (1973). *The interpretation of cultures: Selected essays*. New York: Basic Books.

Grixti, Joe. (2011). Indigenous media values: Cultural and ethical implications. In Robert S. Fortner and P. Mark Fackler (Eds.), *The handbook of global communication and media ethics* (pp. 342–363). Malden: Blackwell.

Gubrium, Jaber F., and Holstein, James A. (Eds.). (2002a). *Handbook of interview research: Context and method*. Thousand Oaks, CA: Sage.

Gubrium, Jaber F., and Holstein, James A. (2002b). From the individual interview to the interview society. In Jaber A. Gubrium and James A. Holstein (Eds.), *Handbook of interview research: Context and method* (pp. 103–119). Thousand Oaks, CA: Sage.

Hall, Stuart. 1989. Ideology. In Erik Barnouw (Ed.), *International encyclopedia of communication* (pp. 307–311). New York: Oxford Press.

Hallin, Daniel C., and Mancini, Paolo. (2004). *Comparing media systems: Three models of media and politics*. Cambridge: Cambridge University Press.

Hanitzsch, Thomas. (2007). Deconstructing journalism culture: Towards a universal theory. *Communication Theory, 17* (4): 367–385. doi:10.1111/j.1468-2885.2007.00303.x

Hanusch, Folker. (2009). A product of their culture: Using a value systems approach to understand the work practices of journalists. *International Communication Gazette, 71* (7): 613–626. doi:10.1177/1748048509341895

Hanusch, Folker. (2012). The visibility of disaster deaths in news images: A comparison of newspapers from 15 countries. *International Communications Gazette, 74* (7): 655–672. doi:10.1177/1748048512458560

Hanusch, Folker. (2013a). Dimensions of indigenous journalism culture: Exploring Māori news-making in Aotearoa New Zealand. *Journalism: Theory, practice and criticism* (pp. 951–967). doi:10.1177/1464884913495757

Hanusch, Folker. (2013b). Charting a theoretical framework for examining indigenous journalism culture. *Media International Australia, 149*: 82–91.

Harawira, Wena. (2008, April 16–18). *Challenges facing indigenous broadcasters.* Paper presented at the Pacific Media Summit, Apia.

Hofstede, Geert. (2001). *Culture's consequences: Comparing values, behaviors, institutions, and organizations across nations* (2nd ed.). London: Sage.

Inglehart, Ronald. (1997). *Modernization and postmodernization: Cultural, economic and political change in 43 societies.* Princeton, NJ: Princeton University Press.

Johnson, John M. (2002). In-depth interviewing. In Jaber F. Gubrium and James H. Holstein (Eds.), *Handbook of interview research: Context and method* (pp. 3–32). Thousand Oaks, CA: Sage.

Ka'ai-Mahuta, Rachael Te Awhina. (2010). He kupu tuku iho mō tēnei reanga: A critical analysis of *waiata* and *haka* as commentaries and archives of Māori political history. PhD diss., Auckland University of Technology.

Kanayama, Tomoko, and Anne Cooper-Chen. (2005). Hofstede's masculinity/femininity dimension and the pregnancy of Princess Masako: An analysis of Japanese and international newspaper coverage. *Keio Communication Review, 27*: 23–42.

Kasoma, Francis. (1996). The foundations of African ethics (Afriethics) and the professional practice of journalism: The case for society-centred media morality. *Africa Media Review, 10* (3): 93–116.

Kim, Yung Soo, and Kelly, James D. (2008). A matter of culture: A comparative study of photojournalism in American and Korean newspapers. *International Communication Gazette, 70* (2): 155–173. doi:10.1177/1748048507086910

Kunelius, Risto. (2006). Good journalism: On the evaluation criteria of some interested and experienced actors. *Journalism Studies, 7* (5): 671–690.

Kvale, Steinar. (1996). *Interviews: An introduction to qualitative research interviewing.* Thousand Oaks, CA: Sage.

Liebling, Abbott Joseph. (1963). *The most of A. J. Liebling.* New York: Simon & Schuster.

Littlefied, Daniel F., and Parins, James W. (1984). *American Indian and Alaska native newspapers and periodicals, 1826–1924.* Westport, CT: Greenwood Press.

Loew, Patty, and Mella, Kelly. (2005). Black ink and the new red power: Native American newspapers and tribal sovereignty. *Journalism and Communication Monographs, 7* (3): 99–142. doi:10.1177/152263790500700301

Maori Television. (2009). Maori television marks fifth on-air anniversary. *Scoop.* Retrieved July 19, 2013, from www.scoop.co.nz/stories/CU0903/S00362.htm

Massey, Brian L., and Chang, Li-jing Arthur. (2002). Locating Asian values in Asian journalism: A content analysis of Web newspapers. *Journal of Communication, 52* (4): 987–1003. doi:10.1111/j.1460-2466.2002.tb02585.x

McGregor, Judy, and Comrie, Margie. (1995). *Balance and fairness in broadcasting news (1985–1994).* Wellington: New Zealand Broadcasting Standards Authority.

McRae, Jane. (2002). 'E Many, Tena Koe!' 'O Bird, Greetings to you': The oral tradition in newspaper writing. In Jenifer Curnow, Ngapare K. Hopa, and Jane McRae (Eds.), *Rere atu, taku manu! Discovering history, language and politics in the Maori-language newspapers* (pp. 42–59). Auckland: Auckland University Press.

Mead, Hirini Moko. (2003). *Tikanga Māori: Living by Māori Values.* Wellington: Huia.

Meadows, Michael, and Molnar, Helen. (2002). Bridging the gaps: Towards a history of indigenous media in Australia. *Media History, 8* (1): 9–20. doi:10.1080/13688800220134473

Metzler, Ken. (1977). *Creative interviewing: The writer's guide to gathering information by asking questions.* Englewood Cliffs, NJ: Prentice Hall.

Middleton, Julie. (2010). Ka Rangona te Reo: The development of Māori-language television broadcasting in Aotearoa New Zealand. *Te Kaharoa, 3* (1): 146–176.

Molnar, Helen, and Meadows, Michael. (2001). *Songlines to satellites: Indigenous communication in Australia, the South Pacific and Canada.* Annandale, NSW: Pluto Press.

Newcomb, Horace M. (1999). Media institutions: The creation of television drama. In Klaus Bruhn Jensen and Nicholas W. Jankowski (Eds.), *A handbook of qualitative methodologies for mass communication research* (pp. 93–107). London: Routledge.

Oakley, Ann. (1981). Interviewing women: A contradiction in terms. In Helen Roberts (Ed.), *Doing feminist research* (pp. 30–62). London: Routledge & Kegan Paul.

Pietikäinen, Sari. (2008). Broadcasting indigenous voices: Sami minority media production. *European Journal of Communication, 23* (2): 173–191. doi:10.1177/0267323108089221

Rankine, Jenny, Nairn, Raymond, Barnes, Angela, Moewaka, Gregory, Mandi, Kaiwai, Hector, Borell, Belinda, and McCreanor, Tim. (2007). *Media and te tiriti o Waitangi 2007.* Auckland: Kupu Taea.

Ravi, Narasimhan. (2005). Looking beyond flawed journalism: How national interests, patriotism, and cultural values shaped the coverage of the Iraq War. *The Harvard International Journal of Press/Politics, 10* (1): 45–62. doi:10.1177/1081180X05275765

Ravitz, Jessica. (2011, September 14). Dumbest question in the universe. *CNN Living.* Retrieved from http://articles.cnn.com/2011-09-14/living/living_miss-universe-question_1_beauty pageant-miss-universe-pageant-miss-brazil?_s=PM:LIVING

Rokeach, Milton. (1973). *The nature of human values.* New York: Free Press.

Salazar, Juan Francisco. (2003). Articulating an activist imaginary: Internet as counter public sphere in the Mapuche movement. *Media Information Australia, 107*: 19–29.

Santo, Avi. (2004). Nunavut: Inuit television and cultural citizenship. *International Journal of Cultural Studies, 7* (4): 379–397. doi:10.1177/1367877904047860

Schwartz, Shalom H. (2004). Mapping and interpreting cultural differences around the world. In Henk Vinken, Joseph Soeters, and Peter Ester (Eds.), *Comparing cultures: Dimensions of culture in a comparative perspective* (pp. 43–73). Leiden: Brill.

Shoemaker, Pamela, and Vos, Tim P. (2009). *Gatekeeping theory.* New York: Routledge.

Siebert, Fred S., Peterson, Theodore, and Schramm, Wilbur. (1956). *Four theories of the press.* Urbana: University of Illinois Press.

Skloot, Rebecca. (2010). *The immortal life of Henrietta Lacks.* New York: Crown.

Smith, Linda Tuhiwai. (1999). *Decolonizing methodologies: Research and indigenous peoples.* London: Zed Books.

Sontheimer, Morton. (1941). *Newspapermen: A book about the business.* New York: Whittlesey House.

Stuart, Ian. (2002). Maori and mainstream: Towards bicultural reporting. *Pacific Journalism Review, 8* (1): 42–58.

Te Awa, Joanne. (1996). Mana news: A case study. *Sites, 33*: 168–175.

Terkel, Studs. (1992). *Race: How blacks and whites think and feel about the American obsession.* New York: The New Press.

Tomaselli, Keyan G. (2003). 'Our Culture' vs 'Foreign Culture': An essay on ontological and professional issues in African journalism. *Gazette, 65* (6): 427–441.

Waitangi Tribunal. (2013). Introduction. *Waitangi Tribunal.* Retrieved July 19, from www.waitangi-tribunal.govt.nz/about/intro.asp

Walker, Ranginui. (2004). *Ka Whawhai Tonu Matou: Struggle without end.* Auckland: Penguin.

Walters, Barbara. (1970). *How to talk with practically anybody about practically anything.* Garden City, NY: Doubleday.

Warren, Carol A. B. (2002). Qualitative interviewing. In Jaber F. Gubrium and James A. Holstein (Eds.), *Handbook of interview research: Context and method* (pp. 83–102). Thousand Oaks, CA: Sage.

Weaver, David H. (Ed.). (1998). *The global journalist: News people around the world.* Cresskill, NJ: Hampton Press.

Wilson, Pamela, and Stewart, Michelle. (Eds.). (2008). *Global indigenous media: Cultures, poetics, and politics.* Durham: Duke University Press.

Winfield, Betty H., Mizuno, Takeya, and Beaudoin, Christopher E. (2000). Confucianism, collectivism and constitutions: Press systems in China and Japan. *Communication Law and Policy, 5* (3): 323–347. doi:10.1207/S15326926CLP0503_2

Xu, Xiaoge. (2005). *Demystifying asian values in journalism.* Singapore: Marshall Cavendish.

Zhou, Xiang. (2008). Cultural dimensions and framing the Internet in China: A cross-cultural study of newspapers' coverage in Hong Kong, Singapore, the US and UK. *International Communication Gazette, 70* (2): 117–136. doi:10.1177/1748048507086908

CHAPTER **4**

Focus Groups

Qualitative research is a contact sport, requiring some degree of immersion into individuals' lives.
—Stewart, Shamdasani, and Rook (2007, p. 12)

Focus groups are a popular qualitative methodology, often used in political communication, advertising, public relations and marketing research. In fact, focus groups account for about 80 percent of the qualitative market research currently being done (Stewart, Shamdasani, and Rook, 2007). Focus groups are used to provide inexpensive and timely information regarding consumer opinions on products, services, issues and policies, and they are also used to gather insights into voter reactions and behaviors. They can generate new ideas, help researchers understand how people use different services and/or products, and help marketers and advertisers to target consumers effectively. Focus groups are routinely used to identify participants' preferences, attitudes, motivations and beliefs, and they also provide researchers with interviewing flexibility and insights regarding group dynamics that product manufacturers and service providers find particularly useful. Considered a user-friendly and non-threatening research method, which participants find stimulating and enjoyable, focus groups are also used to help people express themselves openly about sensitive issues as well as to "bridge social and cultural differences" (Morgan, 2002, p. 141).

A focus group is a directed conversation among several people regarding a specific topic, issue or concern that is led by a trained moderator who facilitates group discussion. The goal of a focus group is to stimulate discussion in order to determine how people think and act individually and within a social group (Berger, 1998). Focus groups are usually recorded, and while there can be from three to fourteen participants per group, eight to twelve members is considered the optimum size for useful group interaction. Participants are usually chosen on the basis of having similar backgrounds, demographics, behaviors and/or attitudes and are brought together to discuss their opinions, practices, preferences and behaviors. Focus group participants are usually paid a small stipend to cover their time and travel costs, and snacks or a meal is often served during focus group sessions.

Most focus groups are face-to-face conversations. However, sometimes they are held via telephone calls or videoconferencing, or in online chat rooms. When focus groups are held through videoconferencing, participants may gather at one location or they may participate from their homes or offices. Telephone focus groups may be transmitted online to a different city, where some or all observers watch the focus group in real time on video monitors. While some moderators find it difficult to build a working relationship with clients who do not attend each focus group, videoconferencing can save money because observers do not have to travel to different locations in order to observe each focus group.

Focus groups are also held on the Internet through blogs, bulletin boards and video web conferences in chat rooms. Although the use of online focus groups saves money, some researchers find a variety of security and research challenges with Internet focus groups. Stewart, Shamdasani, and Rook (2007) suggested that with Internet focus groups a moderator has less control of the participants and cannot adequately assess non-verbal communication, which may reduce intimacy and spontaneity within the group. Greenbaum (1998) found it difficult to stimulate authentic interaction and positive group dynamics in virtual focus groups, and he was concerned that the security of the information and the authenticity of the participants may be compromised.

However, recent technological changes now provide researchers with the opportunity to use tools such as Adobe Connect, a web-based meeting client, to conduct virtual focus groups online in real time. Such focus groups help researchers to provide additional diversity to their groups and to interact with people who might otherwise be difficult to recruit for in-person focus groups. Participants in virtual focus groups use their own tablets or computers and may log on from a place of their choosing. Researchers have suggested that real-time online focus groups may increase participants' willingness to discuss sensitive topics more fully and comfortably. For example, Woodyatt, Finneran, and Stephenson (2016) compared online real-time focus groups addressing the issue of intimate partner violence with in-person focus groups held with gay and bisexual men. They found that, while both types of focus groups produced excellent information on key themes, the online focus group members discussed sensitive topics more completely and candidly.

The Development of Focus Groups

While coffee klatches and sewing circles have been around for hundreds of years, the first media-related research using focused group interviews considered the persuasive appeals and effects of radio programming on audience members. This early focus group methodology was designed by Paul Lazarsfeld, Robert Merton and their associates in an attempt to understand the effectiveness and likability of radio messages. From 1940 to 1945, Merton and Lazarsfeld held focus groups at the Office of Radio Research at Columbia University to consider audience response to CBS radio programming. Lazarsfeld understood the marketing potential of mass media research and had developed an "administrative research" perspective that envisioned communication research being carried out in service of media industries (Hardt, 1998). During these early focus group sessions, audience members were initially asked to press a red button if they heard anything in the program that angered, annoyed or bored them, or made them react negatively to the show. Participants were instructed to push a green button if they heard something that they agreed with or enjoyed, or if the communication messages encouraged them to react positively. Audience members' responses and the timing of those responses were recorded into a product analyzer, a device similar to those still used in media research today.

After the radio program, participants discussed the strengths and weaknesses of what they had heard with the researchers, who focused discussion on the audience members' reasons for their negative and/or positive responses to the radio program. The goal of the focus groups was to gather information from audience members to understand "the group dynamics that affect individuals' perceptions, information processing, and decision making" (Stewart, Shamdasani, and Rook, 2007, p. 9). In addition, the researchers gathered in-depth information on the participants' listening preferences, attitudes, interests and motivations. During World War II, Merton and his associates used focus groups to help train American soldiers and to develop propaganda films for the army, which were intended to boost soldiers' morale. Ultimately, Lazarsfeld and Merton's focus group approach helped researchers to understand the effectiveness of persuasive media messages.

As was discussed in Chapter 1, after World War II, communication researchers began to emphasize a quantitative social scientific approach that emphasized numerical correlations and quantified objective data. The subjective individual experiences of focus group members, which did not yield statistical information that could be measured, became less useful to media researchers, and focus groups were rarely used in media and communication research during this era. However, by the late 1960s and early 1970s, with the rise of marketing and its emphasis on audience reception studies, focus groups began to become popular again. By the time qualitative research methods became an accepted alternative research strategy, focus groups were a useful method for many types of communication and media studies research.

Contemporary Focus Groups

In contemporary media research, focus groups are regularly used to gather preliminary information, to aid in the development of products and to help researchers understand aspects of consumer behavior. Marketers often use focus groups to gather feedback on services and products and to acquire consumer responses to business venues, advertising campaigns, branding and prices. Marketers particularly value the associations and connections that participants make using their own descriptions, and they also consider their direct interaction with consumers as the most compelling aspect of focus groups (Stewart, Shamdasani, and Rook, 2007). Qualitative researchers often find focus groups appropriate for generating research questions, collecting general information about an issue or topic and identifying overarching themes and conceptual frameworks. Scholars often conduct focus groups as a preliminary research step that is later combined with at least one other qualitative or quantitative method.

More recently, qualitative researchers have used focus groups as a primary research methodology. For example, feminist researchers use focused group conversations to "provide women with safe space to talk about their own lives and struggles" (Kamberelis and Dimitriadis, 2008, p. 383), as well as to help raise women's political consciousness and empower them to reclaim their lives.

Focus groups have played a pivotal role in contemporary political campaigns and have been used to gain feedback about candidates and their platform positions. For example, during the 2004 US presidential election campaign, public opinion polls repeatedly indicated that John Kerry was leading George W. Bush by a significant margin. However, from the in-depth conversations held in a variety of focus groups, researchers discovered that Kerry was not connecting with many voters, who were uncomfortable about his identity and uncertain about his policies. Although public opinion polls and media pundits repeatedly indicated that Kerry was winning the presidential debates, focus group members still felt they did not know enough about him to vote for him as president (Stewart, Shamdasani, and Rook, 2007). More recently, during the 2016 US presidential election, candidates used focus groups to evaluate campaign issues and concerns and to connect with and understand key constituencies in battleground states. For example, this chapter's research example is based on eight focus groups conducted with young voters in order to understand the influence of celebrity voter appeals that appeared on social media (Nisbett and DeWalt, 2016).

In general, focus groups that address consumer attitudes or behavior are usually run by a trained moderator and are held in a research facility that includes a one-way mirror and space for researchers or clients to watch each session. When clients watch focus groups they are often in direct contact with the moderator, communicating through an electronic earpiece or new media technology, or updating the moderator during quick briefings held while the focus groups are being run. Qualitative researchers who use focus groups for more general research purposes, tend to hold them in more casual settings such as at participants' homes, work spaces, conventions and coffee shops, and when clients are involved, they usually sit off to the side in the same room.

The Role of a Moderator

A focus group moderator, who is also known as a facilitator, is a key part of each focus group. An experienced moderator manages the entire research process, conceptualizing the project, designing clear research objectives and presenting the research findings. A moderator provides the client or researcher with methodological guidance, helps craft discussion topics and questions, coordinates with the facility being used for the sessions and provides advice on specific logistical issues such as the geographical location for the sessions, the number and types of groups as well as the mix of participants in each group. Perhaps most importantly, a moderator facilitates the actual group sessions, prompts discussion and manages group dynamics. Successful focus group facilitators should be personable, persuasive and energetic, have excellent listening skills, be organized and flexible, communicate effectively and have a great short-term memory. It is important for focus group moderators to be skillful enough to draw out shy participants and to handle difficult ones while encouraging discussion among all members of the group (Fontana and Frey, 1994).

In the fields of political communication, advertising, public relations and marketing, researchers often hire professional moderators who have considerable experience running focus groups. If you plan to hire a moderator to run your focus groups, you should consider the person a key part of your research team. It is important to draw on his or her experiences throughout the focus group process and to talk openly about your goals for the project. In other media-related fields, many qualitative researchers choose to serve as the facilitator for their own focus groups. Whether you plan to hire a professional moderator or intend to facilitate your own focus groups, it is important to consider several aspects of the moderator's role in the focus group process.

In order for a focus group to be successful, a moderator must be able to gain all of the participants' attention and quickly create a welcoming environment of openness and trust. The facilitator should also control the group dynamics so that everyone can share their experiences and interact effectively in a non-threatening environment. At the outset of each focus group, the moderator takes charge of the session, setting rules and procedures and explaining to the participants the topic under discussion as well as the research goals. Focus group facilitators should notify participants that the session will be recorded and, if applicable, should explain that observers will be watching through a one-way mirror in a separate room. It is also important that moderators explain that their role in the focus group is to facilitate discussion among members of the group rather than to share their personal opinions with the group members.

Facilitators' Communication Strategies

Experienced focus group facilitators have both passive and active listening skills. Passive listening, which is also known as non-reflective listening, encourages participants to talk. When a moderator responds by nodding his or her head, or by replying "mm-hmm" to a focus group member's statement, it illustrates the moderator's interest in what the participant has to say and reinforces a sympathetic and nonthreatening environment.

Active listening, or reflective listening, seeks to clarify what a participant is saying. Fern (2001) found four different active listening responses that can aid the communication process: clarifying responses, paraphrasing responses, reflecting responses and summarizing responses. Using the example of a focus group in which members are discussing the future of news, we can describe these four active listening responses. Clarifying responses encourage the participant to explain what she or he has said. An example of a clarifying response that a moderator might make is: "I don't understand what you mean when you say that newspapers are dead." Paraphrasing responses restate key aspects of what a participant has said in order to make sure that the moderator fully understands what the person intended to say. For example, a facilitator might say: "When you say that newspapers are dead, is it correct that you are talking about printed newspapers because you feel that most people these days get their news online?" Reflecting responses are used to determine the feelings that people have regarding a product, issue or concern rather than focus on the content of the statement. For example, a moderator might say: "You seem to feel sad about what you see as the end of newspapers." Finally, summarizing responses reiterate the key statements and/or feelings of a participant in a focus group. A facilitator might say: "The main point I think you are making is that young people no longer have the newspaper habit and newspapers are finding it increasingly difficult to get new subscribers because so much news is available for free online."

Focus group moderators pose questions that are clear and concise and encourage group discussion. Open-ended questions help participants to discuss a topic or issue rather than to respond with a simple yes or no. Questions such as "What did you think when you first saw the car advertisement?" or "How do you feel women are depicted in the music video?" or "What did you learn from the online breaking news story?" are all examples of open-ended questions appropriate to ask focus group members. Focus group moderators often begin with general icebreaker questions that introduce all of the participants and get the conversation going. After focus group members are comfortable, a facilitator introduces the topic and begins to ask open-ended questions to encourage group participation. Probing questions that add depth to the conversation follow the initial focus group questions. Most moderators end their focus groups with a few concluding questions that are intended to summarize key insights and provide final commentary on the topic or issue. It is important that facilitators avoid asking questions that may put participants on the defensive or make them feel embarrassed about their responses. For more information on framing interview questions, see Chapters 3 and 6.

If we use the example of a product-based focus group with cell phone users about iPhones, a moderator might begin general discussion on the topic with a question such as "What is your initial impression of the new iPhone 7?" Depending on the group members' responses, the facilitator could follow up with some probing questions in order to gain additional information. The moderator might ask group members to explain why they feel a particular way about the iPhone, or to expand on their initial comments about the costs associated with the new iPhone 7, or to clarify their feelings about using an iPhone. Asking follow-up questions based on the participants' comments will provide greater depth to the conversation and can help other members to join in. Moderators should not ask questions that reflect their personal perspectives on a topic. "Don't you just love iPhones?" is an example of the type of question that should be avoided because it illustrates a facilitator's personal opinion and can put pressure on a respondent to reply in a particular way. "I can't believe you don't want to own an iPhone" is also an inappropriate statement for a moderator to make because it singles a participant out and it might put him or her in a defensive position, or it might prevent the moderator from getting honest responses.

Experienced facilitators are aware that their tone of voice and the way they word their questions can significantly impact the way participants will respond (Greenbaum, 2000). For example, in a focus group with teenage girls regarding their use of new media, a moderator might respond to a participant with the declarative sentence, "You don't feel email is a relevant communication tool for teenagers anymore." Such a comment is a neutral response that could be used to make sure the moderator understands what the teenager has said. Now if a facilitator's response is in the form of a question, "You don't feel that email is a relevant communication tool for teenagers anymore?" the moderator is asking the participant to explain why she feels the way she does about email. Responding to a participant's comments with a clarifying question is a good strategy moderators often use to aid discussion within a focus group. However, if a facilitator responds to the participant in a tone that indicates surprise ("You don't feel that email is a relevant communication tool for teenagers anymore!"), a participant might feel that the facilitator does not like her response and she may feel that she has been put on the defensive.

Focus group moderators do their best to remain neutral and are careful about their own body language so that it does not influence the conversation. If they remain interested and engaged in the discussion, chances are the participants will too. Facilitators are also aware of the non-verbal responses of the focus group members. When participants are interested or enthusiastic about a conversation, they often sit toward the front of their chairs, leaning forward as if attempting to get into the action. They often seem alert and enthusiastic and may nod in agreement with other members. However, if a participant sits slumped with folded arms across his or her chest looks up at the ceiling or makes disagreeable facial expressions, it is clear that he or she does not agree with what is being said. An alert facilitator will notice the disagreement and use it to engage the participant in the conversation. If a moderator notices that a group member is yawning frequently, repeatedly looking at his or her watch, or has begun doodling, it is a safe bet that the person is tired or bored and is no longer interested in the discussion. A facilitator might take a break, walk around the room or even tell a joke to get all members refocused on the topic at hand.

Experienced moderators use a variety of techniques to encourage discussion and facilitate group interaction. Moderators often use prototypes for new products, advertising concepts and public service campaigns to get participants' first impressions and reactions to new items and services. Facilitators may show group members photographs of individuals using a specific product and ask them to discuss their feelings about the people shown. In some cases, participants are asked to choose which of several pictures best relates to the topic being discussed. Greenbaum (1998) learned that when participants are asked to make "forced relationships" between a product and types of images, the most commonly used categories "are automobiles, colors, and animals, since these appear to have a specific meaning to virtually all consumers" (p. 127).

For example, if a researcher is attempting to understand the reputation of an advertising agency, a moderator might ask focus group participants to write down the type of animal that they associate with the particular agency and to explain why they chose the animal. Greenbaum suggested that while some people may feel the exercise is silly, he found that it provides a variety of perspectives about the issue or topic being addressed, and the choice of animal ultimately expresses a participant's feelings toward the agency. For Greenbaum, the choice of a bear is usually associated with a friendly, caring organization, while those participants who pick a lion see the organization as being powerful but not friendly. Conversely, a turtle references a slow-moving or backward organization, while the choice of a snake or other reptile or a rodent illustrates unpredictability and distrust regarding an institution.

Recruiting Participants

Since the goal of focus groups is to gather information and understand group dynamics, it is important that all members of a focus group feel comfortable with each other and are open to engaging each other in conversation. One common strategy to help group dynamics is to create similar or homogeneous participant groups for each focus group. Bringing together people from similar backgrounds, perspectives and experiences can help focus group members to click. Depending on the research topic, it may be helpful to choose participants on the basis of age, income, education or occupation. Focus group members are also recruited according to their race and ethnicity, gender, socioeconomic status, religion and physical characteristics, including height, weight and attractiveness.

Most professional focus group firms prefer that all focus group members be strangers because they find that strangers tend to speak more freely than groups of people who know each other. However, some qualitative researchers construct focus groups from established special interest groups, work groups, clubs and organizations because recruitment can be easier and groups of friends can provide important context for the discussions. In some cases, one individual is recruited and then asked to persuade his or her friends or colleagues to participate in the focus groups. Stewart, Shamdasani, and Rook (2007) encouraged researchers recruiting focus group members to also consider the issue of social power and how it may influence group dynamics. Those members with greater status and power based on their occupations, education and experiences or even because of the way they dress may be given special treatment by other participants in the group.

Bloor et al. (2001) maintained that homogeneous focus groups are more effective than heterogeneous groups with members who have diverse backgrounds, social or political views or experiences. Concerned with the dynamic interaction during a focus group, that even an innocuous topic may become unpredictable, damaging or even threatening, they explained that when diverse views and experiences are represented in a focus group, a great degree of conflict may occur which can "crush discussion and inhibit debate" (p. 20). For example, Bloor et al. would not recommend putting pro-choice and pro-life participants together in the same focus group or grouping pro-EU and Brexit supporters together – even when the focus group topic is unrelated to their political views. While group dynamics should be considered when constructing focus groups, it is also important to remember that some diversity of opinion is helpful. Sometimes when the focus group participants are too similar, there may be a lot of head nodding in agreement with what one member says, and a moderator may find it difficult to get enough depth to the conversation.

The number of focus groups conducted for any given research study will vary based on a variety of factors, including the research question, group dynamics, diversity of participants and a researcher's preference for homogeneous or heterogeneous groups. Although some researchers conduct large numbers of focus groups, a 2016 study of focus groups focusing on the health behaviors of African American men found that 90 percent of relevant themes were addressed within three to six focus groups. Guest, Namey, and McKenna (2017) suggested that conducting three to six separate focus groups on a topic was sufficient to identify all key themes in a study and that additional focus groups did not provide greater insights.

I am often asked how to go about finding participants for focus groups. There are a variety of databases available from market research companies, and many clubs, organizations and political interest groups have membership lists that they are willing to share. You can also use social networking sites such as Facebook, Google+, BranchOut and LinkedIn to recruit participants. Online chat rooms and email listservs can also provide you with potential focus group members. There are a multitude of online governmental, political, environmental, educational, social and cultural groups and organizations. For example, a list of US government organizations is available at www.usgovinfo.about.com for a variety of issues, including health care, campaign policy reform, labor, immigration and taxes. There are also Internet clubs for sports enthusiasts, hobbyists and gamers, as well as same-name clubs such as "The Bob Club," an online group started in 2003 that now has more than 3,000 members (thebobclub.com). You can also contact people through text, email and telephone, and of course in person by visiting relevant community agencies and groups, local gyms and recreation centers, schools and businesses. A few years ago, some of my graduate students successfully recruited freshmen for their focus groups by posting flyers in the college recreation center locker rooms promising free pizza and cash prizes for those chosen to participate.

Focus group participants are usually paid anywhere from $50 to $200 to cover their time and expenses, and most focus group sessions also include snacks or a meal. Eight to twelve participants is usually considered the optimum size for a focus group. This is because it is difficult to get good group interaction when there are fewer than six participants, and when the group is larger than twelve, it is often difficult for a moderator to maintain control. Researchers usually recruit a couple of additional people for each session just in case there are people who cancel at the last minute. When recruiting focus group participants, it is important to tell them the research topic and to explain that their active participation in the group discussion is necessary.

Dealing With Difficult Participants

Fresh from her 2011 Emmy win for Outstanding Lead Actress in a Comedy Series, Melissa McCarthy portrayed an overly enthusiastic focus group participant during the October 1 episode of *Saturday Night Live*. As Linda, a focus group member desperate to come up with a new slogan for Hidden Valley Ranch salad dressings, she is loud, obnoxious, disruptive and intent on monopolizing the conversation. Several times during the focus group, Linda shouts out, "There's a Hidden Valley Ranch party in my mouth!" and she repeatedly asks the moderator, "Can you garlic ranch blast me now?" She even yells at another participant, "Shut up, Sue, we all hate you." After Linda begins to chug an entire bottle of salad dressing, which playfully cascades down her face, the frustrated moderator offers her $50 just to leave the group. While the skit is played for laughs, it also points out a variety of participant-related challenges that focus group moderators may encounter.

Moderators sometimes have to deal with a dominant focus group member who tries to control the group in any way he or she can. Such an individual may enthusiastically answer every question before others can respond, may interrupt other participants when they try to speak, or may even lecture other group members as to the correct responses to the questions. An overly enthusiastic focus group member can inhibit discussion and disturb group dynamics. Researchers consider the potential for a focus group member to dominate the conversation one of the primary disadvantages of focus groups. Given the potential for a dominant focus group member to destroy group interaction, it is imperative that a moderator respond to such a person quickly and appropriately.

Greenbaum (2000) suggested that moderators use a variety of writing exercises as well as non-verbal and verbal cues to get all members to participate and to minimize the influence of an overly enthusiastic focus group member. Writing exercises, during which a moderator asks all focus group members to write down their opinions on a particular topic and then share them with the rest of the group, encourage all participants to consider how they personally feel about an issue. For example, a moderator for a focus group discussing press coverage of presidential candidates might ask participants to jot down how they usually learn about a candidate's political platform. The moderator would then go around the room and ask all participants to share with the group what they had written down.

Non-verbal cues, such as looking directly at the dominant person but not calling on him or her to speak or holding up a hand to indicate that someone else is speaking, may also encourage that person not to monopolize the conversation. In addition, facilitators should remind focus group members that they have a responsibility to hear the opinions of each member of the group. Greenbaum (2000) noted that if none of the previous strategies works, a moderator should directly address the dominant group member by saying something such as "Bob, I can tell that you are very passionate about this issue, but we really need to hear how the others feel about it" (p. 148). As in the *Saturday Night Live* focus group skit, occasionally a participant is so difficult to deal with that he or she must be removed from the group. In such a case, it is helpful to work with clients, researchers or professionals at the focus group facility to remove the person from the focus group swiftly so that any negative group dynamics are quickly minimized.

Sometimes a focus group member may feel intimidated or become disinterested in the conversation and stop participating in the discussion. If this happens, the facilitator should remind the group that it is the moderator's job to make sure that everyone participates. If the focus group member still does not talk, the moderator should direct a question to the individual to help him or her become engaged in the discussion. If the participant still does not engage with other members of the group, another strategy is for the facilitator to switch to a writing assignment and follow up by asking all participants what they wrote down.

Ethical Considerations

Informed consent is pivotal to the focus group process. All participants must be told the topic of the study before the focus group begins. They must understand that their role in the group is voluntary and that they are free to answer or not answer any or all of the questions. It is also helpful to remind the participants that they may leave the focus group if they become uncomfortable with the process. When one participant is asked to recruit his or her friends or co-workers for a focus group, the use of informed consent can help participants not to feel guilty or obligated to participate in the session.

The issue of confidentiality is more challenging in focus groups, particularly when a researcher chooses to use people in the group who know each other. If requested, a researcher can change the names of the group members and can also allow participants to review focus group transcripts before the sessions are analyzed and presented. Given the "unpredictability and dynamic nature of focus groups" (Bloor et al., 2001, p. 26), focus group discussions may go in many different ways. A moderator should be alert for any signs of discomfort among focus group members and should take action to maintain an open and comfortable environment. If a focus group member becomes hostile or belligerent, it is important for the facilitator to ask the person to leave the session so that the group dynamics are not negatively impacted.

As I mentioned earlier, most individuals receive payment to cover their time and travel expenses when they participate in a focus group. Apart from focus groups, qualitative researchers rarely pay people to participate in their research. While most advertising, public relations, political communication and marketing researchers support paying focus group participants, other academic researchers remain concerned about the implications of paying for participation. They worry that if money is the basis for participation, a study may be "susceptible to manipulation and dishonesty" (Lindlof and Taylor, 2011, p. 104). Other researchers wonder about bringing together a group of strangers to talk about issues, and they suggest that focus group conversations are less natural than other types of interviews. Yet, Morgan (2002) suggested that since all methods are shaped by specific historical and social contexts, a researcher's familiarity with traditional interview techniques might influence his or her response to focus group interviews.

The Focus Group Process
Set research objectives and budget
Choose moderator
Determine criteria for participants
Set location, number of groups
Design interview questions
Recruit focus group members
Hold focus groups
Evaluate focus groups
Present findings

If you wish to use focus groups as a research method, you should begin by determining the research objectives, goals and potential research question for your study. You will need to consider the use of a professional facilitator for the focus groups. If you plan to hire a moderator, it is important to pick one at the beginning of the research process so that you are able to work with the person throughout your research project. You will also want to decide on the criteria that will be used to choose participants, and set a budget for the research project. In addition, you will want to determine the number of sessions that will be held, the geographic location for the sessions and the facility or place where the groups will be held. Quirk's Marketing Research Review (available online at www.quirks.com/direc tory/index.aspx) offers an international directory of market research companies that can help you to identify professional facilities and services, as does Greenbook: The Guide for Buyers of Marketing Research (accessed online at www.greenbook.org).

Because environmental factors may influence a focus group's dynamics, you will want to consider the size and composition of the room when choosing a facility for your focus groups. It is helpful to have a space that is large enough for all participants to sit comfortably around a table so that they can all see each other. Professional focus group facilities tend to be centrally located in popular places such as shopping malls or airports. They generally

include state-of-the-art technology, rooms with one-way mirrors and a separate space for client-observers. If you plan to conduct your focus groups
in a more natural environment, you should make sure the space is large
enough for all members to sit comfortably and that there is a separate space
for observers so that the participants do not feel they are being watched.

After these initial decisions have been made, you will work with your
facilitator to construct interview questions and topic areas for the focus
groups. Moderators should also be given the flexibility to ask follow-up
questions and to revise or change any existing questions during the sessions.

The recruitment and selection of appropriate focus group members is
crucial to the success of your focus groups. You will want to match your
participants to your research objectives. While some marketing studies
may only require focus group participants to have general knowledge or
interest in a product, other research studies may require specific demographic characteristics. For example, for the study "US Teenagers' Perceptions and Awareness of Digital Technology: A Focus Group Approach,"
because the authors were specifically interested in young people's opinions, they recruited eighty middle-school and high-school students for
their focus groups. Their initial plan was to compare the views of students living on the West Coast with those of students on the East Coast,
because they presumed that the locations alone would provide socioeconomic and ethnic diversity. However, they discovered that while the focus
group members from the two locations were ethnically diverse, students
from both regions were equally economically disadvantaged (Hundley
and Shyles, 2010).

During each focus group session you will observe that the moderator
poses questions to the participants in order to keep the conversation flowing. Focus groups are group discussions rather than group interviews; the
moderator asks questions to facilitate the group dynamics and he or she
uses a variety of strategies to encourage group members to fully interact
with each other (Wilkinson, 2011). If you plan to serve as the facilitator for
your focus groups, your topics and questions should be flexible enough to
allow you to engage participants and encourage them to fully explore the
issues and topics.

The evaluation of the focus group sessions varies, depending on the
types of focus groups being held as well as on the researchers' goals for
the research. In public relations, political communication and marketing
research, as well as in other areas in which a professional moderator is used
and clients usually observe the sessions, the evaluation of the focus groups
is done by the moderator and presented to the client. The evaluation is
based on the client's needs, and a moderator may craft a written report
about the focus groups, or he or she may give an oral presentation to the

client. Some moderators meet with clients or researchers immediately after the focus group is finished. Such a strategy allows the moderator to discuss any problems or concerns he or she has with the process, as well as to share initial observations about the group. Post-group discussions between the client and the moderator may also help the research project to evolve and may result in changes to the questions asked to future focus group participants (Greenbaum, 1998).

Academic researchers who use focus groups usually transcribe the audio and/or video recordings of the sessions and then conduct a textual analysis of the focus group transcripts. For more information on textual analysis, see Chapter 8. If you plan to transcribe your focus group sessions, I recommend that you ask the moderator to introduce each participant by name at the beginning of each session. It is helpful for the moderator also to use participants' names whenever possible during the sessions. This is a strategy that will help to personalize the conversation and aid you with the transcription process. You should transcribe all conversation that occurs during the focus group sessions. As Bloor et al. (2001) explained, "[T]he transcript needs to reproduce as near as possible the group as it happened, so that anyone reading the transcript can really 'see' how the group went" (p. 61).

Focus Group Research

At the most basic level the focus group transcript provides information for researchers to use in research reports and presentations. Some focus group analyses are descriptive in nature, summarizing the discussion, while others are analytical, identifying key themes, synthesizing information and interpreting key issues and concepts (Fern, 2001). The following research, "Exploring the Influence of Celebrities in Politics: A Focus Group Study of Young Voters" by Gwendelyn S. Nisbett and Christina Childs DeWalt, illustrated an analytical analysis of focus group research. Note how the final two paragraphs of the introduction described the intention and research goals for the study.

"Exploring the Influence of Celebrities in Politics: A Focus Group Study of Young Voters," by Gwendelyn S. Nisbetta and Christina Childs DeWalt

From *Atlantic Journal of Communication*, 24 (3) 2016, 144–156

Introduction

From presidential campaigns to social awareness crusades, celebrities have increasingly become central fixtures in many contemporary political and social platforms. Big celebrities advocate on behalf of political candidates, policy initiatives, and social activism. Although mixing celebrity and politics is not a new phenomenon, strategically utilizing celebrity influence is increasingly used to target young people. Many of the campaigns are geared toward increasing civic engagement and voting.

Youth get out the vote campaigns have been around for the past few decades—Rock the Vote is an example from the 1990s. However, the collision of social media and celebrity involvement is creating more and more examples of celebrity appeals to young voters. In 2004 and again in 2008, two political campaigns geared toward mobilizing the youth vote emerged: Vote or Die and Declare Yourself. Moreover, other celebrities created social media fueled vote campaigns, like Sarah Silverman's Great Schlep (in 2008) and Samuel L. Jackson's Wake the F*ck Up (in 2012). Snyder (2003) argued that "celebrity permeates all aspects of contemporary American culture: celebrities' presence expresses a defining characteristic of our time" (p. 441). It is not a far-fetched notion to conclude that some young people are turning to film stars and music icons to form and direct their political and social ideologies.

The campaigns are clever and catchy, using flashy media and sex appeal, and enlist the help of some of the biggest celebrities. The campaigns receive coverage from the media and a lot of Internet traffic, Twitter retweets, Tumblr posts, and Facebook likes. But do they really work? Is a comedic shtick and famous face all you need to increase youth civic engagement?

Celebrity political engagement may be considered unconventional or even silly. Certainly there are critics who regard celebrity political speech as mind-numbingly lowbrow (Babcock and Whitehouse, 2005; Weiskel, 2005) and thus potentially harmful to our ability to engage critical rational discourse. Celebrity engagement may even be more beneficial to celebrities and their reputation management (Brockington and Henson, 2015) than it is a benefit and inspiration for people to engage in public civic life (Markham, 2015). Still others have praised the use of celebrity political speech, arguing that it allows for a different type of civic engagement (Street, 2004; Wheeler, 2012) and inspires critical discourse (Goodnight, 2005). Celebrity political speech, even by minor or issue-specific celebrities, has the potential to capture and guide attention to issues or civic engagement movements that would otherwise be ignored (Tufekci, 2013). Moreover, others have argued that celebrity politics is here to stay and it is an important factor of modern politics (Meyer and Gamson, 1995; Street, 2012).

Proponents of celebrity campaigns argue that a key to the resurgence in young voter engagement is due in part to efforts made by campaigns to mobilize them. For instance, Citizen Change, a foundation created by music mogul Sean "P. Diddy" Combs, launched the Vote or Die campaign in 2004 to directly target young voters. Although it is hard to quantify the direct influence of Vote or Die and Rock the Vote with celebrities like Ben Affleck leading the way, the increased use and increased connection between celebrity and youth voter is hard to ignore (Payne, Hanlon, and Twomey, 2007).

The 2004 election was a landmark event for young voter turnout and produced an increase of more than 4 million youth ballots cast (Vargas, 2004). In the 2008 presidential election, Obama inspired youth engagement and captured a majority of youth vote (Pew Research Center, 2008). Despite the gains seen in youth civic engagement in 2008 and prior, current polling suggests that more study is needed to maintain that involvement and interest level. In the most recent presidential general election, the Pew Research Center (2012) found that although the youth vote still turned out, it was not with the same intensity as 2008. The report also found that the disengagement was highest among adults 30 years and younger and that the overall disinterest was not ideologically associated, as it was observed with both major parties (Pew Research Center, 2012). The 2016 presidential season is noted for youth excitement for Bernie Sanders due in part to their general disillusionment with establishment politics and institutions (Bahrampour, 2016). These snapshots show that, although many strides have been made to keep young people interested in politics and social issues, much is still to be discovered about how to maintain and perpetuate that excitement and activism.

The purpose of this project is to better comprehend how young voters are understanding and interpreting celebrity appeals in political and issue campaigns. Of particular interest are identification and platform. The power of identification that an audience has with celebrity influencers should be center to celebrity-driven political speech. Moreover, platform is paramount: It is important to understand how social media is breaking down traditional barriers between famous and ordinary people in an attempt to increase political engagement.

Much of the research on celebrity influence and endorsements has examined information processing and credibility levels of celebrity sources. This project seeks to go beyond mere processing, diving into the thought processing, deliberation, and reflection on how celebrities influence political engagement. This investigative strategy follows a call by John Street (2012) to place greater emphasis on audience analysis through nonexperimental approaches. Focus groups were used to get beyond unidimensional favorability numbers and social media statistics in order to understand how young people are talking about celebrity influence.

In the following literature review and methods sections, the authors offered valuable research and context for their study. Note how their research questions grew out of previous research on the topic. This section also explained the specific focus group procedure used for the research and listed the questions all participants were asked. For this study, a trained researcher facilitated the focus groups.

Celebrity Persuasive Influence

Previous research on celebrities and political engagement suggests that, especially among young voters, people seek political information from nontraditional sources (like celebrities and entertainment media; Hollander, 2005). Moreover, politicians utilize entertainment platforms to appear more approachable (Baum, 2005; Schutz, 1995). Entertainment allows many audiences who would otherwise be alienated or apathetic with the political process a chance to hear political information (Baum and Jamison, 2006). Collectively, young voters are the perfect demographic for celebrity-fueled political appeals.

Celebrity endorsement research is a particular salient area when discussing celebrity political influence. Much of the research on the impact of celebrities speaking on political issues concerns endorsements or social marketing. In this section we first review celebrities in advertising and marketing and then focus on celebrity political marketing.

Celebrity Endorsers

Celebrity endorsements continue to be seen as desirable by marketers and advertisers (Brockington and Henson, 2015). Audience processing of celebrity endorsements is the primary line of research in celebrity advertising. Research focuses on factors such as credibility, issue-congruence, and attractiveness.

A number of trends have emerged. People who find celebrities more attractive also have more positive appraisals and greater recall of endorsed brands (Kahle and Homer, 1985). Celebrity endorsers work best when they are perceived as credible (Ohanian, 1991) or carry cultural credence (McCracken, 1989). People also use both central cognitive and peripheral heuristic processing in evaluating celebrity endorsements (Fleck, Korchia, and Le Roy, 2012). More recent research focuses on information-processing models that examine the affective value of fan attachment in advertising (Hung, 2014) and processing entertainment media influence (Moyer-Guse and Nabi, 2010). Research utilizing processing models suggests that celebrity influence is more intricate and complex than mere attractiveness and issue fit. For instance, Chang (2013) found that message context primes processing when people are ambivalent to a celebrity endorser.

Perceptions of celebrity-brand congruence are also rather complex. Choi and Rifon (2012), influenced by previous work on celebrity-issue congruence and source credibility, examined audience aspiration as a component of connection with a celebrity. They found that when a celebrity exhibits qualities that a person aspires to possess for their ideal self-image, evaluation of the endorsement was more positive. In other words, people want to see the best of themselves reflected in a celebrity. Fleck and colleagues (2012), in modeling celebrity congruence and likeability, found that congruence with a brand is important, but likeability of the celebrity made the congruence stronger or created congruence where there otherwise would not have been. In other words, both congruence and likeability are rather important.

There are some drawbacks to celebrity endorsements of a product, brand, or organization. If a celebrity endorses multiple causes or brands simultaneously, audiences can become confused or unable to recall endorsed material (Kelting and Rice, 2013). Oftentimes the issue or organization may be overshadowed by a celebrity's personal agenda (Meyer and Gamson, 1995). Moreover, an endorser may fall from popularity, decreasing their usefulness (Erdogan, 1999). Should an endorser become embroiled in controversy, steps taken by the organization are not always clear-cut (Carrillat, D'Astous, and Lazure, 2013). Given this, utilizing celebrities in political marketing is a tricky strategy.

Celebrity Political Advocacy

Celebrity political marketing research also tends to focus on audience processing. Research has examined impact on direct voter action (Garthwaite and Moore, 2013), voter attitudes (Jackson and Darrow, 2005), and apathy and involvement (Becker, 2012). Celebrity political activity has also been found to shape voters' views of political parties (Nownes, 2012).

In a study about Oprah Winfrey's support of Barack Obama, Pease and Brewer (2008) found that Winfrey's endorsement did not impact perceptions about candidate likeability and favorability but did influence perceptions of likelihood to win. They also found a link between the endorsement and a greater likelihood to vote for Obama. Similarly, in an analysis of campaign data, Garthwaite and Moore (2013) found a link between an Oprah Winfrey endorsement and greater voter turnout for Obama and increased Obama campaign contributions.

In terms of advocacy, Becker (2013) found the congruence between celebrity and issue was important: Celebrities were seen as more appropriate for less important issues. However, positive reception to celebrity political speech increased with more exposure. Moreover, in an examination of Twitter-based word-of-mouth endorsements, Jin and Phua (2014) found that heuristic cues like followers, celebrity type, and credibility predicted impact of celebrity tweets.

Whether a voter is engaged with an election or issue is also an important factor. Veer, Becirovic, and Martin (2010) found that low politically salient voters were more influenced by celebrity endorsements compared to high politically salient voters. Austin et al. (2008) found a link between celebrity endorsements and political efficacy levels in young people. The influence of celebrity speech led to less political complacency and greater political self-efficacy; both of these potentially lead to greater political engagement. Moreover, celebrity political endorsements can draw attention to and make issues more palatable to younger voters (Jackson and Darrow, 2005).

Overall, this research suggests that there is a connection between celebrity involvement and voter attitudes. It is not clear how the many different factors of a celebrity endorsement work together to influence voters. Given this, the current project examines three areas: perceived credibility of celebrity appeals, perceived influence of celebrities, and the platform used for celebrity political appeals. These are important considerations in evaluating the viability of using celebrities as political spokespeople. Previous research suggests that people process politics in entertainment less in terms of factual information and more in terms of impressions and feelings (Kim and Vishak, 2008; Pfau, Houston, and Semmler, 2007). Thus, a person's overall impression of a celebrity political spokesperson and his or her fit to a message could arguably be more important than the issue information the celebrity is espousing. Moreover, where young people are viewing celebrity political messages should also impact how they interpret and use the information. Given an unclear picture of the usefulness of celebrities as political speakers, the following research questions are considered:

RQ1: Where are young voters seeing celebrity political messages the most?
RQ2: In political and social issue persuasive appeals, how is celebrity credibility interpreted?
RQ3: In political and social issue persuasive appeals using celebrities, how are young voters interpreting the influence of these messages?

Method

Focus groups were used for this project because it was the goal to gain a better understanding of how young people perceive and talk about the celebrities they see in political settings. Moreover, through focus groups, this project provides a framework for future research using a variety of methodological tools.

Participants and Procedure

Eight focus groups were conducted with young voters (n = 30) recruited from a large southwestern university. Of the participants, 73% were female and the average age was 23. In terms of ethnic makeup of the groups, 43% were White, 17% African American, 13% Asian, and 27% were mixed/other. Moreover, 37% identified as Hispanic or Latino (regardless of race).

Focus groups were held in a small conference room with sessions moderated by a trained researcher. Before group discussions began, participants completed a short survey with demographic questions. Session discussions lasted for approximately 1 hr. Each session was recorded and later transcribed for analysis. Transcripts were coded using a thematic analysis method described by Braun and Clarke (2006). The first round used open coding to derive themes, with subsequent rounds analyzing the fit and redundancy of the themes.

Questions for group sessions were designed to include warm-up questions, primary questions, and concluding questions, as suggested by previous focus group research (Krueger and Casey, 2000). Focus groups were asked the following questions with subsequent follow-up questions: (a) What is your interest in celebrity culture? What is your interest in politics? (b) What is your opinion of celebrities' credibility to speak about political issues? (c) Where do you see celebrities speaking about politics (in the media and social media)? (d) How do you feel when a celebrity is trying to persuade you about a political issue? (e) Are the celebrities successful in getting you interested in politics? Do they reflect your values and the values of your community? (f) Do you share links or comments about celebrities in politics in social media?

I found it interesting that, in the next section, the authors derived their definition of "celebrity" directly from the focus groups they conducted. Nisbett and DeWalt's thematic analysis of the focus groups identified four key themes related to the impact of celebrity on young voters that were addressed in the next sections. Notice how the authors used a variety of examples taken directly from the focus group conversations to illustrate each of these themes.

Thematic Analysis

In an attempt to set parameters for this discussion and to derive meaning from the focus group discourse, it is useful to set parameters around the type of celebrity discussed. Research on celebrity politics has often focused on the fluid nature of celebrity. For instance, Street (2004, 2012) argued that politicians can be seen as a type of celebrity (e.g., Barack Obama or Bernie Sanders) who can wield the power of charisma and charm. Other popular political speakers like Jon Stewart and Stephen Colbert also have had a tremendous fan following, but they are arguably a different type of celebrity distinct from politicians and entertainment performers. Still other people may gain notoriety and limited celebrity status within the context of a particular campaign or issue (e.g., Joe the Plumber in the 2008 presidential election). To contribute to the literature on celebrity political activity, this discussion focuses on entertainment celebrities who advocate on behalf of a political or social issue. This is guided by previous research highlighting the influence of these types of celebrities (Jackson and Darrow, 2005).

More important, the participants in the focus groups guided the parameters of this project. To them, celebrity meant the most traditional form of celebrity— actors, music performers, and those famous for being famous. Whereas celebrity politicians and celebrity political commentators have a natural entrée into political discourse, the most traditional celebrity is often perceived as outside of the political system. This group of celebrities is perhaps the most interesting to examine, because people like Kim Kardashian and Jay Z have tremendous followings but their political credibility and influence is rather unclear. Recent survey studies found that celebrities like Oprah do have some influence on voting behavior (Garthwaite and Moore, 2013; Pease and Brewer, 2008). This project examines whether these otherwise nonpolitical celebrities are persuasive speakers within the realm of political discourse.

Seeking a different understanding of celebrity impact, and in addressing the research questions, four themes emerged as the most salient across all eight groups. These themes focused on level of credibility, identification with celebrities, perceived influence of celebrities, and social media as a platform for celebrity political speech.

Credibility and Identification

A major theme to emerge was the link between general perceptions of credibility of a celebrity and the amount of influence that celebrity had on an issue. Meyer and Gamson (1995), in a study about the role of celebrities in social movements, explored the notion of celebrity credibility when speaking about social or political issues. They argued that celebrities, by their very nature as socially constructed elites, have a somewhat limited scope in which they have credibility. Thus celebrities tend to avoid marginalized or stigmatized issues, because they understand their power rests with staying popular. They also suggested that celebrity credibility levels are rather tenuous, resulting in a tendency to support socially acceptable causes and use broad-sweeping language when promoting issues. Findings from this study support this fluid notion of celebrity credibility.

Participant perceptions of credibility were rather complex and intricate. Findings suggest that credibility is influenced by a combination of Meyer and

Gamson's (1995) factors of limited celebrity credibility—including celebrities choosing palatable issues in order to maintain popularity and celebrities hedging about their actual intentions. Perceptions of credibility were also influenced by identification and aspirational identification (i.e., did the celebrity reflect the participants ideal identity or what they aspire to be).

To break this theme down further, subthemes were evident. First, there is a class of celebrity who are considered interesting and entertaining but not the least bit credible in a political context. Although these celebrities may catch attention, they had little to no persuasive credibility. A person like Paris Hilton was a particularly obvious target; as one participant put it, "She's a joke to me. Her life is a joke."

Fandom does not necessarily equate to increased credibility as a political speaker. For instance, one participant who is "obsessed with the Kardashians" had a more thoughtful approach to evaluating celebrity credibility:

> When a celebrity just tweets about some random thing that's happening—I would never take Chris Brown as a credible source because of his background. I guess depending on each celebrity—it would depend on their background, whether they know what they are talking about. Oprah Winfrey more 'cause she's very involved in current affairs; but someone like, I don't know, like Justin Bieber—he can't keep his own life together, so . . .

Second, people are drawn to different celebrities for different reasons, but one clear distinguishing factor surfaced: intention. Motivation for a celebrity's involvement in politics was often questioned and doubted. Participants were rather cynical and often viewed celebrity support of a cause or political position as an avenue for personal gain, be it to increase sales, broaden their appeal, or improve their image. One participant commented, "Celebrities that tweet on Twitter say things just to say things or to get more followers, I don't really consider them a reliable source."

Participants placed celebrities in either a goodwill intention category or a self-aggrandizing intention category. Participants did not make clear distinctions about the type of issue discussed by celebrities, but they were cognizant of a celebrity's intentions (or perceived intentions). One participant questioned, "Is there a genuine concern for something or is it something they hopped on 'cause they thought it was popular?"

Many mentioned goodwill-intending celebrities like Brad Pitt building houses in Hurricane Katrina–ravaged New Orleans, Angelina Jolie working with UNICEF, Oprah Winfrey's general involvement in social issues, and Bono's work with global charities. Intention was also linked with the type of political speech deemed credible and acceptable. Being political just to be political was looked upon with doubt. However, political speech with goodwill intentions, be it to raise money or awareness about an issue, was praised. Another participant shared,

> If a group of celebrities were to do something because they have a political agenda, a lot of it gets thrown up because it's just political speak. But when there's a tragedy or a cause, they do it just to do it. This is what people should be doing to help each other.

Youth voter engagement campaigns like Rock the Vote and Vote or Die were in a distinct category—not viewed as entirely an act of goodwill but not totally discounted either. When intentions were not clear, participants tended to rely more heavily on perceived credibility and identification. In reference to the Vote or Die campaign, participants did not understand why the celebrities were in the campaign, questioned the credibility of the celebrities, and even pointed out that some of the campaign celebrities are "not even registered to vote." For celebrities like Paris Hilton, participants used words like "trashy" and "oversexualized" and "hot mess." One participant summed up the celebrity involvement like this: "Voting is supposed to be bigger than yourself, but this is saying vote or pay attention to me."

Fame alone does not carry the credibility to get young people interested and involved in politics. Just because someone is famous or popular in some regard does not necessarily translate to the political arena. Some celebrities (like Paris Hilton or Kim Kardashian) who are seen as self-serving and not serious can even have a negative impact on perceptions of an issue or political campaign. Previous research supports this notion that more shallow celebrities tend to have more negative appraisals (Spears, Royne, and Steenburg, 2013).

Contrary to research linking the mere presence of a celebrity with changes in political attitudes and voting intentions, these focus group findings suggest the relationship between celebrity, audience, and persuasion is much more intricate. Above and beyond societal notions of a celebrity's credibility, participants were more concerned with identifying with a celebrity—identification is critical.

More than notoriety and fandom as avenues for inspiring political interest, there is a link between identification and inspiration on political and social issues. As one participant shared, "Yeah I look at people similar to me and try to follow them." Another participant commented,

> I'm obsessed with Selena Gomez, like obsessed. . . . I follow her on Twitter, I get her Facebook updates sent to my phone. . . . I'm obsessed. I'm like literally "Oh she's doing UNICEF, I should do UNICEF. Oh she should do this, I should do this."

On the surface, the link between fandom and subsequent political activities or views seems quite simplistic. Upon further discussion, however, this same participant revealed that her attachment to Gomez was based on a high level of identification. They are both from the same geographic region, are the same gender, and come from a similar ethnic and socioeconomic background. The participant further commented, "I relate to her 'cause I grew up in Texas, my parents didn't have that much money. So there's that common link."

Choi and Rifon's (2012) findings on audience aspirational self-image are rather poignantly displayed here. Beyond congruence of issue and celebrity, young people are perhaps looking for guidance on who they aspire to be in terms of their political identities. Identification seemed to override external opinions of a celebrity's credibility and influence. For an individual, if particular celebrities mean something to the individual and the individual looks up to them, then they are considered credible and influential. These findings suggest that perceived credibility is not as critical as the ability of a celebrity to mesh with an audience member's self-image and aspirations.

When a celebrity is viewed as not identifiable, perceptions of celebrity political influence are not very positive. Said one participant, "I look at celebrities similar to me—so not Kardashians or Lauren Conrad—that's a whole different story. That just makes me angry." Moreover, the fit between a celebrity and the issue that celebrity is promoting was important. Previous research found some evidence for negative appraisals when celebrities and political issues are not congruent (Becker, 2013). Participants needed to identify the celebrity with a cause or issue. For example, one participant commented, "Well I remember from the recent campaign, Eva Longoria—she supported Barack Obama and his immigration policy. Being from Texas and being a minority, she was credible in being able to speak about it."

Again, beyond mere congruence, there are subtle notes of personal identification. This participant was also Hispanic and Texan, so these celebrity characteristics became most salient.

Perceived Influence of Celebrities

Participant perceptions of influence on their own attitudes were vastly different compared to the perceived celebrity influence on other people. For influence on themselves, participants initially claimed no influence at all. Offered one participant, "Why should I care? Like I know what I believe in and stand for. Like no matter how much I like them, they won't persuade me about what's gonna benefit me and my family." Added another: "I voted for Obama, but not because Beyoncé told me to or Jay Z said so."

Gradually, however, they offered a more nuanced explanation. The discussion shifted slightly to admit to some influence, but it was mostly influence on exploring new information and different viewpoints. One participant commented on celebrity influence: "I'm kinda open to it. I'm serious about what I believe, but open to different points of view from people." Another suggested that celebrities may "help me to look at something in a different way."

Influence is often manifested in an increased interest in exploring a political or issue position, more so than blindly following the celebrity. One participant offered,

> I don't necessarily follow, but there are people that inspire me. So I check in on them every now and then to see what they're doing. Not necessarily to say "that's what they're doing, I want to do that too."

Another commented,

> To say that they don't influence me would be inaccurate because I take the information they give me and I do my own research to get my own view on it. Me taking what is given to me and analyzing it—if that's influence, then yeah.

Influence, like credibility, is linked to identification—both identifying with a celebrity and the celebrity being identified with an issue. One participant commented, "So for me the celebrities I pay attention to are definitely in tune with me." When identification is low, perceived influence is low. One participant offered, "Celebrities don't deal with life like us—they have all different things. They seem like they are going through what we go through and they try to persuade us, but do they actually know what we are going through?"

In terms of perceived influence on others, participants exhibited signs of third-person perception. Davison (1983) suggested that people assume the media influences other people more than themselves, and previous research on celebrity political endorsements found evidence for third-person perception for out-group endorsements (Brubaker, 2011). Some third-person perception was evident with the focus groups. One participant commented on the influence:

> Not me personally, but definitely see how whatever they say can influence another person just because people look at celebrity as being aspirational. So when they see a celebrity saying something, I can see how that influences people, but not me personally.

Added another participant: "If their favorite celebrity says to vote for Obama, they would; but not me personally."

Whether this higher perceived influence was positive or negative depended on the audience and the perceived motivation of the celebrity. Participants were

particularly concerned about influence on "younger" people who are not as politically savvy. Overall, participants seemed to be in a transitional phase where
celebrity influence may not be as strong as it once was and they are developing
individual political ideologies. One participant summed it up:

> I think maybe celebrity influence is at a somewhat younger age . . .
> maybe the age you're just about to vote . . . moving from teenager world
> to an adult. It's a good time to grasp things and at an older age, you're
> not as affected by celebrities as much.

Participants were also concerned with a celebrity's right to use fame as a
platform for political speech. For example, one participant noted,

> I went to go see a Spanish band called Mana and it was thousands of
> people of all ages. They told the young people to start voting and they
> said how important it was for Hispanics to vote. And I saw how Madonna
> did something with her concert supporting Obama and Katy Perry also.

However, participants questioned, regardless of the right to speak, whether
a celebrity should take advantage of their fame-generated platform to speak out
on political issues. One participant put it this way: "With great power comes
great responsibility. If that person saying something knows others follow him—if
they're saying it, they must believe it."

Social Media

An increasingly relevant question is how the growth of social media usage is
intertwined with the increase of celebrities as political speakers. Social networking sites, and Internet use in general, allow for more audience interactivity and
relativity, in effect bringing the lives of celebrities closer and making the messages of campaigns more direct. Thrall et al. (2008) argued that Internet-fueled
advocacy is inspiring greater attention and discussion of political issues outside
of mainstream political news.

Social media campaigns are a good conduit to connect celebrity influence
with these potential voters. Even in the earliest stages of social networking development and general Internet use, research found that although most traditional
forms of political and social activism failed to connect with young people, Internet-
based initiatives worked to increase political awareness and activity (Owens,
2008). Despite the potential usefulness of social media, Loader, Vromen, and
Xenos (2016) argued that celebrities and campaigns need to use these platforms more effectively to inspire discourse and interactivity.

The media in which young voters are consuming and interacting with celebrities on political issues is an important component of persuasive political speech. Not surprisingly, social media was the most cited medium. This is partially due to the media-use habits of the participants; young people tend to use more social media, and this was the case with the study participants. But social media also seems to be the most efficient venue for celebrities to connect with young voters. As one participant noted, "There's a lot on Twitter, even little subtle things. That's where I picked up and see most of it." Participants explained that celebrities engaged in political speech were particularly suited to social media because it was more personal, interactive, and a direct line to people. One participant commented, "Like during the elections, whenever there was a speech like on TV, you would see all the celebrities on Twitter—'OMG I can't believe that this guy said this'—and I was like 'yeah, I know right.'" Participants seemed to appreciate the intimacy and immediacy of social media political discourse in which they could make commentary along with celebrities. Social media was also linked with more instantaneous responses to current events. Participants noticed that, in comparison to political leaders, many celebrities respond faster (via social media) to important issues.

It was also noted that when a celebrity said something, others circulated their statements, especially through social media and traditional media. One participant said,

> I see it more on social media because people re-tweet or a media outlet will tweet—"Oh, did you see that tweet from so and so." You can take a tweet from Twitter and screenshot it, Instagram, Facebook. I can see more celebrity political statements through these than I see on TV.

This circulation of political statements is a critical component of modern word-of-mouth campaigns. But social media does have a drawback. Campaign planners utilizing social media may think they are being clever and cutting-edge, but it may not have the impact they intend. A common sentiment suggests that there is a glut of political chatter on social media, making it hard to cut through the clutter. "Social media was just everybody," offered one participant. When asked about particular social media examples, one participant replied with "I don't know if I can think of an exact instance." Again, identification with a celebrity meant that participants followed them more closely, thereby carving through the social media flotsam and jetsam.

In the following sections, Nisbett and DeWalt evaluated the evidence that they gathered from their focus groups to address larger issues related to celebrity-driven political campaigns. The authors suggested areas for future research and addressed the strengths and weaknesses of focus groups as a research method.

Normative Implications and Future Research

So why should understanding celebrity influence matter? It matters because celebrity-driven campaigns are a strategy that political leaders, social elites, and campaign marketers have adopted to instigate political action and discourse among young people. A glance at current political campaigns and discourse with young people involves Twitter hashtags, Facebook likes, and gimmicky viral videos. It is flashy and trendy and makes use of the immediacy of social media. This is how our society has chosen to speak to young people about the incredible importance of civic engagement.

This study's most important normative finding is a better understanding of the complex opinion formation process of young voters. They are not lemmings chasing after the latest gimmick trending in social media. Weaving all the themes together, findings suggest that young people are using celebrities as sounding boards and as aspirational figures because celebrities are the ones who stand up and talk about politics (or at least have platforms for engaging in political speech). Political elites are reinforcing this by recruiting celebrities to talk about politics.

Findings suggest that celebrity identity, credibility, and perceived influence are intertwined with an audience member's self-image. A young voter's personal identity—dreams, obligations, and aspirations—dictate how celebrity influence is processed. Beyond finding celebrities who are widely perceived to be credible political speakers (like Oprah and Bono) and matching a celebrity with the correct issue, political elites and social campaigners should recognize that young people are in a phase of opinion formation and civic growth. Instigating greater political and social participation goes hand in hand with developing a young voter's personal aspirations to be civically engaged. If a celebrity is a young person's aspirational role model, then campaigns can be better crafted to attune to these aspirational needs.

Future Research

Future research on celebrities and political influence should focus on this personal interaction between young voters and celebrities. Social media as a platform provides an immediacy and intimacy in a young person's interactions with a celebrity. Some participants regarded celebrities with great personal affection, suggesting a high level of parasocial attachment (see Horton and Wohl, 1956). A parasocial interaction is a one-sided relationship that people can have with celebrities or fictitious characters (Rubin and McHugh, 1987). Parasocial in conjunction with Moyer-Guse and Nabi's (2010) work on the extended elaboration likelihood model and the entertainment overcoming resistance model are potentially useful tools for strategic planners. Using these models takes the aspirational identification aspects of this study and allows for researchers to explore them in more experimental studies.

Another interesting factor to emerge from this study was political social media etiquette. Although not discussed in the context of this study, it is an interesting concept to explore further. There were some participants who expressed reticence with retweeting or posting political social media content. Perhaps, unlike older adults, young voters are taciturn about sharing political opinions because it is seen as too "private" or unseemly and even "offensive." One participant commented, "I don't feel like it's my duty to inform everybody about how I feel about certain issues." This is particularly important given the conventional wisdom of campaign strategists who think that engaging young voters is built on connecting and building networks through social media. Future research could build on the concept of a young voter's personal political identity and their willingness to express political opinions. After all, talking about politics is a key component and stepping stone for further political engagement.

Perhaps political engagement can be measured and expressed in different ways. Participants mentioned their approval of celebrities who support causes, organizations, or products that were socially responsible. Conceivably, understanding the consumption of celebrity political speech may be particularly interesting when thought of in conjunction with conscious consumerism. Ward and Vreese (2011) argued that young people act politically through socially conscious consumerism even if they appear disengaged in more traditional political actions like voting. Future research could examine the link between celebrity political speech and increases in celebrity capital. For young voters uncomfortable with traditional political speech, expressing opinions about conscious consumer activities may be an avenue to further civic engagement.

Limitations

The goal of this project was to explore the strategy of using celebrities as political speakers by better understanding how young people discuss and make sense of celebrity involvement in politics. The participants in the focus groups were actually a strong point in the study. They were slightly older (at an average age of 23 years) and diversity was excellent. One area of improvement is the sex disparity with so many more female participants. A future study should attempt to recruit more male participants. Moreover, this qualitative study was designed to complement the existing literature on celebrity political influence. Although the results are not generalizable, the themes are rather enlightening.

In the concluding section of the research, note how the authors broadened their analysis of the focus group research to consider the implications of persuasive appeals to young people and strategies to engage them in the political process.

Conclusion

Much of the research on celebrity political speech has focused either on celebrity endorsements or the theoretical impact of celebrities being a part of a wider political discourse. Findings from this project suggest that young voter audiences for celebrity political speech are not really processing whether something is a clear endorsement, part of a larger advertising campaign, or a speech act as part of a national political discourse. For the most part, they see celebrity political speech in snippets and blurbs—a tweet here, a quote there. The weakness of celebrity political impact research tends to be a lack of understanding about the dynamics of celebrity influence outside of lab experiments and quantitative data. In a review of celebrity endorsement research, Keel and Nataraajan (2012) called for research beyond endorsements and viewer effects. This project attempted to fill some of those gaps.

Overall, participants seemed to be in a phase of life where they are developing their own political views while bouncing them off friends, family, and cultural influences. At this point in their lives, celebrities function as elite beacons for navigating political and social issues. They are at the point in life where they may be influenced by celebrities they highly respect, but they are also cultivating stronger political convictions. The factors of identification, intentions, credibility, and medium are all incredibly important in stoking this political development.

In terms of influence, campaigns should ask of young people something they are willing to give. A consensus from the groups suggests that changes in attitude are unlikely. Many young voters have ambivalent attitudes about calls to action—from posting on social media to voting. This is partially due to unclear perceptions about celebrities' motivations, be they for personal gain or for true social concern. One concept that emerged and is particularly useful is the notion that celebrities inspire curiosity. When a celebrity has adequate credibility, a bond of identification, and fits with an issue, he or she can motivate people to investigate a social or political issue further, at the very least.

This research aimed to identify if young voters find celebrities to be credible when talking about politics or trying to persuade them about politics. In addition, this study explored the validity of current practices and tactics aimed at young voter turnout: How effective are they, and can they be expected to maintain or possibly grow the current interest level in the civic involvement? Ultimately, this research shows a paramount need to continually evaluate persuasive appeals aimed at engaging young voters. Increasing young voter political and social awareness is a democratic responsibility, and only through exploration of the mediums and means used to attract these young people can we begin to grasp a more complete picture of what is needed to maintain interest levels and engagement.

Focus Group Exercises

1. Observe at least three different groups of people in a restaurant or coffee shop. In particular, take note of the spatial relations, the nonverbal communication and the group dynamics. Explain how a facilitator might use this information to improve focus group interactions.
2. Craft a set of ten questions on a topic of your choice that will help you to learn more about some aspect of new media usage. Try each question out on a couple of your friends and see what types of responses you get. Did your friends understand the type of response you wanted from each of your questions? Ask each friend about the wording of each question—particularly if she or he did not respond to a question in the way you would have liked. Your goal is to make each question open-ended, clear, concise and accessible.
3. Volunteer to be a member of a focus group. Professional focus group facilities often recruit for participants at local malls. During the focus group, pay particular attention to how the moderator facilitates group interaction. If there were any challenging focus group members, explain how the moderator handled them. Did you enjoy being a focus group member? If so, what made the experience enjoyable? If not, what do you think could have made the focus group session more enjoyable?

References

Austin, Erica Weintraub, Vord, Rebecca Van de, Pinkleton, Bruce E., and Epstein, Evan. (2008). Celebrity endorsements and their potential to motivate young voters. *Mass Communication & Society, 11* (4): 420–436.

Babcock, William, and Whitehouse, Virginia. (2005). Celebrity as a postmodern phenomenon, ethical crisis for democracy, and media nightmare. *Journal of Mass Media Ethics, 20* (2–3): 176–191.

Bahrampour, Tara. (2016, February 29). For millennials, Bernie Sanders is cool because he's 74, not in spite of it. *The Washington Post.* Retrieved from www.washingtonpost.com/local/ social-issues/why-bernie-sanders-age-is-not-irrelevant-to-the-millennials-who-love-him/2016/02/28/a74e6db4-da76-11e5-81ae-7491b9b9e7df_story.html

Baum, Matthew A. (2005). Talking the vote: Why presidential candidates hit the talk show circuit. *American Journal of Political Science, 49* (2): 213–234.

Baum, Matthew A., and Jamison, Angela S. (2006). The Oprah effect: How soft news helps inattentive citizens vote consistently. *The Journal of Politics, 68* (4): 946–959.

Becker, Amy B. (2012). Engaging celebrity? Measuring the impact of issue-advocacy messages on situational involvement, complacency and apathy. *Celebrity Studies, 3* (2): 213–231.

Becker, Amy B. (2013). Star power? Advocacy, receptivity, and viewpoints on celebrity involvement in issue politics. *Atlantic Journal of Communication, 21* (1): 1–16.

Berger, Arthur Asa. (1998). *Media research techniques* (2nd ed.). Thousand Oaks, CA: Sage.

Bloor, Michael, Frankland, Jane, Thomas, Michelle, and Robson, Kate. (2001). *Focus groups in social research.* London: Sage.

Braun, Virginia, and Clarke, Victoria. (2006). Using thematic analysis in psychology. *Qualitative Research in Psychology, 3* (2): 77–101.

Brockington, Dan, and Henson, Spensor. (2015). Signifying the public: Celebrity advocacy and post-democratic politics. *International Journal of Cultural Studies, 18* (4): 431–448.

Brubaker, Jennifer. (2011). It doesn't affect my vote: Third-person effects of celebrity endorsements on college voters in the 2004 and 2008 presidential elections. *American Communication Journal, 13* (2): 4–22.

Carrillat, Francois A., D'Astous, Alain, and Lazure, Josianne. (2013). For better, for worse? What to do when celebrity endorsements go bad. *Journal of Advertising Research, 53* (1): 1–15.

Chang, Chingching. (2013). The influence of ambivalence toward a communication source: Media context priming and persuasion polarization. *Communication Research, 41* (6): 783–808.

Choi, Sejung Marina, and Rifon, Nora J. (2012). It is a match: The impact of congruence between celebrity image and consumer ideal self on endorsement effectiveness. *Psychology and Marketing, 29* (9): 639–650.

Davison, W. Philips. (1983). The third person effect in communication. *Public Opinion Quarterly, 47* (1): 1–15.

Erdogan, B. Zafer. (1999). Celebrity endorsement: A literature review. *Journal of Marketing Management, 15* (4): 291–315.

Fern, Edward F. (2001). *Advanced focus group research.* Thousand Oaks, CA: Sage.

Fleck, Nathalie, Korchia, Michael, and Le Roy, Isabelle. (2012). Celebrities in advertising: Looking for congruence or likability? *Psychology & Marketing, 29* (9): 651–662.

Fontana, Andrea, and Frey, James H. (1994). Interviewing: The art of science. In Norman K. Denzin and Yvonna S. Lincoln (Eds.), *Handbook of qualitative research* (pp. 361–376). Thousand Oaks, CA: Sage.

Garthwaite, Craig, and Moore, Timothy J. (2013). Can celebrity endorsements affect political outcomes? Evidence from the 2008 US Democratic presidential primary. *Journal of Law, Economics, & Organization, 29* (2): 355–384.

Goodnight, G. Thomas. (2005). The passion of the Christ meets Fahrenheit 9/11: A study in celebrity advocacy. *American Behavioral Scientist, 49* (3): 410–435.

Greenbaum, Thomas L. (1998). *The handbook for focus group research* (2nd ed.). Thousand Oaks, CA: Sage.

Greenbaum, Thomas L. (2000). *Moderating focus groups: A practical guide for group facilitation.* Thousand Oaks, CA: Sage.

Guest, Greg, Namey, Emily, and McKenna, Kevin. (2017). How many focus groups are enough? Building an evidence base for nonprobability sample sizes. *Field Methods, 29* (1): 3–22.

Hardt, Hanno. (1998). *Interactions: Critical studies in communication, media, and journalism.* Lanham, MD: Rowman & Littlefield.

Hollander, Barry A. (2005). Late-night learning: Do entertainment programs increase political campaign knowledge for young viewers? *Journal of Broadcasting & Electronic Media, 49* (4): 402–415.

Horton, Donald, and Wohl, R. Richard. (1956). Mass communication and para-social interaction: Observances on intimacy at a distance. *Psychiatry, 19* (3): 215–229.

Hundley, Heather L., and Shyles, Leonard. (2010). US teenagers' perceptions and awareness of digital technology: A focus group approach. *New Media and Society, 12* (3): 417–433.

Hung, Kineta. (2014). Why celebrity sells: A dual entertainment model of brand endorsement. *Journal of Advertising, 43* (2): 155–166.

Jackson, David J., and Darrow, Thomas I. A. (2005). The influence of celebrity endorsements on young adults' political opinions. *The Harvard International Journal of Press/Politics, 10* (3): 80–98.

Jin, Seung-A. Annie, and Phua, Joe. (2014). Following celebrities' Tweets about brands: The impact of Twitter-based electronic word-of-mouth on consumers' source credibility perception, buying intention, and social identification with celebrities. *Journal of Advertising, 43* (2): 181–195.

Kahle, Lynn R., and Homer, Pamela M. (1985). Physical attractiveness of the celebrity endorser: A social adaptation perspective. *Journal of Consumer Research, 11* (4): 954–961.

Kamberelis, George, and Dimitriadis, Greg. (2008). Focus groups: Strategic articulations of pedagogy, politics, and inquiry. In Norman K. Denzin and Yvonna S. Lincoln (Eds.), *Collecting and interpreting qualitative materials* (3rd ed., pp. 375–402). Los Angeles, CA: Sage.

Keel, Astrid, and Nataraajan, Rajan. (2012). Celebrity endorsements and beyond: New avenues for celebrity branding. *Psychology & Marketing, 29* (9): 690–703.

Kelting, Katie, and Rice, Dan Hamilton. (2013). Should we hire David Beckham to endorse our brands? Contextual interference and consumer memory for brands in a celebrity's endorsement portfolio. *Psychology & Marketing, 30* (7): 602–613.

Kim, Young Mie, and Vishak, John. (2008). Just laugh! You don't need to remember: The effects of entertainment media on political information acquisition and information processing in political judgment. *Journal of Communication, 58* (2): 338–360.

Krueger, Richard A., and Casey, Mary Anne. (2000). *Focus groups: A practical guide for application.* Thousand Oaks, CA: Sage.

Lindlof, Thomas R., and Taylor, Bryan C. (2011). *Qualitative communication research methods* (3rd ed.). Thousand Oaks, CA: Sage.

Loader, Brian D., Vromen, Ariadne, and Xenos, Michael A. (2016). Performing for the young networked citizen? Celebrity politics, social networking and the political engagement of young people. *Media, Culture & Society, 38* (3): 400–419.

Markham, Tim. (2015). Celebrity advocacy and public engagement: The divergent uses of celebrity. *International Journal of Cultural Studies, 18* (4): 467–480.

McCracken, Grant. (1989). Who is the celebrity endorser? Cultural foundations of the endorsement process. *Journal of Consumer Research, 16* (3): 310–321.

Meyer, David S., and Gamson, Joshua. (1995). The challenge of cultural elites: Celebrities and social movements. *Sociological Inquiry, 65* (2): 181–206.

Morgan, David L. (2002). Focus group interviewing. In Jaber F. Gubrium and James A. Holstein (Eds.), *Handbook of interview research: Context and method* (pp. 141–159). Thousand Oaks, CA: Sage.

Moyer-Guse, Emily, and Nabi, Robin L. (2010). Explaining the effects of narrative in an entertainment television program: Overcoming resistance to persuasion. *Human Communication Research, 36* (1): 26–52.

Nisbett, Gwendelyn S., and DeWalt, Christina Childs. (2016). Exploring the influence of celebrities in politics: A focus group study of young voters. *Atlantic Journal of Communication, 24* (3): 144–156.

Nownes, Anthony J. (2012). An experimental investigation of the effects of celebrity support for political parties in the United States. *American Politics Research, 40* (3): 476–500.

Ohanian, Roobina. (1991). The impact of celebrity spokespersons' perceived image on consumers' intention to purchase. *Journal of Advertising Research, 31* (1): 46–54.

Owens, Diana. (2008). The Internet and youth civic engagement in the United States. In Sarah Oates, Diana Owen, and Rachel K. Gibson (Eds.), *The Internet and politics: Citizens, voters and activists* (pp. 17–33). New York, NY: Routledge.

Payne, J. Gregory, Hanlon, John P., and Twomey, David P. (2007). Celebrity spectacle influence on young voters in the 2004 presidential campaign: What to expect in 2008. *American Behavioral Scientist, 50* (9): 1239–1246.

Pease, Andrew, and Brewer, Paul R. (2008). The Oprah factor: The effects of a celebrity endorsement in a presidential primary campaign. *The International Journal of Press/Politics, 13* (4): 386–400.

Pew Research Center. (2008). *Young voters in the 2008 elections.* Retrieved from www.pewresearch. org/2008/11/13/young-voters-in-the-2008-election/

Pew Research Center. (2012). *Youth engagement falls; registration also declines.* Retrieved from www. peoplepress.org/2012/09/28/youth-engagement-falls-registration-also-declines/

Pfau, Michael, Houston, J. Brian, and Semmler, Shane M. (2007). *Mediating the vote: The changing media landscape in U.S. presidential campaigns.* Lanham, MD: Rowman & Littlefield.

Rubin, Rebecca B., and McHugh, Michael P. (1987). Development of parasocial interaction relationships. *Journal of Broadcasting & Electronic Media, 31* (3): 279–292.

Schutz, Astrid. (1995). Entertainers, experts, or public servants? Politicians' self-presentation on television talk shows. *Political Communication, 12* (2): 211–221.

Snyder, Robert W. (2003). American journalism and the culture of celebrity. *Reviews in American History, 31* (3): 440–448.

Spears, Nancy, Royne, Maria, and Steenburg, Eric Van. (2013). Are celebrity-heroes effective endorsers? Exploring the links between hero, celebrity, and advertising response. *Journal of Promotion Management, 19* (1): 17–37.

Stewart, David W., Shamdasani, Prem N., and Rook, Dennis W. (2007). *Focus groups: Theory and practice* (2nd ed.). Thousand Oaks, CA: Sage.

Street, John. (2004). Celebrity politicians: Popular culture and political representation. *The British Journal of Politics and International Relations, 6* (4): 435–452.

Street, John. (2012). Do celebrity politics and celebrity politicians matter? *The British Journal of Politics and International Relations, 14* (3): 346–356.

Thrall, A. Trevor, Lollio-Fakhreddine, Jaime, Berent, Jon, Donnelly, Lana, Herrin, Wes, Paquette, Zachary, Wenglinski, Rebecca, and Wyatt, Amy. (2008). Star power: Celebrity advocacy and the evolution of the public sphere. *The International Journal of Press/Politics, 13* (4): 362–385.

Tufekci, Zeynep. (2013). 'Not this one': Social movements, the attention economy, and microcelebrity networked activism. *American Behavioral Scientist, 57* (7): 848–870.

Vargas, Jose Antonio. (2004, November 9). Vote or die? Well, they did vote: Youth ballots up 4.6 million from 2000, in Kerry's favor. *The Washington Post.* Retrieved from www.washingtonpost. com/wp-dyn/articles/A35290-2004Nov8.html

Veer, Ekant, Becirovic, Ilda, and Martin, Brett A. S. (2010). If Kate voted conservative, would you? The role of celebrity endorsements in political party advertising. *European Journal of Marketing, 44* (3–4), 436–450.

Ward, Janelle, and Vreese, Claes de. (2011). Political consumerism, young citizens and the internet. *Media, Culture & Society, 33* (3): 399–413.

Weiskel, Timothy C. (2005). From sidekick to sideshow: Celebrity, entertainment, and the politics of distraction. *American Behavioral Scientist, 49* (3): 393–409.

Wheeler, Mark. (2012). The democratic worth of celebrity politics in an era of late modernity. *The British Journal of Politics and International Relations, 14* (3): 407–422.

Wilkinson, Sue. (2011). Analysing focus group data. In David Silverman (Ed.), *Qualitative research: Issues of theory, method and practice* (3rd ed., pp. 168–184). London: Sage.

Woodyatt, Cory R., Finneran, Catherine A., and Stephenson, Rob. (2016). In person versus online focus group discussions. A comparative analysis of data quality. *Qualitative Health Research, 26* (6): 741–749.

CHAPTER **5**

History

*He who controls the past controls the future. He who controls the present
controls the past.*
                                            —George Orwell (1948/1950), *1984*

History is about the achievements, challenges, failings and mysteries of our
lives. Using stories to provide glimpses into the past, historians help us to
understand what it means to live at a particular place and time. They offer
us guidance about what to value, what to avoid, how to spend our time and
how to make sense of our world. Contrasting the past with the present,
historians focus on the context associated with people, events and issues
in an effort to explain the human experience. Some historians see their job
as bringing an authentic recounting of the past to life by crafting accurate
narratives that are based on the most relevant historical evidence. Others
maintain that while historical evidence is created in the past, we can only
evaluate this evidence in the present. What this means is that for these historians, we cannot comprehend the past as it actually was; at best we are
able to understand aspects of the past from a contemporary perspective.

   History is the oldest qualitative method, and ancient cultures drew on
historical evidence to create social narratives about their lives. For example, the Greek historian Thucydides, who is generally regarded as the
father of history, crafted a detailed political and military account of the

Peloponnesian War in the fifth century BCE. One of the earliest Chinese historians, Confucius, introduced ethics into history and suggested that discussions about the past could teach people how they should conduct their lives (Donnelly and Norton, 2011). For thousands of years, historians have crafted oral and written stories to explain, enhance and justify the actions of a culture.

These days there are all kinds of historians who do many different types of history. There are researchers who focus on the history of a particular subject or field such as journalism history, military history or economic history. Some researchers do history from the top down, focusing on the lives of kings, presidents, industry leaders or other elites, while other researchers do history from the bottom up, stressing the role of everyday people in the historical process. Some historians specialize in a specific time period or event such as World War II or 1920s social history. There are comparative historians, who study different societies that existed at a similar time; labor historians, who focus on the labor movement; and intellectual historians, who address the development of ideas in human thought. There are also antiquarians, who narrowly focus on historical periods and facts to evaluate ancient objects of science and art, and there is even a field of study known as historiography that deals with the actual writing of history as well as the philosophical issues related to the craft of history.

Historian John Tosh (2009) suggested that contemporary researchers are motivated by four somewhat contradictory attitudes toward history. Some historians aspire to learn what it was like to live at a previous time and place, envisioning historical research as a type of "detective enquiry, or a venture in resurrection" (p. 2). Some historians seek to uncover the progress of human destiny, while other researchers showcase history within the political or ideological interests of a society. Finally, there are historians who draw on the historical record as a "cautionary tale" (p. 8) to help us to learn from the past.

Traditional vs. Cultural History

In this chapter I distinguish between two different types of historians; while they are known by many different names, I refer to them as traditional historians and cultural historians. Traditional historians study the past from a positivist or post-positivist paradigm that regards evidence as elements of reality. In contrast, cultural historians who come from a constructivist or critical theories philosophical orientation focus on "the domain of the lived" (Hall, 1989, p. 26), which is the way people actively engage with, experience and interact within elements of culture within the historical process. In Chapter 1 I discuss the differences between these paradigms, and how during the twentieth century, scientific research protocols and procedures influenced all types of research, including the study of history. Some historians began to envision the stories of the past as generalizable facts while others reacted against a scientific focus, critiquing the influence of culture and ideology within the narrative structures of history (Brennen and Hardt, 2011).

Although Thucydides was one of the first historians to differentiate literature from history (Donnelly and Norton, 2011), to this day researchers continue to debate the relationship between history and literature. Cultural historian Hayden White envisioned the writing of history as a type of fiction that was more like literature than science, due to its content and narrative form. Yet, he suggested that most historians chose to ignore the fictional aspects of their work, believing that by following specific guidelines and rules to evaluate their evidence, historians were somehow transcending fiction. For White (1978), while historians often focus on events with "specific time-space locations" and novelists rely primarily on "imagined, hypothetical or invented" (pp. 121–122) events, they both used the same forms and techniques in their narratives, striving to provide an image of "reality" that corresponds with authentic human experience.

Often incorporating a commonsense understanding of history as the story of the past, traditional historians present historical evidence as chronological reconstructions that address names, dates and places. Focusing on the quantity of facts rather than the quality of information, this type of historian addresses catastrophes, crises and ruptures that are measured and evaluated as outliers from the norms of continuity and progress. While traditional historians attempt to reconstruct the past by emphasizing the collection and description of evidence, their evidence often remains untouched by theory, analysis or interpretation. Other historians have taken issue with this type of history, referring to it as "pseudo-history." As political theorist Fredric Jameson (1971) has sarcastically noted, this type of history has been characterized as an "obsession with historical rise and decline, the never-ending search for the date of the fall and the name of the serpent" (p. 324).

Traditional historians present their narratives as fact-based objective explanations of events, issues and problems. However, cultural historians maintain that researchers cannot remain neutral about historical evidence—that they interpret the past using relevant concepts and theories in order to understand the evidence that they are able to access. Cultural historians suggest that researchers must go beyond reconstructions of the past to consider people's experiences in culture. For cultural historians, connections are drawn between historical figures, events and issues and the relevant social, political and economic developments in society. Rather than emphasizing facts alone, they evaluate evidence as it interacts with the relevant historical context, looking at the challenges and struggles and envisioning progress as a contradictory notion. They see history as a living process, including issues of continuity and discontinuity as well as instances of evolution and of revolution. In addition to placing an emphasis on crisis, catastrophe and oppression, cultural historians also address the challenges, changes, oppositions and regenerations that occur within societies (Williams, 1989).

Media History

The development of media history began with the invention of the printing press and other communication technologies. Journalism historians initially focused on crafting stories about famous editors and publishers, whom they saw as working to ensure the fourth estate function of the press. Their biographies were augmented with institutional histories that recounted the development of newspapers in democratic societies.

In 1974, cultural theorist James Carey called for the creation of cultural media history as an alternative to traditional journalism history. Carey (1974) found the existing Whig or progressive view of journalism history, with its emphasis on progress, "something of an embarrassment" (p. 3). He suggested that its accounts of the struggles between good and evil and its focus on the growth and progress of freedom, democracy, liberalism and knowledge had become an exhausted genre. At that time, traditional media history emphasized a search for facts, yet historians often excluded the interpretation and contextualization of those facts. Critical theorist Hanno Hardt (1989) noted that historical facts were usually presented chronologically as a linear tale providing "overwhelming evidence" (p. 119) to support the growth of newspapers as well as a particular notion of freedom of the press within democracy.

In contrast, Carey noted that cultural media history, with its emphasis on the emotions, motivations, values, attitudes and expectations of people involved in historical events, could offer journalism history a fresh perspective. Cultural media history emphasizes the collective process of people connected with communication within specific economic, political and cultural environments. From this perspective, a consideration of media would address the development of specific technologies as well as view them as social practices and cultural forms. When media history focuses primarily on the specific technological inventions, it privileges the tools, making the technologies seem more important than those who use them. Understanding how people accept or reject new technologies, along with considering the reasons for their incorporation and how people use those technologies, reinforces human agency in the communication process (Williams, 1974).

Carey's call for cultural media history prompted considerable debate about the field of journalism history. While some researchers have embraced Carey's suggestions, others maintained that the field of journalism history should be expanded further to consider all aspects of media and communication history. Communication historian David Paul Nord determined that an emphasis on individuals and how they interacted with elements of communication neglected important structures of power within mass media institutions. Noting that a focus on history from the bottom up is difficult, since media messages are constructed from the top down by those in charge, Nord (1988) insisted that it is important to remember that the "'consciousness' embedded in the language of journalism is the product of large institutions" (p. 10).

Sociologist Michael Schudson (1991) has outlined three contemporary approaches to the study of communication history: institutional history, macro-history and history proper. Institutional history focuses specifically on the development of media properties. This is a popular approach: there are many historical studies of newspapers, advertising agencies, broadcast stations and public relations firms as well as biographies and memoirs of publishers, editors, reporters and photographers that have been published. Relying on the availability of organizational and government archives and records, institutional histories rarely address larger issues regarding the role of communication in human experience or social change. As Schudson (1991) explained, institutional media histories "too often become a parade of personalities and organizational reshufflings" (p. 179). Nord (1989) referred to this type of history as "hagiography," which is the study of the "saints" of journalism like Joseph Pulitzer, William Randolph Hearst and Rupert Murdoch, all of whom helped to build media empires. Nord suggested that institutional media history remained primarily a-theoretical in nature apart from "a vague faith in progress" (p. 309).

Schudson's second approach to communication history, macro-history, considers the relationship between communication and human nature. Often focusing on issues of development, progress and modernization, macro-history has helped to legitimate communication as a relevant field of study. History proper is Schudson's third contemporary approach to media history. Akin to Carey's understanding of cultural history, history proper considers the relationship of media to the larger social, economic and/or political history. It seeks to understand how changes in media influence society, as well as how changes in society impact the communication process. As Schudson explained, while macro-history focuses only on what communication illustrates about some aspect of human nature, history proper looks at what media say about society or what society reveals about the communication process.

The Method of History

As with other qualitative methods, historians pick their topics and craft their research questions on the basis of their interests, receiving guidance from their theoretical frameworks and conceptual orientations. See Chapter 2 for more information on the crafting of qualitative research projects. After historians have chosen their topics, they gather as much documentary evidence as possible and evaluate that evidence for reliability and authenticity. They interpret the significance and meaning of the evidence and finally craft stories about their findings.

Historians maintain that it is important for all researchers to immerse themselves in the general history as well as the published research in their area of interest before crafting their research questions. For example, if a researcher is interested in the development of the blurring of broadcast news and entertainment, it is imperative for him or her to gain background knowledge about how the conception of news began to change during the nineteenth century, as well as to understand the larger issues of media conglomeration and concentration. It is also important for the historian to immerse him- or herself in general broadcast media history and to be knowledgeable about theories of communication and society. Once a researcher is familiar with the general history in his or her interest area and has a good grounding in the relevant theory, the crafting of research questions should follow naturally. Historical research questions should be open-ended and flexible, allowing a researcher to revise a question if needed during the research process. Research questions should also be clearly stated, unambiguous and precise. In recent years, some media and communication historians have begun to consider relational questions that address the complex interactions between aspects of media, culture and society.

There is a huge amount of historical evidence available on some media history topics, and if you pick one of these, you will find it necessary to narrow your topic and research question so that you are able to immerse yourself in the literature. However, you may find that there is very little evidence for some historical topics that you might be interested in researching. If this is the case, you may need to broaden your topic and/or consider collecting different types of evidence or conducting oral history interviews, which are discussed at length in Chapter 6. For example, if you were interested in an historical research project on the development of Edelman Public Relations during the 1950s and 1960s, you would quickly be able to find many different types of evidence for your research project. As one of the world's largest PR firms, Edelman has been written about extensively. Its website alone includes six decades of information about its offices, clients and campaigns. However, if you were interested in learning about labor issues in public relations firms during the 1950s and 1960s, you would have to get creative and consider using novels, films and memoirs, or even doing your own oral history interviews with PR professionals, because there has been only limited historical research done in this area.

Collecting Historical Evidence

Until recently, doing historical research usually meant traveling to historical archives that were housed on university campuses, in libraries or at historical societies. These days, considerable historical material is available online through electronic archives, databases, organizations and a variety of other publications. For example, the Library and Archives Canada includes all types of historical materials, in a variety of formats, related to the cultural, economic and political development of Canada. The collection may be searched electronically and many items may be viewed online. Library and Archives Canada showcases government records, books, journals, research papers, audio and video recordings, films, architectural plans and drawings, maps and nearly 30 million photographic images. It also houses a large collection of daily newspapers throughout Canada, which includes student newspapers and community newsletters.

The Electronic Records Archives (ERA) houses approximately 10 billion US federal government records online at the National Archives at www. archives.gov/era/. This searchable archive includes photographs, videos, films, interviews, letters, news articles, federal agency records and many other types of historical material. The archive also promotes a variety of featured exhibits in its Digital Vaults on significant historical events such as the American Revolution, the influenza epidemic of 1918 and the Civil Rights March on Washington. The ERA includes many types of historical materials, including World War II propaganda posters, images of Americans working from the mid-nineteenth century throughout the twentieth century, online copies of the Declaration of Independence, Edison's light bulb patent, Apollo 11's flight plan and even a letter from Jackie Robinson to President Dwight D. Eisenhower. The site also includes an online Archival Research Catalog, searchable by name and number, referencing all types of collections held by the National Archives.

These days many newspaper archives are now available online; each year, more collections are becoming fully indexed and searchable. Historical societies throughout the US and Europe have uploaded a variety of different types of historical documents and digital photograph collections, and community libraries often include online county historical archives. There are online archives for many different types of history, including women's history, labor history, presidential history, military history and ancient and medieval history.

Considerable biographical material on many public figures is also now available online, and more documents are being uploaded every day. For example, the Hebrew University of Jerusalem has digitized its entire collection of 81,500 items related to the life of Albert Einstein, and the entire collection can be retrieved electronically. The archive includes scientific and non-scientific documents, correspondence, travel diaries, personal materials, photographs, films and sound recordings. The research portal offers many of Einstein's commentaries on his physics research, including his theory of relativity, as well as private correspondence with family members and friends, fan mail he received, and letters regarding his commitment to social issues ranging from nuclear disarmament to civil rights.

Even when historical materials are not available online, many archives have uploaded searchable indexes that researchers can use to get a sense of their holdings. Archivists are also available to talk with researchers about their collections. Several years ago I was writing a book chapter on the development of the American Newspaper Guild, and I worked with a wonderful archivist from the Archives of Labor and Urban Affairs at the Walter Reuther Library who helped me to locate key historical documents for my study.

Types of Historical Materials

In their research, historians evaluate many types of primary and secondary source material. Traditional historians define primary sources as "eyewitness testimony" (Smith, 1989, p. 321) by a person, video or still camera, or other recording device that was present at an event and documents it for the purpose of leaving an historical record. The format or presentation style of an eyewitness record is of less importance to historians than its time frame and content. While some primary sources include commentary regarding an event or issue, other primary sources do not. Traditional historians also distinguish eyewitness testimony about an event from historical documents that were created for other purposes. They use the term "records" to define primary source material about a topic that was intentionally produced and was intended to be seen and distinguish "relics" as primary source materials that are relevant to a study but were actually created for some other reason. Records include news accounts, memoirs, autobiographies, letters, diaries, films, photographs, oral testimony, and some industry and government documents, while relics are things like business financial records, treaties, tools and equipment, local customs, and some government documents. Historians also evaluate paintings and sculptures, advertisements, cartoons, pamphlets, maps and other cultural artifacts to help us understand the social customs and values.

Unpublished primary source documents can provide historians with a more detailed record of an issue or event than published reports or official documents. Historians draw on unpublished papers, memos, letters, tweets and email correspondence to help them understand people's motivations and intentions for their actions. They understand that published materials often document decisions that were taken, rather than discuss the reasons behind the decisions (McDowell, 2002). For example, the unpublished minutes from a corporate media board meeting might provide additional context and information regarding the reasons the board instituted a new international news policy than would be available in the company's published annual report.

While traditional historians remain wary of using poems, novels, songs and other fictional materials as primary sources of evidence, cultural historians, who see history as a creative endeavor, reject distinctions between history and fiction based upon differences between real evidence and imagined material. Instead, they focus on the relevance of the evidence to their specific research projects.

Secondary sources of evidence are created after an event has happened and they often involve the restatement of primary sources of information that have been presented somewhere else. Individuals who craft secondary sources rarely witness the actual events. However, secondary sources are often important sources of evidence providing historians with contextual information about the topic. Most secondary sources include interpretation of the evidence, and these accounts and interpretations tend to change over time. Books, recordings and journal articles on the historical topic are usually considered secondary sources of evidence. While many traditional historians primarily use secondary sources to begin their research projects, drawing on the existing research to provide context and to help them frame their research questions, cultural historians tend to draw on a mixture of primary and secondary sources through their research.

Evaluating Historical Evidence

On November 22, 2011, to commemorate the forty-eighth anniversary of the assassination of President John F. Kennedy, filmmaker Errol Morris created a short documentary, *The Umbrella Man*, in which he addressed the interpretation of historical evidence. The film highlighted an interview with the author of *Six Seconds in Dallas*, Josiah (Tink) Thompson, who discussed the story of the one man who stood under an open black umbrella at the time and place where President Kennedy was assassinated. The question of why a man stood holding an open black umbrella on a lovely warm day in Dallas has initiated numerous theories of an assassination conspiracy. Some maintained that the umbrella man was the real assassin, while others insisted that his opening of the umbrella, as the motorcade approached, signaled the actual marksman or marksmen. As Thompson explained, the umbrella man became a sinister fact that signaled conspiracy. No one was able to interpret the open umbrella as anything but peculiar and evil.

In 1978 the umbrella man, Louis Steven Witt, came forward and testified before the House Select Committee on Assassinations. Witt said that he had held the open black umbrella as a visual protest against Kennedy's father, Joseph P. Kennedy, and his support for Britain's appeasement policies when he served as ambassador to the Court of St. James's in London in 1938 and 1939. For Witt, the umbrella represented the former prime minister of the United Kingdom, Neville Chamberlain, who was known for carrying a black umbrella.

Thompson found Witt's explanation wacky enough to be true, and he suggested that the umbrella man offered a cautionary tale regarding the way we interpret information. When we attempt to understand seemingly sinister things that occur in life, it is important for us to remember that there may be a logical or reasonable interpretation. The umbrella man also reminds us of the active role that researchers play in the interpretation of historical evidence. Historians do not merely record the names, dates and places of events that occur. Through their selection of information, their evaluation of documentation, their analysis of facts and their interpretation of evidence, researchers construct specific historical narratives.

After historians have collected all relevant source material, they analyze the evidence they have obtained for its authenticity and credibility. While most documents held in archives and depositories have already been authenticated, other historical information will need to be evaluated for intentional and accidental errors, which might indicate that the documents are forgeries or otherwise unreliable. Historians also assess the credibility of historical information, considering personal letters, photographs, diaries, interoffice memos and other historical artifacts to be more credible than memoirs, news reports and unsigned memos. The credibility of historical material is often enhanced when it can be corroborated by several other independent sources.

In their evaluations of historical evidence, historians consider the type of information they have obtained and when and where the evidence was produced, and they assess the creator of the evidence as well as his or her intention, original purpose and intended audience. They evaluate evidence for inconsistencies, omissions, contradictions and/or distortions and attempt to verify the information from other sources. In addition, historians also consider the language used in the historical evidence. Because the definitions of words change over time, it is important for researchers to understand the meanings of words within their proper cultural and historical contexts.

Traditional historians evaluate evidence for its reliability and integrity. They look for accidental and intentional errors of fact, forgeries and cases of plagiarism, and they worry about the misuse of evidence and information that is taken out of context. Traditional historians also consider the loss and/or suppression of evidence and problems with identity, motives and the origin of documentary evidence. In their evaluation of evidence they privilege the original over the copy and value the expertise of the document's author and the level of confidentiality, suggesting that government documents and official sources often provide the "best" evidence (Nevins, 1963).

However, from a cultural history perspective, historical research is based on more than the collection of factual information; it involves the interplay between the evidence and the evaluation, and interpretation of this evidence by historians. In their efforts to understand the past, it is important for historians to consider the relationships between one event and a broader pattern of events. Unfortunately, there is not one definitive text on history, or a standard compilation of historical facts or even one interpretation of key historical events. The past is no longer fully available to us; the observations that survive may have misrepresented or misunderstood elements of the past, or taken them out of their proper context. Firsthand observers may have documented some events considered of minor relevance when they first occurred. If the documentation was saved, historians may have studied these events, and their historical narrations may have increased the events' significance. In their efforts to understand the relevance of past events within a society, historians systematically evaluate evidence of the past, doing their best to distinguish authentic from inaccurate reports. While historians cannot completely reconstruct the past, they can provide "penetrating insight into snapshots of past events" (McDowell, 2002, p. 29).

Cultural historians see evidence not merely as facts but also as cultural practices, created by people at a distinct place and time, that may provide insight into the values, beliefs and experiences of a society. Finding that all types of cultural products may contain relevant historical evidence, cultural historians go beyond surface evaluations to consider the style, language, structure and absences and other latent meanings of the evidence.

While traditional historians usually evaluate evidence as "particles of reality" (Kellner, 1989, p. 10) from which a factual story of the past can be constructed, cultural historians encourage researchers to consider historical materials as cultural artifacts that can help us to make sense of how people lived their lives at a particular place and time. In addition, cultural historians attempt to study their own cultures as "alien" cultures and to see those who lived at a particular place and time as the "other." As cultural historian Robert Darnton (2009) explained, "We constantly need to be shaken out of a false sense of familiarity with the past, to be administered doses of culture shock" (p. 325).

After historians have evaluated historical evidence for its authenticity, integrity and significance, they select relevant evidence, compare it with other information gathered from primary and secondary sources, and they analyze and interpret the evidence. Finally, they craft stories and attempt to understand the significance of their historical research.

Ethical Considerations

The assessment of historical evidence raises some ethical challenges for historians. Researchers find it challenging to understand people's motivations for their attitudes, beliefs and actions. They also find it difficult to determine the accuracy of historical sources and to determine which information is based on observation, which is grounded in opinion and which evidence has been created or fabricated. For example, in 2012 Ira Glass, host of the National Public Radio program *This American Life*, pulled one of its shows after he learned that key evidence had been fabricated. The thirty-nine-minute radio episode was based on Mike Daisey's one-man theater show depicting Apple's manufacturing processes in China. Daisey justified his invention of some events and characters by insisting that theater was not journalism and that his fabrications were created "in service of a greater narrative truth" (Carr, 2012) about people's suffering in China.

However, Glass noted that although the goal of the show was to raise people's consciousness about offshore manufacturing, it was important to share accurate information with the American public.

Historians craft stories that are meant to be interesting, well written, dramatic and compelling, and it is this narrative emphasis that may lead to "simplifications or exaggerations" (Berger, 2000, p. 135) of the historical record. While most historians see history as "part art and historians part artist" (Nerone, 1993, p. 150), it is important for researchers to do their best to present the historical evidence they obtain accurately, clearly, completely and within its proper context.

Research Using History

Historical research is usually presented in narrative form, recounting one or more stories that are built from a researcher's interpretations of historical evidence. Some historians use a chronological framework for their narratives, tracing a variety of issues or ideas over time, while others tell their stories thematically. In the following historical study, Allissa Richardson used a thematic approach to showcase early twentieth-century collaborative news partnerships between the black press and African American Pullman porters as examples of networked journalism. Pullman porters served as news aggregators, distributors and writers, and their news partnerships with the black press helped to create a black political imaginary among writers and activists.

"The Platform: How Pullman Porters Used Railways to Engage in Networked Journalism," by Allissa V. Richardson

From *Journalism Studies*, 2016, 1–17

Introduction

When African-American soldiers returned to the United States from World War I in 1918, they soon discovered that another battle—for their civil rights—had just begun. Soldiers came home to find the Jim Crow system of institutionalized racism still intact. Lynching was at its height. Respectable jobs were scarce—save that of the Pullman porter, whose travels across the railroads of the United States provided the worldly exposure that African-American men had only just begun to glimpse abroad during the Great War. Despite harsh working conditions, a job as a Pullman porter was considered the very best post to which an African-American man could aspire. Pullman porters were black America's itinerant scholars who used the railroads to transmit the news and public opinion of the day. It was the Pullman porter—and his contact with US presidents, foreign dignitaries, and wealthy people traveling to and fro—that informed African-American newspapers and, arguably, helped shape the black political imaginary that reverberated throughout the works of Harlem Renaissance writers and early Civil Rights activists alike after the Great War. In his subservient position as an attendant aboard the nation's luxurious sleeper-train cars, the Pullman porter was an invisible man, privy to all manner of information. He was a clandestine news gatherer and subversive news distributor, often tossing black newspapers off their trains in between scheduled stops across the South. As such, he served as a vital node in what modern journalism scholars now call "networked journalism." Networked journalism refers to a twenty-first-century style of reportage that leverages the efforts of a broad range of people to tell a story, from local amateurs acting as citizen journalists to professional journalists working for official news outlets (Beckett and Mansell, 2008; Van der Haak, Parks, and Castells, 2012). This essay re-frames the news partnerships of Pullman porters and African-American newspapers as an example of networked journalism that functioned efficiently for decades, well before the Information Age. The Pullman porters and African-American newspapers used the railways as an antecedent to computerized social networks to achieve modern notions of information crowdsourcing and collaborative news editing, which helped shape and convey black political thought in dangerous times. This essay also recasts the Pullman porter as more than a servile laborer, but rather as a progressive agent of socially conscious participatory journalism who added a daily, working-class voice to black newspapers.

I specifically examine the Pullman porter's alliances with five prominent African-American newspapers from 1914 (at the start of the Great War) to 1939 (the end of the Harlem Renaissance): *Baltimore Afro-American*, *Chicago Defender*, *New York Age*, *New York Amsterdam News*, and *Pittsburgh Courier*. This essay follows in three parts. First, I review the existing literature to explain how the post-World War I racial climate fostered an environment for Pullman porters to act as unifying nodes in the network of antebellum black thought. Then, I present primary sources, from the digital archives of the five newspapers, to highlight the porters' contributions to journalism—as news gatherers, distributors, and authors; secondary sourcing of relevant books and journal articles round out this analysis. Finally, I conclude with a survey of Pullman porters who left the industry eventually to pursue full-time journalism careers.

In the following sections, note how Richardson provided important context on the early twentieth-century racial climate and offered readers a history of the development of Pullman porters. She also addressed the rise of the Harlem Renaissance, identifying Pullman porters as ideal emissaries of a post–World War I "black political awakening."

Coming Home

It was hardly a hero's welcome. Wilbur Little stepped off the train in his home-town of Blakely, Georgia on April 10, 1919, wearing the khaki military dress uniform that the United States Army issued to him during the Great War. Local whites ordered the African-American soldier to remove it at the station or face arrest. Little explained that he did not have any civilian clothes with him and the men allowed him to go home. Several days later, Little continued to wear the uniform in public, despite anonymous written threats to take it off. When he refused, a mob gathered in the center of town and beat him to death ("Georgia soldier," 1919). When African-American soldiers began to return to the United States from World War I in 1918, many of them met Wilbur Little's fate (Williams, 2010). The black press filed anguished reports of African-American soldiers in uniform, hanging from trees, burned alive or cut into pieces by racist mobs—betrayed by the country they fought to protect abroad during the Great War ("Lynchers shoot," 1919; "Nine ex-soldiers," 1920). Black rage reached fever pitch in the summer and early fall of 1919, when race riots erupted in more than two dozen cities across the country, claiming the most lives in Chicago, Washington, DC and Elaine, Arkansas, where blacks retaliated violently against white provocateurs. James Weldon Johnson, field secretary for the National Association for the Advancement of Colored People (NAACP), called the season the "Red Summer of 1919" and told Baltimore's Afro-American newspaper on October 24:

> The Negro came back from the Great War disillusioned: thousands died for what to them is a lie, and the whole race, galvanized into thought, is going after what it is entitled to and what it is going to get—unlimited American democracy.
>
> ("Thousands die," 1919)

The specter of lynching meant that the struggle for racial equality could not be fought openly. White supremacists were convinced that blacks were America's greatest problem. One contemporary author, Dr. Robert W. Shufeldt wrote:

> The negro is too grossly and hopelessly ignorant to recognize the ruin his presence among us entails . . . At no historical time have two such

distinct races, each numbered by its millions, the [white] one repre-
senting the highest stage of civilization and advancement, the [black]
other practically but a day removed from savagery and cannibalism,
been thrown together in the same geographical region and not sepa-
rated by any political or natural barriers.

(Shufeldt, 1915, p. 274)

Shufeldt was a United States Army Major in the Medical Corps. His urgent
manifesto called for the wholesale deportation of blacks to Africa, or social control through lynching whenever emigration was not possible. As he was a deco-
rated soldier and a lettered academic who was a member of more than a dozen
medical honor societies, his writing would have been very influential at the time.
The volatile racial climate that white supremacists like Shufeldt instigated is,
paradoxically, what birthed the porter profession. The African-American railroad experience began in slavery, where blacks dug roadbeds and lay trestle for
tracks. Working on the railroad was dangerous and often fatal. Countless slaves
died in train collisions, premature dynamite explosions, and site cave-ins. The
14-hour workdays left their bodies susceptible to disease too—malaria, cholera,
and scarlet fever were common ailments along the track. The end of the Civil
War in 1865 left four million newly emancipated black men looking for paid
work. Most of the railroad jobs in the immediate antebellum period involved
loading and unloading freight as a depot hand. Other jobs involved maintenance
of the South's 8784-mile (by 1861) rail network where black men served as
brakemen, firemen, and switchmen (Kornweibel, 2010). The more prestigious
posts of engineer and conductor were off-limits to black men. Ironically, it was
George Pullman, the man who literally lifted the city of Chicago from its mal-
odorous bogs, who lifted the social status of the black man in the antebellum
South—albeit unintentionally.

Pullman arrived in Chicago from New York in 1859 to help the city build its
first sewage system. He reinvested the proceeds from this contract to fund a
new venture in 1867: luxury sleeper trains. Prior to Pullman's vision of a hotel
on wheels, train travel was uncomfortable and dangerous. It was not uncommon
for bandits to rob trains in the antebellum South and Old West, as the cargo
typically included corporate payrolls and other cash shipments. The culture of
train robbery sprouted from the Southern whites who had fought in the Civil
War as Confederate soldiers and faced destitution after their side lost. In fact,
notorious train robber Jesse James was a Confederate veteran (Stiles, 2003).
Pullman endeavored to counter this criminal element of the railway experience.
He envisioned opulent quarters where passengers could relax with their families, dining and drinking until they reached their eventual destinations. Such
an experience would be incomplete without the sense of being waited on, hand

and foot, however. Pullman needed a fleet of workers with whom wealthy whites would feel comfortable. They must be willing to work roughly 400 hours per month, sleeping only for three to four hours per day. They must be part-butler, part-concierge, part-babysitter, part-security guard, part-housekeeper, part-chef, part-raconteur, and part-minstrel. They must be willing to toil with no promise of a salaried wage. Their main recompense would come in the form of passenger tips ("Pullman Porters' Average," 1925). They must be strong enough to lift heavy cargo, but diminutive enough in spirit to disappear among the train's furnishings when necessary. Pullman saw in the four million newly emancipated slaves this ideal servant. Railway historian Theodore Kornweibel has noted:

> To what extent Pullman coldly calculated that ex-slaves, under the prod of economic necessity, would willingly become passengers' servants cannot be definitely resolved. Clearly, he believed that blacks were temperamentally suited to serve others. That he was nobly inspired to offer a helping hand to a newly liberated race is doubtful.
>
> (Kornweibel, 2010, pp. 114–116)

If the Pullman porters were one key to the company's success, the other was high-profile marketing. George Pullman's first high-profile passenger was the deceased President Abraham Lincoln, whom he transported back to Illinois after the funeral on one of his luxury trains. Pullman later appointed Lincoln's son, Robert Todd, to serve as the company's general counsel. Robert became the president of Pullman Co. when Pullman died in 1897. Ironically, the younger Lincoln's politics diverged from his father's, however, and he was one of the most vocal opponents to African-American racial equality. During his tenure, Robert Lincoln paid the porters exploitatively low wages and maintained oppressive labor policies. A former Pullman porter wrote a book that lambasted Lincoln (Anderson, 1904). According to Kornweibel (2010), at the height of Pullman's monopoly on the sleeper car industry, his company boasted more than 2000 cars crisscrossing the country along the rails. Pullman Co. was worth $62 million in 1893 (worth roughly $1.4 billion today).[1] In 1918, right after Great War veterans began to return home, the average Pullman porter wage was $1410 per year (roughly $22,000 today). Pullman's rationale for his low-wage policy was that he was uplifting a formerly beleaguered group of people. He fancied himself doing blacks a favor by employing them when no one else in the antebellum South would do so.

Despite the exploitative pay and demeaning work, the stately, crisp porter uniforms conveyed a cosmopolitan elegance that stood in stark contrast to the dirty denim overalls one would be forced to wear as a Southern sharecropper or some other form of agrarian peon ("Hundreds leave," 1921). Moreover, the promise to leave the confines of the oppressive South, to see other parts of the country, must have stirred the souls of black men too, for they entered the profession in droves. To the white passengers they served, they were menials. To their black communities, however, they were men of élan and influence. Those who left the porter profession had their pick of top jobs in the service industry, historians note. They often "graduated" to fine hotels and restaurants. Some porters even attracted the attention of US Presidents who invited them to work as White House staff. John W. Mayes, for example, went on to serve as the barber for Presidents William McKinley, Theodore Roosevelt, William Howard Taft, Woodrow Wilson, Warren Harding, Calvin Coolidge, Herbert Hoover, Franklin D. Roosevelt, and Harry S. Truman ("Hundreds leave," 1921). Another porter, James B. Newsome, who served for 52 years and traveled 5.8 million miles during his tenure, told the *Chicago Defender* (1922) that he served many of the pioneers of the West Coast, which included "Wild Bill" Hickok, the Morton family (which founded the salt company that still exists), the Stanford family (for which the university is named), and publishing magnate William Randolph Hearst's family.

Despite his close encounters with the wealthy, the first generation of Pullman porters fathered black men who still were not free. Yet, at the turn of the century, black and white leaders alike urged them to take up arms to defend American democracy. In a July 1918 essay entitled "Close Ranks," W. E. B. Du Bois (1918), a staunch integrationist and cofounder of the NAACP, attempted to rally African-American men to fight in the Great War through the pages of the group's official organ, *The Crisis* magazine. Although Du Bois agreed that the racial status quo in America for blacks was excruciatingly stagnant, he disagreed that blacks should leave America. He argued that instead they should stay, get an education, and assimilate their way into powerful leadership roles. When black soldiers returned home, however, and faced the same intense bigotry and Jim Crow legislation that they had left behind, black America splintered into several nodes of thought, each represented by its own bold journalistic enterprise. The canon of advocacy journalism that came out of this era expressed the "New Negro" ideology, in which black intellectuals debated publicly about how best to improve the quality of life for the race (Locke, 1925; Hickmott, 2011).

First, Du Bois reversed his patriotic position with his diatribe "Returning Soldiers," which ran in *The Crisis* in May 1919 (Du Bois, 1919). He railed against lynching and disenfranchisement but urged blacks to stay in America to fight for their rights. At the other end of the spectrum, Marcus Garvey founded *Negro World* newspaper in August 1918, and in it proposed total emigration to Africa. By June 1919, more than two million readers became card-carrying members of his organization, the Universal Negro Improvement Association and African Communities League (UNIA-ACL). In the metaphorical middle—between Du Bois's call to integrate and Garvey's call to emigrate—stood A. Philip Randolph and Chandler Owen, who began to publish *The Messenger* magazine in 1917. They touted their publication as, "The Only Radical Negro Magazine in America" and spouted Marxist rhetoric, so as not to disappoint. They idolized the Russian Bolshevik protests and urged blacks across America to take up arms. They believed, as their early writings reflect, that the black proletariat could defeat the white bourgeoisie with force and civil uprising, but not by convening docile meetings or academic conventions, or by leaving America for Africa. All of these intrepid thinkers and community organizers were impassioned, eloquent, and prolific writers. They formed the vanguard of what history would later call "The Harlem Renaissance." Some of these men, such as Du Bois, were Ivy League-educated. Others had married "into money," and so enjoyed a relatively privileged social status. For example, A. Philip Randolph's wife, Lucille Campbell, was a hair stylist and protegé of Madame C. J. Walker, the first black woman millionaire. Campbell was wealthy in her own right too, and funded *The Messenger* in its infancy (Anderson, 1973). What the black public sphere lacked, then, was a working-class voice from beyond the Ivory Tower. The Pullman porter, at the dawn of a post-war era of black political awakening, was anointed the ideal emissary.

Pullman Porters Were Educated, Yet Relegated

In the summer of 1923, a train careened off its track in a heavy storm, tossing Pullman porter James Owens and other passengers into the pitch black night. When Owens woke from unconsciousness, he crawled through the wreckage to find the conductor. The two then stumbled through the iron detritus to extricate passengers from twisted bits of metal. Although Owens became a hero, his fellow porter colleague, Theodore M. Seldon, was not as fortunate. His body was so disfigured that the train employees could identify him only by his Phi Beta Kappa Key, which he had earned at Dartmouth College earlier that spring (Kornweibel, 2010). Second-generation Pullman porters had benefited greatly from the sleepless nights of their fathers, who finally had scraped together enough money to send their children to some of the most prestigious colleges in the land. Many Pullman porters were impeccable savers and the black press published dozens of news stories about their relatively large estates. My favorite story is an *Afro-American* (1921) piece that describes family members creating fraudulent wills when they discover a recently deceased porter left $15,000 cash to his heirs. A 1939 *Defender* piece about a high school teacher who inherited $57,000 from her porter father—which would be worth $956,000 today—was equally impressive.

The black press often reported that most porters who came to the profession in the 1920s were college-educated, yet could not find employment after graduation, due to discriminatory hiring practices or outright Jim Crow-enforced segregation. An article that ran in the *Afro-American* (1924) highlighted 100 Howard University students who entered the profession as summer employees. By the mid-1920s, historians estimate that 30 percent of black medical school graduates were ex-porters (Kornweibel, 2010). They used their tips to pay for tuition and studied while passengers slept. John Baptist Ford was a Pullman porter who rose to national prominence after a white business school professor at Dartmouth took notice of his impeccable service and invited him to the university to deliver three keynote addresses. The *Pittsburgh Courier* (1924) reported that Ford told the audience, "I know a couple of doctors—brothers—who stayed ten years in the service after they'd taken their degrees. They were saving money all the time. When they'd got enough, they set up in practice."

The assumption that a Pullman porter was uneducated often worked to his advantage. He could appear submissive as needed. His unassuming demeanor made wealthy whites feel comfortable—while the train was rolling. The incongruity of the racial realpolitik of the time dictated that when the train came to a stop, the same black Pullman porter who had been entrusted to handle the white passenger's bag of heirloom jewelry could not stay in the same hotel as the family who had offered him a tip. Pullman porters soon learned, then, to take advantage of the non-traditional education they received through interaction with the country's most influential people. Collectively, Pullman porters served roughly 35 million passengers annually, including celebrities and tycoons such as Cornelius Vanderbilt, J. Pierpont Morgan, John D. Rockefeller, Buffalo Bill Cody, Mrs. Will Rogers, and Mrs. H. J. Heinz, to name a select few (Kornweibel, 2010, p. 128). Every train ride reinforced to Pullman porters what life was like for the other half. This scared some whites of the time. Raymond Patterson wrote:

> That is to say, a Pullman porter who has run from Mobile to Montgomery, and then to Atlanta or Chattanooga, the end of his run being evidently a little further north with every change he makes. In this way, they tell me, the railroad negroes are shifting North slowly but surely day by day, and in the only way they could do it without directly buying a ticket and moving wife and family.
>
> (Patterson, 1911, p. 21)

Patterson further argued that such a migration would disrupt the natural social order of America, and that policies should be enacted to keep blacks as separate from whites as possible. Although the tone of this book is incredulous to modern audiences, his observations were prescient. Pullman porters did help spread the word about migration to the North, especially to Chicago, as secret distributors of the *Chicago Defender* newspaper, as we will discuss later in this essay. We should note for now, however, that Patterson was an influential white journalist of his time, penning pieces for the *Chicago Tribune* and for the *Washington Post* (Church and Goodman, 1909). Moreover, the foreword of his manifesto, *The Negro and His Needs* (Patterson, 1911), is written by the future US president William Howard Taft, who was his classmate at Yale University. Prominent separatist voices such as Patterson's perhaps made the Pullman porter arguably all too willing to participate in subversive acts of news production that would offer a counter-narrative of black American life not as full of problems, but full of promise.

Drawing on primary sources from five newspapers available from digital archives, as well as secondary sources from relevant books and journal articles, in the next sections Richardson detailed the experiences of Pullman porters as news gatherers, news distributors and as authors. For me, the story of Robert Abbott's alliance between the *Chicago Defender* and Pullman porters was a fascinating example of the creative ways the black press gathered news and shared it with their readers.

The Pullman Porter as News Gatherer

Gossip was a porter "specialty," journalist Larry Tye explained in his book *Rising from the Rails* (Tye, 2004), adding, "They picked up tidbits about everything from politics to finances, and knew which to keep alive and which were privileged." For example, porters on President Franklin D. Roosevelt's sleeper car knew he was battling the debilitating effects of polio long before the public did, and waited on him diligently as he slowly lost his ability to walk (Tye, 2004, p. 183; "Grand Old Man," 1937). In the modern networked journalism model, professional journalists work with amateurs to create a news story that could not have been realized without that partnership. These kinds of collaborative efforts are facilitated by new forms of convergent media platforms, such as the mobile phone, which allow speedy newsgathering. So it was at the end of the Great War too. The advent of the electric telegraph in the 1830s already had replaced homing pigeons and the Pony Express to transmit information more swiftly over the vast expanse of the country (Thompson, 1947). By 1918, as more railroad tracks continued to be laid across the land, telegraph lines often ran alongside it in an increasingly sophisticated network. Unionized telegraphers were stationed at depots along the nation's railways, regularly dispatching news and directing train traffic. Professional journalists from mainstream daily newspapers relied on updates from these telegraphers acting as amateur news gatherers to provide stories for its primarily white audiences. Many of these telegraphers became indispensable members of the newsroom (Rasmussen, 1998). As telegraphy was not a field typically open to black men at the time, the black press relied instead on the Pullman porter.

Perhaps the most famous alliance between the Pullman porters and the black press is that of the *Chicago Defender*. Robert Abbott, who founded the paper in 1905, enlisted the help of Frank P. George to collect newspapers and magazines that wealthy passengers left behind on the trains. At the end of George's Boston-to-Chicago runs, he brought back bundles of periodicals. He frequently clipped stories from the *New York Times*, *New York Herald Tribune*, the *Wall Street Journal*, and the *Saturday Evening Post* (Tye, 2004). The *Defender* staff pored over every periodical that George aggregated, scouring its pages for out-of-town news on African-Americans. Soon George realized he needed help, and he groomed Pullman porter Alexander O. Taylor to bring in papers too (Ottley, 1955). Taylor picked up newspapers between Cleveland and Chicago. He summarized what he clipped and heard on train cars in a near daily news brief entitled, "Ohio State News." Taylor eventually become a social secretary of sorts for the *Defender*, gathering news about Cleveland's black middle class and its relative prosperity. He aggregated information about the dinner parties of well-to-do blacks, with careful attention to detail. In one such holiday edition of his dispatch, he noted that a Miss Lucy Manson had exhibited "exceeding hospitality" to a large dinner party of family and friends, and that one of her guests treated the group to a ride in one of his luxury cars. Taylor (1915) also wrote that he was a proper host too, serving a "16½-pound fowl" from his family's Virginia farm. No news seemed too small for Taylor to collect. His briefs were filled with praises for well-delivered church sermons, job opportunities, profiles of black professionals who were returning from glamorous summer vacations, and news of divorces, deaths, and births. In his later years, Taylor quit Pullman Co. to become a full-time distributor of the *Defender* for the Cleveland area (Young, 1955).

Rounding out Abbott's newsgathering team was Frank "Fay" Young. In 1914, Young joined the *Defender* staff as a sports writer, working for the publication for free, just like all of the other contributors. By day, Young was a dining car waiter aboard the Chicago & Northwestern Railroad, quietly collecting news items that he would send back to the *Defender* too. Eventually Abbott came to rely on Young so much, he offered him a full-time job for the newspaper, but Young initially declined. Historian Roi Ottley explained:

> He asked Fay Young to resign from his railroad job and work for the paper, but Young was reluctant because Abbott offered him only fifteen dollars a week, less than he earned as a dining car waiter; moreover,

joining the *Defender* meant a reduction in social status, as railroad men were among the sought-after figures in Negro society, and news-papermen were considered merely hustlers.

(Ottley, 1955, p. 115)

Young eventually did accept Abbott's employment offer. He became the managing editor in 1918, the year that the Great War came to an end. He remained at the *Defender* as a sports writer for the rest of his life, from 1914 until 1957 (Cowans, 1957). Frank P. George spent his whole life gathering news for the Defender too. His obituary, which ran in the *Defender*, read: "His shears were as faithful as his eye. He read by glance and sweep. He fell at his post" (Simmons, 1922).

In addition to curating news second-hand, Pullman porters were privy to real-time breaking news too. It was a Pullman porter who broke the news of race riots in Nebraska, for example. The *Afro-American* (1929) reported: "First news of the Platte, Nebraska race riot in which hundreds of colored people were driven from their homes was brought to H. J. Pinkett and the Omaha branch NAACP by a Pullman porter." This early news tip allowed local blacks to organize and contact the governor that night to seek prosecution for members of the mob. This was a rare occurrence, as many lynchings occurred at night and were not discovered until morning, when the mobs already had dispersed. Although no arrests were made, the victims were able to return to town safely with their homes still intact. In this manner, the Pullman porter not only had the ability to get "the scoop," as journalists say in newsroom parlance, but he had the power to be a swift, invisible grassroots organizer. Every day, he saw the world go by at 50 miles per hour, after all, and he could carry news back and forth with unmatched speed.

The Pullman Porter as News Distributor

By the end of World War I, roughly 1.5 million African-Americans had migrated from the rural South to the industrialized North. Pullman porters were responsible, in part, for what came to be known as the Great Migration. At the time, in the *Chicago Defender*, Abbott called it the Great Northern Drive. He advertised it in a full-page spread ("Northern drive," 1917), urging Southern blacks to move to Chicago to take advantage of the growing job market. At the same time, Pullman porters were growing increasingly disgruntled with their working conditions. They still worked 18–20-hour shifts with only an average of 25-cent tips per passenger. Pullman Co. also expected its porters to pay for their own service supplies, such as shoe shine, which cut into their earnings even further. Hostile race relations brewed aboard the train too, and the porter had to be prepared to deal with verbal insults from or physical altercations with white passengers and train conductors alike. For example, some whites called all Pullman porters "George," or referred to them as "George [Pullman's] boys," rather than call them by their actual names. It was a tradition that harkened back to slavery, where slaves were named after their masters. In 1914, a lumber baron named George W. Dulany created the Society for the Prevention of Calling Sleeping Car Porters "George" to feign indignation that his name was associated with black porters. The organization grew rapidly, however, and at its height it boasted a membership of more than 30,000 men, which included celebrities and aristocrats, such as George Herman "Babe" Ruth, the United Kingdom's King George V, and Georges Clemenceau of France (Santino, 1991; Tye, 2004, p. 2).

By 1925, the porters began to organize themselves into a union. They approached A. Philip Randolph, publisher of *The Messenger*, to become their president. Their goal was to win higher wages for the porters and more reasonable working conditions. Randolph accepted the invitation to lead the men and began to convene meetings in major cities where Pullman porters lived. Whenever the porters convened, Pullman Co. planted moles to spy on the group's operations (Bates, 2001). In 1926, for example, Claude Barnett, the founder of the Associated Negro Press, took money from the Pullman Co. to publish a weekly black newspaper called *The Light and Heebie Jeebies*, which aimed to discredit the Brotherhood of Sleeping Car Porters (BSCP) and A. Philip Randolph. Barnett's news service provided stories to 112 other black member newspapers in America when he accepted this bribe. When the porters discovered his alliance with the Pullman Co., therefore, it stung them deeply and fostered years of distrust of the black press. To counter the porters' leeriness—and to convince them to distribute the *Chicago Defender* newspaper south of the Mason-Dixon line—publisher John Abbott appealed to the porters with promises of stipends and editorial flattery. First, Abbott launched a column entitled "Sparks from the Rail" to highlight porters' human-interest stories (Winston, 1914b). He chose John R. Winston, an active porter and leader in the union movement, to write it weekly. By all published accounts, Winston was a "porter's porter" who represented the very best of the profession. He was a founding member of the Brotherhood of Train Porters of America in 1914, which was a precursor to the BSCP (Winston, 1914a). A *Chicago Defender* (1911) article reported that Winston was "known throughout the United States by the railroad men." Another *Defender* profile noted that he was an effective orator and toastmaster ("John R. Winston made," 1915). Yet another *Defender* piece reported that Winston battled rheumatism after a two-week leisurely vacation, but never failed to continue filing stories with the newspaper while ill ("John R. Winston indisposed," 1912).

John R. Winston became a staple at the Defender and the nation's black porters finally were at Abbott's disposal. The porter—*Defender* networked journalism distribution model then worked like this: Abbott paid the porters to bundle

Defenders before each trip, the porters stored the papers in their lockers at the train station, and then they left them with contacts along their routes. The Pullman porters were responsible for deciding the best places to deliver the *Defender*, and they often chose stops near black barbershops and churches across the South. In his March 14, 1914 "Sparks from the Rail" column, Winston thanked the Pullman porters for their inaugural run as newspaper couriers. He wrote:

> The *Chicago Defender* is indebted to the vast army of railroad men for their pride in its efforts for the good of the race and their creditable work in extending its circulation. Through them it has reached the remote parts of the world.
>
> (Winston, 1914b)

By 1920, the *Defender* had a paid circulation of about 230,000, two-thirds of it outside of Chicago (Tye, 2004, p. 82).

The Pullman porters helped to distribute the *Pittsburgh Courier* too. In 1921, Robert Vann, its owner-editor, competed openly with Robert Abbott for the mantle of top black press editor, and he emulated the *Defender's* practice of using Pullman porters as couriers. Vann, who had served as a summer porter from 1906 to 1910 between semesters of law school, hired Pullman porters to drop his paper across the South, Midwest, and West in the early 1920s. In return, Vann changed his position on the porters' efforts to unionize by publishing more favorable editorials about the BSCP's progress. When the porters eventually published their list of demands in *The Pullman Porter* in 1927, the pamphlet was bundled with the *Pittsburgh Courier* to facilitate its shipment around the country (Brotherhood of Sleeping Car Porters, 1927). Vann also launched a column entitled, "Real Heroes," which valorized Pullman porters when they committed brave acts on behalf of their passengers (Winston, 1938). Lastly, Vann worked with the porters to urge black migration to the North too. He published stories of job opportunities in his city's coal, iron, and steel industries. This led to an influx of blacks primarily from Alabama, where these same industries were based on peonage or a convict-lease system (Dickerson, 1986; Blackmon, 2009). Vann then reported in the *Pittsburgh Courier* (1923), that Georgia had lost $27 million amid the mass black exodus and that 46,674 homes were left vacant. The black population of Pittsburgh bloomed at the height of the *Courier's* popularity, from 10,357 people in 1890 up to 54,983 in 1930. Scholars note that 87 percent of this growth was due to migration from the South, while the remaining growth was attributed to new births from existing black residents (Gottlieb, 1996). Additionally, the porters' newspaper distribution efforts paid off too: circulation rose to 250,000 by 1937, making the *Pittsburgh Courier* the most popular black newspaper of its day.

The Pullman Porter as Author

If anyone had a yarn to spin in black America, it was the Pullman porter. Tye noted:

> Porters had dipped their toes in the Pacific *and* the Atlantic, walked the promenades in New York City and Chicago, and traveled to fifty states with Wall Street barons and baseball gods. They were men with stories to tell, and everyone listened.
>
> (Tye, 2004, p. 77)

One of the largest concentrations of Pullman porters—nearly 2000 men—lived in New York near the Grand Central and Penn terminals. Some of them contributed regularly to the *New York Age* and the *New York Amsterdam News* for several years. Both publications had storied beginnings and colorful leaders who most likely enthralled the porters. *The New York Age* actually began in 1880 as *The New York Globe*. By 1884, the editors changed the title to *The New York Freeman*, settling finally in 1887 on the *Age* (Thornbrough, 1966). T. Thomas Fortune, who was born into slavery in 1856, was its firebrand editor-in-chief who wrote bold invectives about race relations in the United States. He was a close friend and ghostwriter for Booker T. Washington, who was also a silent owner of the publication and its regular financier until his death in 1915 (Adams, 1902). While Washington was an accommodationist who did not believe in challenging the racial status quo in America—he thought blacks should simply learn trades and work within the segregated system to accumulate economic security—Fortune's *raison d'être* was openly condemning anti-lynching. During his tenure, Fortune hired prominent writers such as James Weldon Johnson (who later served as field secretary for the NAACP), W. E. B. Du Bois, and Ida B. Wells-Barnett, whom he personally invited to the staff after local white supremacists in her hometown of Memphis, Tennessee burned her newspaper's office to the ground (Alexander, 2008; Curry, 2012). Fortune encouraged his writers to include their bylines with their pieces, which was a sharp departure from black newspapers like the *Chicago Defender* or the *Pittsburgh Courier* that often published stories anonymously. While the *Age*'s influence grew, Fortune battled quietly with mental illness and alcoholism. He sold his stake of the newspaper in 1907 to Fred Moore, who became its new editor. Under Moore, the newspaper began to adopt more of Booker T. Washington's philosophies and began to lose its credibility as a publication dedicated to the uplift of black people (Wintz and Finkelman, 2004). Even after Washington's death in 1915, the *Age* struggled to stay afloat. It courted readers, however, using the same formula that had worked for both the *Defender* and the *Afro-American*: catering editorially to the Pullman porter.

Perhaps the most famous *New York Age* Pullman porter columnist was James H. Hogans, who penned the column on "Things Seen, Heard and Done Among Pullman Employees" (Hogans, 1929). His editorials on life along the railroad and the effort of porters to unionize during the 1920s earned him a loyal readership. The *Baltimore Afro-American* offered him a full-time job as a columnist in 1936, and he left the porter profession altogether. Hogans wrote nearly 100 editorials for the *Afro-American*, occasionally contributing to the *Chicago Defender* too. In it, he highlighted births, deaths, successes, and failures of porter union organizing, election results for union chapters, and profiles of Pullman porters who rose to prominence. In one column, for instance, Hogans shares the story of Pullman porter Stewart H. Holbrook who was featured in *Esquire* magazine in 1939. He quotes Holbrook as saying that the status of the Pullman porter rose to that of "colored teachers, doctors, lawyers and top businessmen." Hogans (1939) added that the porter now "sends his children to high school, quite often to college" and "lives in the best parts of colored communities."

When T. Thomas Fortune rebounded from his departure from *New York Age*, he began writing and editing at his former rival publication, the *New York Amsterdam News*. He found himself among other radical thinkers, such as Claude McKay, who was a former Pullman porter. McKay wrote his popular 1928 novel, *Home to Harlem*, during his breaks aboard the Pullman sleeper cars. Editors of the *Amsterdam News* granted him a column in 1937. In it, McKay reported hard news about authoritarian regimes throughout Europe, including that of Adolf Hitler in Germany and Benito Mussolini in Italy. He offered scathing commentary about the European scramble to colonize Africa. The column was so popular, it was syndicated in the *Afro-American* too (McKay, 1939). McKay also argued in favor of self-imposed segregation in the United States. He suggested blacks follow the communal example set by Jewish immigrants to create their own economies, schools, and infrastructures. He wrote in a column: "In fact, [the Jews] have broken down 100 percent barriers of American prejudice and discrimination by building up institutions inferior to none and which are a credit to the entire American nation" (McKay, 1937). Aside from politics as prose, McKay also offered commentary through poetry and allowed the black press to syndicate it as well. His most famous poem, "If We Must Die," ran in the *Pittsburgh Courier* on July 14, 1927. In the poem's penultimate line, McKay challenges readers to "face the murderous, cowardly pack/pressed to the wall, dying, but fighting back!" McKay seemed to be speaking not only to black men in America who faced murderous mobs, but also to African men across the vast continent who faced colonial rule. In this manner, McKay was a forerunner in this genre of international ethnic journalism that investigated the plight of black people around the world.

Robert Vann watched the rise of the Pullman porter-cum-global journalist model and decided to emulate it in 1935, sending former porter Joel Augustus Rogers to Ethiopia to cover its war with Italy. Vann was the only black editor who could afford to send a foreign correspondent abroad and *Pittsburgh Courier* readers were thrilled to hear about an African nation resisting the onslaught of European colonization (Calvin, 1935). Rogers had already developed a following with readers after he self-published his seminal novel, *From Superman to Man* in 1917. In it, a black Pullman porter spends a cross-country train ride trying to dissuade a white Southern politician from being racist. Excerpts from the book ran in the *Pittsburgh Courier*, the *Defender*, and in the *New York Amsterdam News* (Asukile, 2010). Rogers retired from the porter profession in 1919, dabbling in art studies and freelance writing for the *Chicago Defender*, Marcus Garvey's *Negro World*, *The Messenger* magazine, and the *New York Amsterdam News*. As a former Pullman porter, he definitely was not a stranger to travel. His writing, however, sometimes reflected the melancholy he felt when riding the train as a free man across Europe. On those foreign tracks, he was a passenger, not a servant. In a *New York Amsterdam News* column entitled "Ruminations," Rogers wrote:

> The more I travel, or meet people, or engage in historical research the firmer grows my belief that humanity is one, and that so-called race really counts for very, very little. The greatest barrier to a better understanding among peoples is that so many of us see others as Baptists or Methodists or Catholics; American, German, English or Chinese; black or white and a thousand and one other distinctions first and then as human beings like ourselves next.
>
> (Rogers, 1934)

In the final section, Richardson went beyond the recounting of historical evidence to evaluate and interpret the meanings of the information she had gathered. In her conclusion, she also discussed the decline of Pullman porters, connecting it to the construction of highway systems developed through the Federal-Aid Highway Act of 1956.

Ending an Era, Forging a Legacy

The story of the Pullman porter always has been shared in terms of race relations. Heretofore this may have been an adequate frame, since America has had such historical struggles with reconciling a safe place for the black man to live, dream, and grow. What we may have overlooked, however, is that the porter was always in control of crafting his own story—and he secretly used the black press to do so. The Pullman porter aggregated, wrote, and distributed news in an incredibly sophisticated system of networked journalism that kept the black press in tune with the black working class and its needs after the Great War. Amid the volatile and violent antebellum era, Pullman porters also helped black newspaper publishers highlight Southern atrocities and Northern possibilities. These partnerships convinced millions of blacks to leave behind agrarian peonage in search of more meaningful work. The Pullman porters' collective bargaining win for higher wages in 1937 also inspired blacks to continue to challenge institutionalized racism in America (Berman, 1935). BSCP president A. Philip Randolph went on to organize the campaign to desegregate the American military during World War II with the first March on Washington in 1941. C. L. Dellums, who served as BSCP's vice-president after being fired in 1927 from Pullman Co. for unionizing, continued to wage labor battles in Oakland, California for the rest of his life (Dellums, 1966). The Pullman porters also inspired future freedom fighters such as Thurgood Marshall, who was the son of a porter; E. D. Nixon, who co-organized the Montgomery, Alabama bus boycotts in the 1950s while still working as a porter; and Malcolm X, who wrote about his time observing race relations aboard the train as a dining car waiter in his autobiography (Christian, 2008).

Former Pullman porters and their children also entered the field of professional journalism in remarkable ways after World War II. Gordon Parks, who began his career as a Pullman porter, found a magazine while working aboard one of his trains that featured Farm Security Administration (FSA) photos of Depression-era poverty. He said that the dust-bowl imagery of poor women and children haunted him (Sloan, 2003). Parks eventually joined the FSA photography collective in 1942 and rose to become the first black photojournalist at *Life* magazine.

Ethel Payne brings our analysis of Pullman porters as journalists full circle. This daughter of a Pullman porter came to be known as the "First Lady of the Black Press." She began working as the national correspondent to the *Chicago Defender* in 1948. She eventually covered the Civil Rights era meticulously, interviewing luminaries such as Dr. Martin Luther King, Jr. and then-Senator John F. Kennedy. She was the first black female commentator for radio and television at CBS and the first black journalist to report on the Vietnam War (McGrath Morris, 2015).

The system of Pullman porter networked journalism began to decline in 1956, when President Dwight D. Eisenhower signed the Federal-Aid Highway Act. This law authorized the construction of 46,876 miles of highway systems that connected the continental United States (Weingroff, 1996). Parts of the country that were once accessible only by train suddenly opened up to everyone. American Airlines established the first domestic flights aboard its Boeing 707 jets on January 25, 1959 (Proctor, Machat, and Kodera, 2010). In just 10 years, by 1969, Pullman Co. was out of business after more than 100 years of service. To preserve what remained of the train industry, Congress passed the Rail Passenger Service Act in 1970, which allowed all remaining train companies in the country to consolidate, forming a for-profit company that is backed by the US government. This entity, now known as Amtrak, did not hire Pullman porters to serve people among its train cars. Consequently, the *New York Times* reported on March 5, 1978 that the BSCP union was effectively defunct (Sheppard, 1978). Though the Pullman porters no longer greet passengers aboard America's trains, the archives of leading black newspapers of the post-Great War period—*Baltimore Afro-American, Chicago Defender, New York Age, New York Amsterdam News*, and *Pittsburgh Courier*—are a treasure trove of journalistic contributions from these distinguished men. The only thing more remarkable than their daily participation in the news production process may be their daily negotiations of identity as an act of self-preservation: they wore the mask of obsequiousness to survive, but bundled their true aspirations, fears, and desires in the newspapers that they smuggled, to *thrive*. In this manner, the railway platform was their *platform*. Whenever they glided onto it, with their sable hats, crisp jackets, and spotless gloves, they spoke volumes, without even saying a word.

Acknowledgments

I would like to thank my late great-grandfather, Willie Harris, for his service aboard America's railways as a train operator for nearly 50 years. He loved his work at the Pennsylvania Railroad Depot so much that he suggested that his granddaughter (my mother) share its initials. He named her Pamela Ruth Downing. Great-grandfather Willie had a second grade-level education, but believed in high-quality schooling for his children and grandchildren. He helped send my mother to Howard University to become the first in the family to earn a college degree. Although he did not live to see my mother eventually earn her doctorate—or to see me in pursuit of mine—our family indeed stands on his shoulders every day.

Note

1   All estimations of monetary value in today's market were computed by using the online calculator at MeasuringWorth.com. To find out more about the calculator functions, see Williamson (2011).

Historical Methods Exercises

1. Pick a journal article based on historical research. Look at all of the footnotes, endnotes and references and evaluate the types of evidence that were used. How does the author use primary and secondary source material? What concepts or theoretical framework does the author draw on to help frame her or his story?
2. Spend a day at a community archive and try to find as much research as possible on a local event that has been celebrated for at least twenty years.
3. Choose a topic that you are interested in studying. See what types of records are available through online archives.

References

100 Howard students Pullman Porters. (1924, June 20). Afro-*American*. Retrieved from http://search.proquest.com/docview/530598666

Adams, Cyrus Field. (1902). Timothy Thomas fortune: Journalist, author, lecturer, agitator. *Colored American Magazine*, 4: 224–228.

Alexander, Shawn Leigh. (2008). *T. Thomas Fortune, the Afro-American agitator: A collection of writings, 1880–1928*. Gainesville: University Press of Florida.

Anderson, Charles Frederick. (1904). *Freemen yet slaves under 'Abe' Lincoln's Son or service and wages of Pullman Porters*. Chicago: Press of the Enterprise Printing House.

Anderson, Jervis. (1973). *A. Philip Randolph: A biographical portrait*. New York: Harcourt Brace Jovanovich.

Asukile, Thabiti. (2010). Joel Augustus Rogers: Black international journalism, archival research, and black print culture. *The Journal of African American History*, 95 (3–4): 322–347.

Bates, Beth Tompkins. (2001). *Pullman Porters and the rise of protest politics in Black America*. Chapel Hill: The University of North Carolina Press.

Beckett, Charlie, and Mansell, Robin. (2008). Crossing boundaries: New media and networked journalism. *Communication, Culture and Critique*, 1 (1): 92–104. doi:10.1111/j.1753-9137.2007.00010.x

Bequeathed $57,000. (1939, October 7). Chicago *Defender*. Retrieved from http://search.proquest.com/docview/492540940

Berger, Arthur Asa. (2000). *Media and communication research methods: An introduction to qualitative and quantitative approaches*. Thousand Oaks, CA: Sage.

Berman, Edward. (1935, August 21). The Pullman Porters win. *The Nation*, 141: 3659.

Blackmon, Douglas A. (2009). *Slavery by another name: The re-enslavement of Black Americans from the Civil War to World War II*. New York: Anchor Books.

Brennen, Bonnie, and Hardt, Hanno (Eds.). (2011). *American journalism history reader: Critical and primary texts*. New York: Routledge.

Brotherhood of Sleeping Car Porters. (1927). *The Pullman Porter*. New York: Brotherhood of Sleeping Car Porters. Retrieved from http://hdl.handle.net/2027/uc1.b4274673

Calvin, Floyd J. (1935, November 30). Race eager for Rogers' Ethiopian War news. *The Pittsburgh Courier*. Retrieved from http://search.proquest.com/docview/201989148

Carey, James W. (1974). The problem of journalism history. *Journalism History*, 1 (1): 3–5, 27.

Carr, David. (2012, March 20). Theater, disguised as real journalism. *New York Times*. Retrieved from www.nytimes.com/2012/03/19/business/media/theater-disguised-up-as-realjournalism.html?scp=1&sq=ira%20glass&st=cse

Christian, Margena A. (2008, June 2). Remembering the Pullman Porters. *Jet Magazine*.

Church, Leroy, and Goodman, Edward. (1909). *The Standard, 57* (13). Retrieved from http://hdl. handle.net/2027/nyp.33433003180555

Cowans, Russ J. (1957, November 2). Fay Young, former sports editor, dies. *The Chicago Defender.* Retrieved from http://search.proquest.com/docview/492890040

Curry, Tommy J. (2012). The fortune of wells: Ida B. Wells-Barnett's use of T. Thomas fortune's philosophy of social agitation as a prolegomenon to militant civil rights activism. *Transactions of the Charles S. Peirce Society: A Quarterly Journal in American Philosophy, 48* (4): 456–482. doi:10.2979/trancharpeirsoc.48.4.456

Darnton, Robert. (2009). From *The great cat massacre and other episodes in French cultural history.* In John Tosh (Ed.), *Historians on history* (2nd ed., pp. 324–330). Harlow, UK: Pearson Longman.

Dellums, C. L. (1966, June 14). *Thanks from FEPC: Los Angeles Times.* Retrieved from http://search. proquest.com/docview/155390863

Dickerson, Dennis C. (1986). World War I and the black migration to Western Pennsylvania, 1916–1930. In *Out of the crucible: Black steel workers in western pennsylvania, 1875–1980* (pp. 27–54, Chap. 2). Albany: SUNY Press.

Donnelly, Mark, and Norton, Claire. (2011). *Doing history.* London: Routledge.

Du Bois, W. E. B. (1918). *Close ranks. The Crisis, 16*: 3. Retrieved from ttp://hdl.handle.net/2027/ hvd.32044011044658

Du Bois, W. E. B. (1919). *Returning soldiers. The Crisis*: 19–21. Retrieved from http://hdl.handle. net/2027/hvd.32044010524130

Georgia soldier lynched for wearing U.S. uniform. (1919, April 11). *Afro-American.* Retrieved from http://search.proquest.com/docview/530435430

Gottlieb, Peter. (1996). *Making their own way: Southern Blacks' migration to Pittsburgh, 1916–30.* Champaign: University of Illinois Press.

Grand Old Man of Pullman Porters sees many things. (1922, December 30). Chicago *Defender.* Retrieved from http://search.proquest.com/docview/491969492

Hall, Stuart. (1989). Cultural studies: Two paradigms. In Tony Bennett et al. (Eds.), *Culture, ideology and social process: A reader* (pp. 19–37). London: Batsford in association with the Open University Press.

Hardt, Hanno. (1989). The foreign-language press in American press history. *Journal of Communication, 39* (2): 114–131.

Hickmott, Alec Fazackerley. (2011). 'Brothers, Come North': The rural south and the political imaginary of new Negro radicalism, 1917–1923. *Intellectual History Review, 21* (4): 395–412. doi:10.1080/17496977.2011.623881

Hogans, James H. (1929, November 30). Things seen, heard and done among Pullman employees. *The New York Age.*

Hogans, James H. (1939, November 11). Among railroad and Pullman workers. *Afro-American.* Retrieved from http://search.proquest.com/docview/531234205

Hundreds leave South to escape Peonage rule. (1921, May 14). Chicago *Defender.* Retrieved from http://search.proquest.com/docview/491882953

Jameson, Fredric. (1971). *Marxism and form.* Princeton, NJ: Princeton University Press.

John R. Winston appointed manager bachelors' club parlor. (1911, June 24). Chicago *Defender.* Retrieved from http://search.proquest.com/docview/493259622

John R. Winston indisposed. (1912, December 14). Chicago *Defender.* Retrieved from http://search. proquest.com/docview/493209478

John R. Winston made toastmaster. (1915, December 4). Chicago *Defender.* Retrieved from http:// search.proquest.com/docview/493254804

Kellner, Hans. (1989). *Language and historical representation: Getting the story crooked.* Madison: University of Wisconsin Press.

Kornweibel, Theodore. (2010). *Railroads in the African-American experience: A photographic journey.* Baltimore: The Johns Hopkins University Press.

Locke, Alain. (1925). Enter the new Negro. *Survey Graphic, 6*: 631–634.

Lynchers shoot and burn victim in Louisiana Sunday. (1919, September 5). Afro-*American.* Retrieved from http://search.proquest.com/docview/530423016

McDowell, William H. (2002). *Historical research: A guide.* London: Longman.

McGrath Morris, James. (2015). *Eye on the struggle: Ethel Payne, the first lady of the Black press*. New York: Amistad Press.

McKay, Claude. (1937, June 5). No! Claude McKay, noted author, argues. *New York Amsterdam News*. Retrieved from http://search.proquest.com/docview/226129958

McKay, Claude. (1939, October 28). Don't be fooled, Il Duce is with him until he gets another slice of Africa, says Claude McKay. *Afro-American*. Retrieved from http://search.proquest.com/docview/531241254

Nerone, John. (1993). Theory and history. *Communication Theory, 3* (2): 148–157.

Nevins, Alan. (1963). *Gateway to history*. Chicago, IL: Quadrangle.

Nine ex-soldiers lynched in the South. (1920, January 3). Chicago *Defender*. Retrieved from http://search.proquest.com/docview/493379599

Nord, David Paul. (1988). A plea for journalism history. *Journalism History, 15* (1): 8–15.

Nord, David Paul. (1989). The nature of historical research. In Guido H. Stempel III and Bruce H. Westley (Eds.), *Research methods in mass communication* (pp. 290–315). Englewood Cliffs, NJ: Prentice Hall.

Northern drive to start. (1917, February 10). Chicago *Defender*. Retrieved from http://search.proquest.com/docview/493324050

Orwell, George. (1948/1950). *1984*. NY: Penguin.

Ottley, Roi. (1955). *The lonely warrior: The life and times of Robert S. Abbott*. Chicago: Henry Regnery Company.

Patterson, Raymond. (1911). *The Negro and his needs*. New York: Fleming H. Revell Company.

The Porter and his tip. (1924, April 19). Pittsburgh *Courier*. Retrieved from http://search.proquest.com/docview/201844280

Porter left $15,000. (1921, August 19). Afro-*American*. Retrieved from http://search.proquest.com/docview/530537578

Proctor, Jon, Machat, Mike, and Kodera, Craig. (2010). *From Props to Jets: Commercial Aviation's Transition to the Jet Age 1952–1962*. North Branch: Specialty Press.

Pullman Porter Brot first news of Nebraska riot. (1929, August 10). Afro-*American*. Retrieved from http://search.proquest.com/docview/530758498

Pullman Porters' average tip is 25c per passenger. (1925, December 19). Afro-*American*. Retrieved from http://search.proquest.com/docview/530607414

Rasmussen, Fred. (1998, May 5). James B. MacNees, 81, telegrapher, reporter. *The Sun*. Retrieved from http://search.proquest.com/docview/406360625

Rogers, Joel Augustus. (1934, January 31). Ruminations: Parallels in diverse peoples. *New York Amsterdam News*. Retrieved from http://search.proquest.com/docview/226288711

Santino, Jack. (1991). *Miles of smiles, years of struggle: Stories of Black Pullman Porters*. Champaign: University of Illinois Press.

Schudson, Michael. (1991). Media contexts: Historical approaches to communication studies. In Klaus Bruhn Jensen and Nicholas W. Jankowski (Eds.), *A handbook of qualitative methodologies for mass communication research* (pp. 175–189). London: Routledge.

Sheppard, Jr., Nathaniel. (1978, March 5). As their Union dies, Pullman Porters recall a proud and bitter era. *New York Times*. Retrieved from http://search.proquest.com/docview/123809890

Shufeldt, Robert W. (1915). *America's Greatest Problem: The Negro*. Philadelphia: F.A. Davis Company.

Simmons, Roscoe. (1922, April 1). The week. *The Chicago Defender*. Retrieved from http://search.proquest.com/docview/491940274

Sloan, Lester. (2003, June 15). Photographer Gordon parks turns 90. *Neiman Reports*. Retrieved from http://niemanreports.org/articles/photographer-gordon-parks-turns-90/

Smith, Maryann Yodelis. (1989). The method of history. In Guido H. Stempel III and Bruce H. Westley (Eds.), *Research methods in mass communication* (pp. 316–330). Englewood Cliffs, NJ: Prentice Hall.

South stands to lose many million [sic] over migration. (1923, August 11). Pittsburgh *Courier*. Retrieved from http://search.proquest.com/docview/201831859

Stiles, T. J. (2003). *Jesse James: Last Rebel of the Civil War*. New York: Vintage Books.

Taylor, Alexander O. (1915, January 2). Cleveland letter. *Chicago Defender*. Retrieved from http://search.proquest.com/docview/493301820

These men served President Roosevelt's party on cross country trip. (1937, October 16). Chicago *Defender*. Retrieved from http://search.proquest.com/docview/492588416

Thompson, Robert Luther. (1947). *Wiring a continent: The history of the telegraph industry in the United States, 1832–1866*. Princeton: Princeton University Press.

Thornbrough, Emma Lou. (1966). American Negro newspapers, 1880–1914. *The Business History Review, 40* (4): 467–490. Retrieved from www.jstor.org/stable/3112124

Thousands die for a lie. (1919, October 24). Afro-*American*. Retrieved from http://search.proquest.com/docview/530423100

Tosh, John. (2009). Introduction. In John Tosh (Ed.), *Historians on history* (2nd ed., pp. 1–16). Harlow, UK: Pearson Longman.

Tye, Larry. (2004). *Rising from the rails: Pullman Porters and the making of the Black Middle Class*. New York: Henry Holt and Company.

Van der Haak, Bregtje, Parks, Michael, and Castells, Manuel. (2012). The future of journalism: Networked journalism. *International Journal of Communication, 6*: 2923–2938.

Weaver, Frederick. (1933, August 5). White House Doorman works from 8 to 4:30. *Afro-American*. Retrieved from http://search.proquest.com/docview/531027848

Weingroff, Richard F. (1996). Creating the interstate system. *Public Roads, 60* (1): 10–17.

White, Hayden. (1978). *Tropics of discourse: Essays on cultural criticism*. Baltimore, MD: Johns Hopkins University Press.

Williams, Chad L. (2010). *Torchbearers of democracy: African-American soldiers in the World War I Era*. Chapel Hill: The University of North Carolina Press.

Williams, Raymond. (1974). *Television: Technology and cultural form*. London: Fontana.

Williams, Raymond. (1989). *Resources of hope: Culture, democracy, socialism*. London: Verso.

Williamson, Samuel H. (2011). Seven ways to compute the relative value of a US dollar amount, 1774 to present. *MeasuringWorth*. Retrieved from www.measuringworth.com/uscompare

Winston, John R. (1914a, January 31). Railroad men organize. *The Chicago Defender*. Retrieved from http://search.proquest.com/docview/493318018

Winston, John R. (1914b, March 14). Sparks from the rail. *The Chicago Defender*. Retrieved from http://search.proquest.com/docview/493291733

Winston, H. W. (1938, August 6). Real heroes. *Pittsburgh Courier*. Retrieved from http://search.proquest.com/docview/202046977

Wintz, Cary D., and Finkelman, Paul. (2004). *Encyclopedia of the Harlem Renaissance: KY* (Vol. 2). New York: Routledge.

Young, Fay. (1955, August 13). People who helped Abbott make defender great. *The Chicago Defender*. Retrieved from http://search.proquest.com/docview/492835025

CHAPTER **6**

Oral History

Who built Thebes of the seven gates? In the books you will find the name of kings. Did the kings haul up the lumps of rock? And Babylon, many times demolished. Who raised it up so many times? In what houses of gold-glittering Lima did the builders live? Where, the evening that the Wall of China was finished, did the masons go?
—Bertolt Brecht, "Questions from a Worker Who Reads"

Until the twentieth century, the study of history focused primarily on the lives and the struggles of the powerful. Historians chronicled the experiences of religious, military, economic and political leaders while the lives of ordinary working people were rarely considered.

Even when historians tried to understand the point of view of workers, it was often difficult to access information about their lives. While all kinds of documentary evidence, such as legal records, letters and diaries, described the experiences of the wealthy and powerful and were held in archives and libraries, most of the written records about everyday people were not saved. For example, the thousands of letters written by John and Abigail Adams have been carefully preserved as part of the Adams family papers and are housed in the Massachusetts Historical Society in Boston. David McCullough (2008) used these letters along with family papers and diaries for his *John Adams* biography and the subsequent HBO mini-series.

In contrast, most of the correspondence of non-famous colonist families is no longer available because these documents were not saved, preserved and/or archived.

While historians may lack sufficient archival documentation about the experiences of everyday people, the method of oral history helps us to recover important information about their lives. Through the use of open-ended depth interviews that are usually recorded, oral historians collect "reminiscences, accounts and interpretations of events" (Hoffman, 1996, p. 88) that can go beyond official records to give us a more nuanced understanding of the past. In addition, during the interview process, oral historians often recover photographs, news articles, letters and other documentary evidence that people have saved over the years. Because most of these materials have not been archived, they are often unknown to historians; yet, this documentary evidence can provide important research information as well as relevant context for the life stories of working people who lived at a specific place and time.

The method of oral history was initially used to augment existing archival research and to fill in the gaps in the life stories of elite members of society. However, during the 1960s social historians began to raise important questions about the role of history, and a populist vision of the past from the perspectives of the "bottom up" emerged. Oral history began to be used to preserve the life experiences of individuals who did not have the time or the ability to write their own stories in order "to radically alter historical practice by bringing ordinary people into the study of history" (Grele, 1991, p. 243). Since the 1960s, oral history has been used to give voice to otherwise voiceless individuals and groups in society. According to Paul Thompson (1990), in his seminal book *The Voice of the Past*, oral history not only challenges the official version of history, but by emphasizing the stories of "the under-classes, the unprivileged, and the defeated" (p. 6) it may also create a richer, more diverse and more authentic construction of the past.

For most of the twentieth century, historical work in media studies primarily focused on institutional aspects of the field, chronicling the histories of major newspapers, magazines, broadcasting stations, advertising agencies and public relations firms. These studies were augmented with biographies of founders, owners and publishers of media properties. While these histories emphasized media holdings and ownership, they did not tell us much about the writers, reporters, photographers, copywriters and others who worked for these media outlets (Hardt and Brennen, 1995). However, in recent years oral histories have been used to help us understand the working conditions, expectations and experiences of rank-and-file media workers and to provide us with a more complete understanding of the field.

These days, while researchers still focus on its emancipatory potential, the method of oral history is also being used in popular culture to provide historical reference points for popular entertainment. For example, to celebrate the tenth anniversary of Justin Timberlake's number one hit, "Sexy Back," *Entertainment Weekly* published an oral history with Timberlake and his collaborators, which addressed the creative process and inspiration for the "genre-busting dance-club banger" (Goodman, 2016, p. 43). *Entertainment Weekly* also showcased an oral history project with the stars and directors of the eight Harry Potter films the week prior to the opening of the final film of the franchise, *Harry Potter and the Deathly Hallows—Part 2* (Markovitz, 2011).

Technique of Oral History

At the most basic level, oral historians ask people questions in order to learn about their lives. Oral historians must be excellent interviewers; they need to learn strategies to establish trust and to help interviewees understand that their experiences are worthwhile and should be saved for posterity. Oral history is a time-consuming method, but if you are willing and able to put in the effort, oral histories may provide you with important insights about all types of individuals and groups who lived at a particular place and time in society.

If you are interested in using oral history interviews in a research project, as with other qualitative methods the first step is to frame a research question—what is it you would like to learn and how might oral history interviews help you to answer your question? Your research question might grow out of past research you have done or it may be based on some new topic or issue you are interested in understanding. For example, my oral history project *For the Record: An Oral History of Rochester, New York, Newsworkers* (Brennen, 2001) was based on an interest in learning more about the routines, expectations and working conditions of journalists who had worked in Rochester, New York. My curiosity helped me to frame the research question for the project: "What was it like to work for Gannett as a journalist in Rochester, New York, during the first half of the twentieth century?"

My past research in this area had revealed that there was limited published information chronicling the lives of rank-and-file reporters, and I decided to use oral history interviews to help fill in the research gaps. I chose Rochester, New York, as the research site not only because at that time I lived close to Rochester but also because I thought it would be interesting to focus on a city with more than one newspaper owned by the same person, group or company. The project taught me a lot about the method of oral history, and throughout this chapter, where it is relevant I draw on aspects of my Gannett research project to help illustrate key aspects of doing oral history.

Once you have crafted a research question, the next step is to begin your background research. The more background information you gather, the better understanding you will have of the issues and concerns related to your topic. For the Rochester oral history project I learned about the local media business and I gathered historical and contemporary information on the Gannett Company and the two daily newspapers it had owned in Rochester, the *Times Union* and the *Democrat & Chronicle*. The research provided important context that was invaluable to me throughout the interviews as well as during the writing process. In addition, I read local histories of Rochester, New York, including one written by Henry Clune (1947), whom I later had the privilege of interviewing for the oral history project. I was also fortunate to meet with the public service director for the Gannett Rochester newspapers, Tom Flynn, who graciously provided me with a list of retired Gannett journalists.

After your background research is under way and you have a clear idea for an oral history project, you should start to identify potential interviewees (also known in oral history as narrators) whom you would like to interview for the study. You may come across the names of relevant people to interview in your background research, or you may only know about potential interviewees by their titles or job descriptions and will need to do some digging to find out their names. After you have an initial list of contacts, your first challenge will be to establish rapport with the potential narrators. I recommend taking an old school approach and sending each person a written letter introducing yourself, explaining your research project and asking him or her to participate. It is important to explain how each person can contribute to your study; potential interviewees may have doubts about their ability to contribute to the research project and it may take some time and reassurance to convince them that you are really interested in their experiences. That initial letter should be followed up with an email and/or phone call during which you will attempt to set up a first meeting. Be sure to keep track of all of your contacts because it may take a while to connect with potential narrators in order to set up a first meeting.

The initial meeting is an opportunity for you to "sell" the research project to the prospective narrator and to get to know more about the person. This meeting may be held in person or over the phone. At this point it is important to begin to establish rapport between you and the interviewee. Shortly after I began my Rochester oral history project, I started to think about my perceptions of the elderly and I wondered how challenging it might be to establish trust with them. I soon realized that my own journalistic experience, coupled with my commitment to the project, were great icebreakers that helped me to establish trust with each of the interviewees.

Assuming the first conversation goes smoothly, you will be able to arrange a time and place to conduct your oral history interview. It is important to schedule the interview in a place that is quiet and without interruptions; remember that a ringing telephone or a television set on in the room can be heard on a recording and can potentially impede the interview process. Oral history interviews are lengthy, and it is helpful to allocate an entire day for each interview so that you will not need to leave midway through a session. However, sometimes an interviewee will tire, or have another appointment, and you may find that it is necessary to schedule a follow-up interview.

Interview Strategies

To become a successful interviewer, a researcher needs to become a great listener and to have a strong understanding of human relationships. Unlike other types of interviews, where an interviewer maintains control throughout the process, oral historians shift power to those they interview. It is the narrator's stories and not the interviewer's interests that are most important. Oral history interviewers should be flexible and they should allow the narrator to take the interview in the direction he or she wants to go. However, interviewers still remain active participants in the interview process. An interviewer needs to know when to be quiet and when to ask follow-up questions, when to probe more deeply and when to switch topics. While reporters and law enforcement officials sometimes use silence to force a non-compliant source to speak, the use of silence in oral history interviewing is mainly used to help give a person additional time to gather his or her thoughts.

It is important for an interviewer to ask brief and open-ended questions that encourage an interviewee to talk and to provide examples and stories to illustrate his or her experiences. After some small talk and a few general icebreaking questions, it is helpful to remind the narrator about the purpose of the project. The beginning of the recorded interview should include your name, the narrator's name, the date and location of the interview and the purpose of the project. Ask for the narrator's oral consent to participate in the research and to record the interview.

I recommend starting with a broadly based general question that is followed by more focused questions. For my oral history research, a general question such as "How did you get started in the news business?" or "Tell me what it was like to be a cub reporter on the *Democrat & Chronicle*" elicited far more information than when I asked a simple yes/no question like "Was your first job at the *Times Union*?" or "Did you enjoy working on the *Democrat & Chronicle* better than the *Times Union*?"

Once a narrator becomes comfortable talking about his or her career, it is useful to ask follow-up questions to clarify and expand on his or her experiences. Start with easy questions that are simply stated and do your best not to become confrontational. The questions you ask and your responses to the narrator's comments will help to build trust between you and the narrator. Valerie Raleigh Yow (2005) has suggested that "positive appraisal of the narrator's work in the interview contributes to the narrator's motivation to continue and to cooperate in the endeavor" (p. 97). It is important to reassure each interviewee that he or she is providing you with useful information. It is also helpful for interviewers to jot down key concepts or ideas that come up during each conversation so that they can follow up with related questions later in the interview. Feel free to use photographs, news articles, commentary from other conversations and other documents to spark an interviewer's memory and to help focus the interview on a particular issue or topic. Other interviewing strategies are discussed at length in Chapters 3 and 4.

While a narrator may be comfortable talking about most aspects of his or her life, there may be issues, concerns and/or topics that are difficult for a person to address. Remember that oral history is a collaborative process; if your background research indicates challenging areas, or if an initial question is met with resistance, tread lightly and come back to it later in the interview.

For example, during my background research for the Gannett oral history project I learned that there had been challenges over the years between the reporters and editors regarding the role of the Newspaper Guild at Gannett. While some reporters had been active in the Guild, others distanced themselves from any type of union activities because they felt that journalists were not the same as other workers and should not be part of a labor union. Although I wanted to know whether each person had been a member of the Guild, I was careful not to begin to explore the topic with that question. Instead, I asked general questions about relationships between reporters and editors, which often sparked a comment about the role of the Newspaper Guild. When a narrator mentioned the Guild, I would follow up on the comment and ask about his or her views of the Guild. If an interviewee did not bring up the Guild, I would later ask what he or she thought was the role of the Newspaper Guild at Gannett and follow up that question with more specific probing questions.

In crafting your questions, it is important to be aware of the words you use. Be careful to use neutral words and try not to ask leading questions. While we all know the problems associated with asking a leading question such as "Do you still beat your wife?", many interviewers still ask questions that encourage narrators to give them information they want, rather than offer information they would like to share. A cooperative narrator may give you the requested answer to a question like "Do you think all copy editors are just frustrated writers?" However, this type of leading question should be avoided because an interviewer does not really learn anything new from this interview strategy. In addition, asking leading questions can affect the power relations of the interview: it can take control of the interview away from the narrator and it may encourage a narrator to shut down or even end an uncomfortable interview.

Pulitzer Prize-winning author Studs Terkel was one of the preeminent interviewers of the twentieth century. His extended conversations with rank-and-file workers, politicians, labor organizers, artists and entertainers chronicled American life and provided important insights into significant challenges, events and changes people faced during the twentieth century. Terkel maintained that oral history interviews differed from traditional journalistic interviews in key ways. In his first collection of oral history interviews, *Division Street: America*, Terkel (1967, p. xxi) explained the differences:

> I realized quite early in this adventure that interviews, convention-ally conducted, were meaningless. Conditioned clichés were cer-tain to come. The question-and-answer technique may be of value in determining favored detergents, toothpaste, and deodorants, but not in the discovery of men and women. It was simply a case of making conversation. And listening.

Learning to Listen

Terkel first learned the value of listening as a child when he lived in a men's hotel that his mother owned; throughout his career, he insisted that lis-tening helps to bestow dignity on people. During your interviews, careful listening will help you to understand how people feel about their lives; it will also provide you with insight on potentially interesting new topics and issues.

Sometimes it is difficult for interviewers to actually sit still and lis-ten. Anderson and Jack (1998) outlined three listening strategies to help researchers understand a person's story from his or her perspective: first, consider a person's moral language; second, listen for meta-statements; and third, follow the logic of the narrative. When we consider self-evaluative statements, through moral language, we can examine relationships between individuals and accepted cultural norms—"between how we are told to act and how we feel about ourselves when we do or do not act in that way" (Anderson and Jack, 1998, p. 166). Similarly, meta-statements are evaluations or judgments made by the narrator during the interview that may indicate a discrepancy between what is said and what you might expect to hear. The third listening strategy—assessing a narrative's logic—refers to considering the consistency and/or contradictions in the interview as well as focusing on the way recurring themes brought up by the narrator may relate to each other.

While listening to an interviewee, it is important to also consider his or her non-verbal body language and other signals, as well as to be aware of your own non-verbal responses. A person who stretches or yawns may be tired and need a break. If your interviewee crosses his or her arms and legs and refuses eye contact, he or she may be uncomfortable with the interview or may feel hostile to you as the interviewer. Be aware of your own responses to each narrator's commentary. If you take issue with something that has been said, be careful not to show judgment because your responses can negatively impact the interview. Try not to interrupt the interviewee, but feel free to use non-verbal cues to encourage a narrator: smiling, nodding, shaking your head affirmatively and maintaining eye contact are supportive responses that can help to build trust between you and the narrator.

During one of my interviews for the Rochester oral history project, the narrator began to make racist comments. I was shocked by the intensity of his commentary but I knew that race was an important issue that was not covered by the newspapers until after the 1964 Rochester riots. I wanted to understand his beliefs and I felt that if I responded negatively to his comments, the interview would end abruptly. I literally bit my lip to keep my emotions and body language in check. After a few minutes the narrator said, "The blacks have taken over the city and destroyed it. Now everything I say from here on makes me a racist pig" (quoted in Brennen, 2001, p. 64). In this case the narrator's self-evaluative statement helped me to understand his frustration with changes in his community. My strategy of keeping quiet helped the narrator to feel comfortable enough to open up and share his views with me.

As you prepare for your oral history interviews, it is helpful to practice interviewing and to work on learning to listen. While interviewing and listening are important skills to acquire, Charles T. Morrissey (1998) reminded researchers not to let the tools and procedures of oral history overwhelm them because it is also important to rely on their own intuition during the interviews. Morrissey suggested that oral historians should remain flexible, understanding and open to the unexpected.

Given that human memory can be faulty and subjective, some researchers have questioned the reliability and validity of oral history interviews. As with other types of qualitative research, Terkel (1997) explained that the goal of oral history is not to uncover plain unvarnished facts but rather to try to understand the deeper meanings and feelings about those facts. While individuals construct feelings at a particular time in history, within a particular cultural context, oral history not only focuses on individuals' recollections of events but also inquires into the collective memories of a society. The experiences that we share with others influence us to forget some things and to remember other experiences and to interpret those shared experiences in particular ways. Yow (2005) suggested oral historians consider the relevant cultural context for the interviews as well as the potential influence of shared experiences and collective memories on each individual's interview.

There are also a variety of ways to verify the factual information obtained from oral history interviews. During each oral history interview it is possible to check the interviewee's memory by asking for specific names, dates and places. Be sure to ask the narrators for the correct spelling of their names as well as the spelling of the names of others they mention. Factual information can also be verified through other interviews that you complete and from other types of primary source material, archival evidence and historical records. Oral history interviewers should be skilled enough to be able to approach the same issue or topic from a variety of approaches or to ask similar questions in different ways to determine whether a narrator's answers are consistent.

The Editing Process

All interviews should be recorded so that they can be transcribed. While some oral historians prefer to video record their interviews, I would suggest that even when video is used, it is still important to record the audio separately, in order to aid the transcription process. Each oral history interview should be transcribed in a timely manner. There are individuals and professional services that specialize in transcribing interviews; however, they are costly. Also, even if you are able to pay transcription costs, learning to transcribe an interview is a good skill to acquire, so I would encourage you to try it at least once. Some researchers maintain that oral historians should transcribe their own interviews because the transcription process allows them to become more familiar with the material.

Voice recognition software is now available to help transcribe interviews. Basic speech recognition programs come with Windows Vista and Microsoft Office for the Macintosh. Dragon NaturallySpeaking works with any Windows program and, with some training, it learns to correct mistakes and can approach 99 percent accuracy. Dragon Dictate for the Macintosh uses the same Dragon recognition technology and is considered fast and accurate. However, a major challenge with the current technology is that at this point none of the voice recognition software can recognize more than one voice. While most oral historians await the development of voice recognition software capable of recognizing multiple voices, Jennifer L. Matheson (2007) developed a cost-effective voice transcription computer technique using a digital voice recorder and an MP3 player, along with voice recognition and transcription software. Although the process requires listening to an interview through headphones and speaking the words into a microphone, the technique is cost-effective and less time-consuming than other transcription techniques.

After an interview has been transcribed, the editing process begins. The interviewer should be the first person to edit the written transcript. If you listen to the recorded interview while you read the transcript, you will often catch a variety of errors that have been made during the transcription process. False starts and duplications should also be removed during the editing process but all other conversation should be included. Once transcripts have been edited, they should be sent to the interviewees for their corrections and feedback. At this point in the process, some interviewees may wish to change information in their interviews to clarify previous remarks. Reading the transcript can spark new memories, and narrators may provide you with additional stories and commentary. It is possible that some interviewees may become concerned when reading their remarks and they may ask you to edit portions of their transcripts. Remember that it is their stories that you want to tell, not yours, and it is important to respect their wishes.

During the *For the Record* editing process, one of the reporters I had interviewed became uncomfortable with his commentary after he read the transcript of his interview. He wrote to me that he felt his statements "rambled" and that some of the information he shared with me was "incoherent." Deciding that he was not a "good interviewee," he returned the transcript of his interview with several sections crossed out. His cover letter said he did not wish to embarrass his friends or former colleagues or to question the business that he had loved and respected many years ago, and he asked me if it was possible to "forget the whole thing." Out of respect for his feelings I decided to pull his interview from the project. While I was disappointed by his request, this experience actually helped me to understand more fully the goal of oral history and how challenging it can be to incorporate the perspectives of ordinary people into the historical record.

Oral historians will use the final corrected transcripts for their research, and copies of final transcripts should also be sent to the interviewees for their files. After each oral history project is complete, it is appropriate to consider archiving the recordings and the final transcripts for future use.

While transcripts remain of central importance to oral historians, in our digital age oral history interview materials are easily shared, saved and searched on the web. Previously, oral history recordings were primarily housed in restricted archives, which made it difficult for most people to interact with the recordings. These days, complete collections of oral history interviews are posted online, on websites and in archival collections and are made instantly accessible to people throughout the world (Frisch, 2016). The sharing of oral histories online may be seen as "an exceptionally powerful means of democratizing the content, process and audience for history" (Shopes, 2014, p. 258). Yet, researchers have cautioned that oral history interviews still need to be verified, evaluated and interpreted.

Ethical Considerations

Given the nature of oral history, it is imperative to receive informed consent from each interviewee. All narrators should understand the purpose of their interviews, the planned use of the transcripts and audio or video recordings and their right not to answer any questions they find objectionable. They should be reminded that they may withdraw from the project at any time. Narrators should also be informed that the purpose of the interviews is to elicit in-depth commentary about their experiences and that they should tell their stories in as much detail as they feel comfortable sharing. Because of the importance of identity and context in the construction of oral history, interviewees are usually identified by name in the interviews. However, if necessary it is possible for a narrator to choose to be anonymous, and that option should be discussed with all interviewees.

The "General Principles for Oral History" (2010) created by the Oral History Association remind interviewers to respect the interviewees' authority and their right to answer questions on their own terms and in their own style and language. Oral historians should also avoid misrepresentations or the use of stereotypes and should be careful not to manipulate narrators' words or take them out of context. Other specific guidelines regarding oral history principles, best practices for pre-interview preparation, professional and technical standards and the preservation of interviews are also available on the Oral History Association website: www.oralhistory.org.

Research Using Oral History Transcripts

Researchers use oral history transcripts in a variety of ways. One strategy is to present the complete life histories of individuals without assessment; the interview transcripts are reprinted in full without additional editorial commentary or scholarly analysis. At most, an editor provides an introduction to the life story or reorganizes the interview transcript around topics and themes. A second strategy involves researchers choosing to group life history excerpts from a variety of interviews around common issues, themes and concerns. This approach usually provides a broader historical explanation and often integrates critical analysis and commentary into the research. A third approach used by researchers is to utilize information gathered from oral history interviews just like any other historical evidence. Researchers incorporate interview quotations with other evidence that is analyzed, critiqued and woven into an historical narrative. All three approaches are appropriate ways to use oral history transcripts and can help to tell important stories about the rank and file. But no matter how you plan to use your oral history interviews, it is important to make sure that any quotations used in the research are put in the proper context and that the quotations that are selected do not misrepresent a narrator's commentary.

The following excerpts from *For the Record* illustrate the second strategy outlined above as a way to use oral history transcripts in media studies research. In crafting the research project, I drew extensively on the oral history interviews I had completed with the Gannett journalists and combined lengthy quotations with critical analysis, relevant contextual information and commentary. For this project, I incorporated Raymond Williams's concept of structure of feeling, which describes the actively felt and lived meanings, experiences and values of a society. Williams (1977/1988) suggested that structure of feeling is often found in the documentary culture of a society, in its novels, music, films and newspaper stories, and in other elements of popular culture. My research used oral history interviews from journalists to provide evidence of a specific structure of feeling that was illustrated on the Rochester, New York, *Times Union* and the *Democrat & Chronicle* during the first half of the twentieth century.

The research project began with a brief biography of Frank Gannett and provided information regarding the development of the Gannett media empire. This background provided important historical context in which to place the journalists' stories. While most of the information in the first excerpt came from traditional historical sources, information from my interview with Henry Clune also provided relevant historical context.

From *For the Record: An Oral History of Rochester, New York, Newsworkers*, by Bonnie Brennen

Frank Gannett's introduction to the newspaper business began in 1885 when the 9-year-old began delivering copies of the Rochester *Democrat & Chronicle* to his neighbors in Blood's Depot, New York. Forty-three years later, the *Democrat & Chronicle* became the thirteenth in his newspaper group when Gannett purchased the paper for $3.5 million.

After graduating from Cornell University, where he had received a four-year scholarship, Gannett was hired as city editor at the *Ithaca Daily News*. In 1906, Gannett purchased a half interest in his first newspaper, the *Elmira Gazette*, for $20,000. The *Gazette* was an established daily newspaper with shopworn and outdated equipment located in an industrial railroad town of 30,000 people.

According to Frank Tripp, who was a *Gazette* reporter at the time and later became general manager and chairman of the board of Gannett Newspapers, in 1906 the *Gazette* plant was "rickety, dingy, poorly ventilated; it had creaking stairs, splintered floors, a tiny freight elevator which periodically dropped three floors, and pied type forms in the basement. The press was powered by a natural gas engine whose cough could be heard for blocks" (quoted in Merrill, 1954, p. 17).

After the purchase, Gannett immediately took editorial control over the *Gazette* while his co-owner, Erwin R. Davenport, focused on the business aspects of the newspaper.

From this modest beginning, Gannett began building his media empire. In 1918, Gannett and Davenport set their sights on the Rochester market. Rochester was a thriving city in upstate New York that was proud of its heritage as a "flour city" (Brandt, 1993, p. 33). Rochester was complete with mills powered by the Genesee River and supplied by locally grown wheat, and it was a city that at the beginning of the twentieth century was suspicious of outsiders. As the locally famous Rochester columnist Henry Clune (1994b, p. 8) recounts:

> There was a social hierarchy here, controlled by maybe a hundred people, just as there was in New York City, where Ward McCallister formed the Four Hundred. There was a woman here named Mrs. Warren Whitney, and she was the social leader of the town. There was a woman on

the *Post Express* named Emily Mond, and she ran a social column. It was like a social registrar. If you didn't belong to the right clubs, she never mentioned you.

In 1918 there were five daily newspapers competing for readership in Rochester; three of them were staunchly Republican and two served Democrats' interests. The Republican *Democrat & Chronicle* and the Democratic *Herald* were published in the mornings, while the afternoon newspapers included two Republican newspapers, the *Post Express* and the *Times*. The head of the local Republican Party, "Boss" George W. Aldridge, was one of the owners of the *Times*. The Democrats' *Union & Advertiser*, also published in the afternoon, had begun on October 15, 1826 as the *Daily Advertiser*, and was the first daily newspaper published between the Hudson River and the Pacific Ocean. After a merger in 1856 it became the *Union & Advertiser*.

Interested in controlling the afternoon market in Rochester, Gannett and Davenport purchased the *Times* and the *Union & Advertiser* and promptly merged them into the *Times Union*. On March 9, 1918, the *Union & Advertiser* ran a prominent advertisement on page 7 which notified readers of the change in ownership:

> The oldest and the newest are now brought together, consolidated into one GREAT NEWSPAPER under new and progressive management and united for A GREATER AND BETTER ROCHESTER. [Signed] Frank E. Gannett, president and editor; Woodford J. Copeland, vice president; E. R. Davenport, secretary-treasurer and manager. First issue out Tuesday. Order early.
>
> (quoted in Brandt, 1993, pp. 36–37)

The *Times Union* initially fashioned itself as an independent alternative in a city of political party organs. Gannett opposed the strong-arm political tactics of men like Boss Aldridge and, together with George Eastman, the founder of Kodak, fought successfully to change Rochester's city government from strong-mayor form to a city manager form (Zeigler, 1983, p. 16). The *Times Union* quickly became Gannett's flagship newspaper, and Gannett's presence was regularly felt in his suggestions to the editorial staff regarding such things as the wording of headlines, or the way a specific news story should be played. The *Times Union* was the only Gannett newspaper that consistently carried Frank Gannett's editorials and that listed his name in the staff box as editor (p. 23). Six years after purchasing the *Times Union*, in 1924, Frank Gannett bought out his partners and, as controlling owner of six upstate New York newspapers, formed the Gannett Company. Over the next few years Gannett would double his holdings.

In 1928 Gannett purchased the *Democrat & Chronicle*, long considered the city's premier newspaper. The *Democrat & Chronicle* began in 1834 as the *Daily Democrat*, and after a merger with the *Daily Chronicle* in 1870 the *Democrat & Chronicle* was established. Frank Tripp, Gannett's general manager, initially opposed the purchase because he felt it would "weaken the influence of both papers and jeopardize the reputation of the publisher" (Zeigler, 1983, p. 22). Yet, Gannett had learned that William Randolph Hearst was interested in purchasing the *Democrat & Chronicle* and he feared Hearst's growing influence in the Rochester market. Hearst had purchased the *Post Express* in 1923 merely for its circulation list and subsequently had established his own *Sunday American* and the *Evening Journal* in Rochester.

When Hearst's empire began to falter in 1937, Gannett bailed Hearst out of his financial problems in Albany and in the process acquired the presses and equipment of Hearst's Rochester *Journal* and *American*. Gannett closed both of Hearst's newspapers and established a monopoly in Rochester through his ownership of the two remaining newspapers in town, the morning *Democrat & Chronicle* and the afternoon *Times Union*. Gannett exercised daily control over the newspapers as an active, hands-on manager/owner.

In the next excerpt, Mitch Kaidy's experience as a political reporter provided important context regarding the *Times Union*'s editorial policy. Commentary from his oral history interview was quoted in full in the next part of the brief biography of Gannett.

Under Gannett's leadership, the *Times Union* began as an independent newspaper; however, over the years its editorial policy began to shift and the paper became staunchly Republican. The *Democrat & Chronicle* was always a Republican paper and under Gannett's control it soon became increasingly right-wing. As *Democratic & Chronicle* Political Reporter Mitch Kaidy explains:

> The Gannett newspapers were always right-wing. As a matter of fact, if you know anything about Frank Gannett, you know that he ran for president. He was one of the very early militant ideologues on the right; Gannett hated Franklin Roosevelt with a vengeance. I've read all this, that's how I know about it. He was certainly one of the first to organize the public to oppose a president's policies. He founded the Committee for Constitutional Government. I believe that was the earliest pacesetter for many other political action committees that would come along later. It was intended to mobilize public opinion

against Roosevelt's policies, especially Roosevelt's attempts to pack the Supreme Court.

Frank Gannett himself was far to the right of his editorial staff and far to the right of his editorial writing staff. The editorial writers and the editorial staff were separate. As a matter of fact, it's probably true, as a lot of people have observed, that young reporters generally are idealistic. Generally they tend to be on the left of the political spectrum. Not far on the left. They exaggerate about how leftist the young reporters are. They're reformers at heart; they're not radicals.

However, in Frank Gannett's day he was very paternalistic. That word was made for Frank Gannett. He used to give out turkeys and have parties and picnics. His wife and he used to come and he treated us as his family. We didn't think in those days that he was looking down on us, or patronizing us. We accepted that in good faith and we cherished it. But paternalism is rejected out of hand these days. I don't think we rejected it in those days.

(1994, p. 8)

Criticism regarding Gannett's newly fashioned media monopoly in Rochester was quick and sustained. Gannett vowed that the two newspapers would maintain separate staffs and would operate independently—a promise that he kept throughout his life. When Gannett purchased the *Democrat & Chronicle*, it was located on Main Street and the *Times Union* was housed in the current Gannett Rochester Building on Exchange Street. It was only years later, when Allen Neuharth ran Gannett, that the *Times Union* and the *Democrat & Chronicle* staffs and facilities were merged.

Landing my first interview with Henry Clune became a defining moment for this research project. Initially, most of the former Gannett journalists were resistant to participate in the oral history project. Some suggested they were too old, others felt that their experiences were ancient history and still others felt that they wouldn't be interesting subjects to interview because they had not become editors or publishers. Clune was the most senior Gannett journalist who was still alive and residing in the Rochester area in the 1990s; his experience spanned most of the twentieth century and it provided me with important context about how journalism was practiced in Rochester. The other Gannett reporters revered him, and once they heard he was part of my oral history project, several of them became willing (and even anxious) to participate. In addition, Clune provided me with the names of other former Gannett newsworkers, and a few of them eventually participated in the project.

I have always been interested in how people got interested in journalism, and for the Gannett oral history project I asked each narrator about how he or she got started in the field. As the following excerpt illustrates, I chose to focus on each narrator's first journalistic experiences as a strategy to transition from the Gannett historical context into the individual journalists' stories. This section also provided examples of relevant background information on the narrators whose stories were featured throughout the rest of the book project.

Several of the journalists interviewed suggested that during the 1950s and 1960s the *Times Union* and the *Democrat & Chronicle* were at the peak of their influence in Rochester. The *Times Union* was considered Gannett's flagship paper, and Paul Miller's influence as publisher and editor gave the newspaper strong leadership and increased its visibility. Allen Neuharth became general manager of both Rochester newspapers on February 1, 1963, and brought with him a philosophy of hands-on management as well as very specific views about the publishing of daily newspapers.

During this era, most newsworkers began their journalism careers at small newspapers or as copyboys or gofers on larger publications like the *Times Union* and the *Democrat & Chronicle*. Clune, who provided the earliest stories for this oral history project, began his sixty-year newspaper career in 1910 as an unpaid sub-reporter on the Rochester *Democrat & Chronicle*. As Clune explains:

> When I first started in the newspaper business, I worked for a city editor who was a man named Morris Adams. Mr. Adams was about the best newspaper executive I've ever known. He was an utterly dedicated man; he didn't get married until he was in his seventies and he was a wonderful person to start under. [While I was still a sub reporter] he told me that I wasn't suited for what I was trying to do and told me I'd ought to try something else. I'd been a kind of a failure as a youth and I wanted to succeed. I pleaded with him. I wasn't getting paid except with street car tokens so he let me stay on and finally—I think it was in April and I started there in June of 1910—in April of 1911 they started to pay me a little. That's the first time I really joined the staff. I started at eight dollars a week. I don't believe they would allow that today. The union wouldn't stand for keeping a man working there for eight months without any money, any pay.
>
> (1994a, pp. 4–5)

Clune's determination to succeed in the newspaper business is echoed by other Gannett newsworkers, particularly when they speak about how they got started in journalism. While their reasons for becoming interested in the newspaper business vary, as did their initial experiences, what remains consistent is the journalists' perseverance and genuine interest in writing. Their experiences getting started in the newspaper business certainly still provide guidance for aspiring journalists.

From the time he was 6 years old, Art Deutsch wanted to become a newspaper reporter:

> I used to drive my mother crazy because in those days I would spend a nickel on a day's circuit of newspapers and have them send me the papers so I could compare how they treated the story. I would get the *Pittsburgh Press*, and the *Post Gazette*, the *Philadelphia Inquirer*, and I'd get the *New York Post* and the *New York Herald Journal*, and the *Cleveland Plain Dealer* when it was a national story, just to see how they did it.
>
> (1994, p. 8)

Deutsch, who worked as an investigative reporter for the *Democrat & Chronicle* from 1956 through 1964, began his journalism career while he was still in high school as a copyboy for the *Philadelphia Inquirer*. Each day he would take the number 37 trolley into Philadelphia from Chester. Deutsch remembers:

> The great managing editor of those days was there, the original front-pager, Eli Z. Dimitman. Oh boy! He was a terror. Dressed like a father and was as earthy a man as you could find. And he had rules. The copy boy had to put out one dozen number two pencils, all drilled to a point. And copy paper, this and that, a carafe of ice water. One day there was a big fire in the Frankfurt section, the industrial section of Philadelphia, and all the reporters were sent out. It was pretty late. And he said, "Hey, come here kid, go down there and grab a hold of the nearest phone and don't leave it. Don't let anybody else use it, except our guys." I got a hundred nickels from the grocer, and I went down there and I kept the phones open for our people.
>
> In those days they had the *Evening Record*, the *Afternoon Record*, they had the *Courier*, the *Daily News*, the *Bulletin* morning, the *Bulletin* evening. God, there must have been eight newspapers. Finally, I'm calling in and a guy on the phone in rewrites said, "Dimitman says to come back in." I got on the trolley and went back. Dimitman said, "Hey kid, grab a phone. You told me once you wanted to write, so write whatever they call in." I said, "I have to tell my mother I'm going to be late." I told my mother about working late because of the big fire. Then I took the story from the phone and checked whatever I could.

When it was all done, time to go, it was about six in the morning. We were exhausted. We all smelled the smoke and it was fun. It was very heady stuff for a kid. Dimitman said, "I suppose you think you're a newspaperman." I didn't say anything. He said, "You won't make a patch on a newspaper man's butt." And I felt dreadful. Friday was payday, you got paid in cash, in little envelopes. I went down there and the cashier said, "Sorry to tell you this, you're through." My face must have fallen down to my ankles. She then said, "No, no, you got a five dollar raise."

(1994, pp. 8–9)

As a junior at the Rochester Institute of Technology, Floyd King became disillusioned with engineering and decided to quit school. King, who remained an active journalist for more than sixty-five years, explains how he decided to embark upon a journalism career shortly before the Great Depression began:

I was walking down the street in Rochester thinking, "What in the world am I going to do with my life? I don't know what I want to do, I haven't the slightest idea." And then just like it came out of the blue, just as if it was from heaven, I remembered what a fifth-grade teacher said to me. She said, "Floyd, I don't know what you're going to make of your life, but I think you ought to make writing a part of it. I think you have a gift for it." It was as if everything opened up immediately. That was the answer. Rochester had three newspapers at the time.

Now, keep in mind that I'd never written a news story in my life. I didn't even know how to start it. I applied at the three newspapers for a job. I guess two of them offered me jobs, the *Times Union* and the Hearst paper, the *Journal*. They both offered me jobs, and the Gannett *Democrat* said, "We just haven't anything now, but keep us in mind. You seem to have a talent." I took the job at the Hearst paper. How did I get it? I don't know but it just seemed that I could do it.

I was a reporter when the financial editor walked out of the financial room and he said, "The stock market has just crashed in New York City. People are jumping off the skyscrapers, going right down." I thought to myself, "What the hell, that doesn't mean anything to me. I haven't any money to speak of in the stock market." I went back to typing and everybody else went back to typing. Within two weeks we were all out of a job. The Hearst paper couldn't get any advertising.

I went over to the *Times Union* where the managing editor had been very good to me. I told him what happened, and he said, "Floyd, we just haven't got a thing in Rochester. Maybe you would like to go down to the Elmira paper [also owned by Gannett]. They need somebody for the summer, and you never know what could happen if you go down there and get a start." I thought, "Geez, I can't lose. I don't have a job anyway." I went to Elmira and got a job as a reporter for the *Star Gazette*. I suppose that I was lucky because I didn't know anything about reporting, but on a small-town paper like that I could pick it up kind of fast, and I did.

One day I was working late and we got word a big freight crashed just outside of Elmira and at least four men were dead. The boss said to me, "Get going and cover the story." I got going and it was just towards night, not quite yet, but there was a great big full moon up there. Steam engines puff when they're standing still. This engine had a dead man at the throttle and a dead man at the break. Both of their hands were still on it and the engine was going "sho, sho, sho." The engine was buried in the caboose. There was a train that hadn't gotten far enough off the track and had killed two men in the caboose also.

The damn story just had everything. I mean, that beautiful full moon, and there were very few people there. I had it all to myself. I went back to the paper and wrote the story. Now it was just one of those lucky things that has happened to me all my life. While I was doing this, L. R. Blanchard, who was then the supervising editor of all the Gannett newspapers, happened to be visiting down there. He never said one damn word about my story. I knew it was a good story and it hurt my feelings. He didn't say one single word. Next week I got a letter from Blanchard in Rochester inviting me to join the *Democrat & Chronicle* as a reporter. I did and I've been there ever since.

(1994, pp. 1–3)

As a senior at St. Andrew's Seminary, Tom Flynn decided that he wanted to become a newspaper reporter. Flynn, who has spent his entire career with Gannett, explains how his persistence eventually landed him his first job as a copyboy for the *Times Union*:

I remember the first Monday I walked in; I had sort of carefully hatched this plan—naïvely, as it turned out, even in 1957—that I would walk in, fill out the job application and as soon as I was available, they would hire me. I showed up in my black seminary suit and white shirt and my black briefcase, and filled out the job application. I was told there were no openings but that they would keep me in mind. Of course, I was still in school, so it was okay because I figured that in June this would be a fait accompli. Someone had told me that that it was important for people to remember who you are, so I came down every week and became a kind of fixture/pest. In any event, that process went along and I was told the same thing each week, that there was still no opening.

In June, when school concluded and I waved good-bye to St. Andrew's Seminary, I was then working part time, as I had for a couple of years, for Schmitt's Meat Market on Joseph Avenue, picking up sides of beef. There was no job at the newspaper in the summer of 1957. But in August of 1957, I got a call that if I was interested, I could start in September at one dollar an hour as a copyboy, and of course I was.

I walked into this building on September 9, 1957, and except for having worked at the original *Democrat & Chronicle* building on Main Street, I've never left. I dutifully enrolled at the University of Rochester and tortured my way through approximately six and a half years to get my BA degree in English. I have no affection for the University of Rochester. It's not their fault. But when you're running in and out of a school at nine o'clock at night and are taking classes under those conditions, it isn't like going to college. It was kind of like going to the dentist.

One dollar an hour, forty dollars a week, thirty-two dollars and eight cents after tax. It seemed like a lot of money, but of course it wasn't. As an editorial clerk, or copyboy, in those days there were no computers, of course, and we would get a lot of information, routine information like birth lists and statistical data, because the *Times Union* has always been the paper of record of sorts in this community. We who were clerks would go to the county clerk's office, or the real estate offices, and gather up [the information], or sometimes essentially take the information down. There was a responsibility there to get it right, and that was good training.

We ran stories on deadline from the newsroom to the composing room, which was, depending on various changes in the building, either on the third floor or the fourth floor—we were always a floor off. A lot of running page proofs to the editors because a lot of things had to be done quickly and things checked. There was some routine typing and some input.

There was pasting-up stocks; the stock quotations would come in every afternoon by a ticker-tape process from New York when the market closed. The *Times Union* had the complete closing stock list in its "Blue Streak" edition, which was a very popular final edition because we had a much larger street sale. Because factory gates were traditional, crowds would pour out of there at four o'clock. There was an urgency to get the stocks listings, which then were pasted up on streets in the exact order as they came in. And you dared not mess it up. Then they were literally typeset in a very short time in the composing room by a number of compositors who were waiting to do this. The new pages were matted, the lead plates cast, and on to the press, and the *Times Union* "Blue Streak" was onto the street no later than 4:00 P.M. It was eagerly grabbed up by downtown commuters, and bus traffic was much heavier, a much greater downtown presence than today. There was a substantial sale of that edition and that was one of the clerical things that we would do.

Sometimes you would go out on deadline to the home of a family who just lost somebody in an accident to negotiate the picture, which was an interesting early experience in diplomacy because most of the time you were in an ugly situation. I found then, and later as a police reporter, that the family members generally were the least of the problem. They were eager, in a semi-shocked state, to talk to you and to provide information. It was the well-meaning neighbor or the nosy brother-in-law who wanted to beat your brains out for stepping into their tragedy. Like all things, I had heard stories about reporters snatching photos when the family wasn't watching. I never did that. I did have to sweet-talk a number of people and in fact, occasionally personally drive back with the photo because it would have been awful if something had happened to it. They accepted the word that the newspaper wanted to present a photo and took us in good faith. I think that's a major part of our responsibility.

I know I got a very good early opportunity at these newspapers because even in 1957 it was not normal that someone who had not had some experience or college education would be allowed to start reporting. I was working for the *Times Union* in a daytime situation as a copyboy or a wire photo operator and [undertaking] various clerical newsroom duties, and I would practice writing news briefs on Saturday afternoons when the *Times Union* still published a Saturday afternoon paper. It was a thrill to see some of those published, of course anonymously, as a clerk.

About eighteen months into that experience, the job in the night library, or news morgue as it was called, became available. It meant more money and it meant more flexibility for school hours. I applied and got it, and worked in the news library for about nine months. I had, by dint of that, become friends with the *Democrat & Chronicle* crowd, which, of course, was mostly a nighttime workforce, and which had recently moved into this building which had expanded to bring them from the Main Street facility. I had made my ambitions known to a number of those people.

(1994, pp. 1–3, 8–10)

As you can see from the previous excerpt, which described how four of the Gannett reporters got started in journalism, the oral history interviews included considerable information about the craft of journalism. The interviews also produced helpful background information and interesting stories about media practices in the early twentieth century, as well as providing important context for the rest of the book. The following chapter summary connected Gannett's institutional history with information on newsroom routines and the training of journalists. These themes were explored more fully throughout the rest of the book.

Flynn's experiences both as a *Times Union* copyboy and as a clerk in the Gannett morgue not only illustrate the extensive job training that many Gannett journalists received, but also reveal the level of determination that newsworkers maintained throughout their apprenticeships. Although copyboys and cub reporters alike often endured routine, repetitive tasks like clipping and filing articles, and even filling paste-pots, their desire to prove themselves and succeed in the business carried them through the most boring of tasks.

Before the 1960s, educational requirements for journalists were minimal and some Gannett newsworkers began their journalism careers while still in high school. During the first half of the twentieth century a college degree was not required for men aspiring to a career in journalism; however, women, who had always had a difficult time gaining access to the newsroom, generally found that earning a college degree was a valuable asset. Rather than pursuing a formal education, young people who wanted to become journalists needed to possess a flair for writing, a sense of adventure and a willingness to work extremely long hours for little or even no pay. Most reporters worked their way up in the field, beginning as correspondents or cub reporters for smaller papers and then moving on to larger daily newspapers like the *Times Union* or the *Democrat & Chronicle*. A newsworker who was able to land his or her first job on a metropolitan daily newspaper usually began as a copyboy, or in Clune's case as a "sub" reporter.

Fred Fedler suggested that during the late nineteenth and the early twentieth centuries, rather than seeking out formal education, journalists often taught themselves by reading, comparing, and analyzing articles published in the major US newspapers (2000, p. 19). Several Gannett journalists spoke of rewriting newspaper articles to teach themselves how to write. Like Deutsch, who felt the pull to journalism from the age of six, these aspiring newsworkers frequently compared the coverage of national stories in a variety of urban daily newspapers.

Frank Gannett's own rise to power from delivery boy to media mogul also reflects this spirit of self-reliance, as well as his particular determination to produce newspapers suitable for all members of his community. When Gannett's

ownership of the *Times Union* and the *Democrat & Chronicle* created a monopoly situation in Rochester, Gannett vowed to keep each newspaper independent
and competitive—a promise that he kept throughout his life. The competition
between newspapers was lively, heated and sometimes hostile, and not only
encouraged excellence but also helped to keep the citizenry informed. The
newsworkers interviewed for this project frequently bemoaned the company's
decision to combine the editorial staffs of the two newspapers, and several accurately predicted the subsequent demise of the *Times Union*.

The background research that I completed for the Gannett oral history
project indicated that during the first half of the twentieth century, women
reporters faced a variety of gender-based challenges in the news industry.
During each interview I asked specific questions about the role of women
in the newsroom and followed up each answer with more probing questions on the topic. Not surprisingly, the female journalists never waited for
me to ask gender-related questions and volunteered commentary on specific challenges that they faced in a male-oriented work environment. The
next excerpt focused on the views of male journalists who worked for Gannett. Although it offered specific information about working conditions for
women reporters, it also provided insight into the prevailing early twentieth-
century (male) philosophy about the role of women in the newsroom.

While women worked on both the *Democrat & Chronicle* and the *Times Union*
throughout the twentieth century, many of the reporters interviewed suggested
that until at least the mid-1960s, women were treated differently than their
male counterparts. Pulitzer Prize-winning reporter Kaidy, who covered labor and
politics for the *Democrat & Chronicle* for fifteen years, echoes the sentiments of
several male reporters when he observes:

> In the 1950s and 1960s we had on the editorial staff a strict quota for
> women. There's no question that women played a back seat in those
> days, that they had some kind of a written or unwritten quota. They had
> good female reporters, no question about it. But it was sort of a given
> that journalism was a male occupation.
>
> (1994, p. 21)

Women were often seen as a necessary obligation rather than as equal members of the editorial staff. Some reporters, like Robert Beck, suggest that one

reason there were few women journalists on the newspaper staff at that time is that they were not as "sophisticated" as their male counterparts:

> During the war, because of the absence of men, they had to hire a few. You had old-time Hearst people like Ruth Chamberlain, who was a fashion and society editor. She made all the others look like car-hops. A real tough broad. A nice girl. One of the reasons they didn't have many women at newspapers in those days is that women were not as sophisticated as they are today. They had no concept of the double entendre, for example. We had a reporter named Elizabeth Keiper and she wrote a garden column. A lovely person, about seventy years old. I remember hearing the expression, "Stop the presses!" and it had to do with one of her stories. It was a picture of a garden with a rooster on a fence behind it, crowing at the dawn. Three columns wide with the headline: "The Big Red Cock Greeted the Morning Dawn."
>
> (1994, pp. 10–11)

Other Gannett newspapermen described the few women who worked news-side as hard-bitten, cigarette-smoking old maids. The one woman who worked in a Rochester newsroom during the 1920s was in charge of society news. According to Clune:

> She was a kind of a fussy old woman, but she had a good following and, being the only woman in there, she was subjected to certain jokes and things, but she was all right. Augie Anderson was her name, Augusta Anderson. She was a general reporter, but the clergy were fond of her and the woman's clubs, and she was a favorite of the people that ran the amateur theatricals. There were a lot of people who thought a good deal of Augusta Anderson.
>
> She was a fine woman, a little absent-minded. I saw her go out one February night; of course she worked like the rest of us until midnight or after. It was below zero and she went down to get the streetcar without her coat.
>
> Later there were girls who first came in to work for the women's department, for society. They finally got a society editor, a women's editor. That began to open the door for them and the woman society editor always had an assistant who was always a woman, although I was the assistant society editor for a brief period in the 1920s.
>
> (1994a, pp. 13–14)

> She wasn't identified, we had no bylines in those days. There were no bylines.
>
> (1994b, p. 2)

By the 1950s, more women began working in the *Times Union* and the *Democrat & Chronicle* newsrooms. Other male reporters echo Luckett's perception that female reporters were pleased with their treatment at Gannett:

> Sally Ann Watts [Sarah Watts] and Margaret Goetz were very attractive female reporters. Elizabeth Keiper, who was a copy editor, was in a sense a prototypical old maid. She was a spinster lady. Her father had been a well-known patent attorney in Rochester. Betty Keiper was very deaf, had two hearing aids, and all the reporters lived in fear of having her stalk over to your desk with a piece of copy and a question about something, because you were pretty sure you weren't going to be able to answer whatever the question was, and if you could, you probably couldn't make Betty hear what your answer was.
>
> Ruth Chamberlain was the society editor and Peg Doyle was her assistant. And that was really it. There were a handful of women. I think that there was a young woman who was a sort of secretary for the city desk, sort of a gofer-type person. There were some copygirls carrying copy around. I don't think that there was any discrimination. Who knows? I'm a male, but it may have been perceived by the women certainly, in terms of the assignments they got from the city desk. I don't really remember a lot of griping from Sally or from Marge. They may have been seething internally; I'm not sure.
>
> (Luckett, 1994, pp. 10–11)

During the course of his interview, Art Deutsch described a few women on the *Democrat & Chronicle* during the 1950s and 1960s who challenged prevailing notions regarding women in the newsroom:

> One woman that we worked with, Gail Sheehy, covered women's stuff. Against the wall were the women's desks. Gail sat there. I used to listen to her talk. Her first husband at that time was going to medical school here and she turned phrases neatly; I noticed that. I said to Red Vagg one day when we were having lunch, I said, "Geez, why don't you put Gail on city side? She can write." "Ah, of course, she's a goddamn woman. You know they're nothing but a pain." After Gail made it pretty big one day [Sheehy is the best-selling author of *Passages*], I bought a paperback and I sent it to Red Vagg. I said, "This is from me and

relates to the girl who didn't know what to do in the city room." He called me up and said, "Deutsch, you're a son of a bitch!" I said, "I know it." He said, "But you were right."

We had others who were good. We had a gal named Connie Gunthers who came from San Francisco. She led a charmed life. She had never been to New York, to the United Nations, so she decided to take a day off and go through it. That's the day that Stevenson and Khrushchev met. She writes a first-person story. She was there. Another time she's coming home from San Francisco, the plane lands in Chicago, O'Hare. Plane collapses, burns, four people dead, one from Rochester, and she files a first-person story. I said, "Jesus Christ, how does that happen? It never happened to me."

We had some pretty good female writers over the years. Jean Walrath, who is dead now, wrote everything in the paper. She did theater, she did women's garbage, society stuff, which she hated, but she also was a good hard news reporter. And I loved that. Jean retired long ago. I covered stuff with her, the opening of the Seaway, that kind of thing. Hard-nosed, [would] take no guff from any one reporter. To me, it doesn't matter if you're a homosexual, a lesbian, or a male or female, what difference does it make? Can you do the job? I see this all the time. People say, "Oh, she can't do that," or "he can't do that," or "he is a pussy cat, I wouldn't send him out now," except that he can write rings around you.

(1994, p. 21)

According to Fradenburgh, there were always women working in the *Times Union* newsroom. What Fradenburgh found difficult to accept, however, was Gannett's decision in the 1960s to put women on the police beat:

I think one of the major changes that happened was we made the decision to let women cover the police beat. A lot of thought went into that because you're going into some areas that you might consider dangerous and there was a lot of soul searching. Now, of course, it's commonplace. One of the most difficult things for me was when the dress code began changing and the women and girls began to come in with jeans on instead of skirts. This is horrible when you've been brought up to see women dress up. This is old school, isn't it? I questioned women going out to meet the public like that. I remember going into my managing editor, John Dougherty, and telling him my concerns. He just said, "Forget it." So I forgot it.

(1994, p. 16)

Flynn also remembers women working in the newsroom throughout his career:

I've worked with women all my life here. I remember strong women that I observed when I was a copyboy on the *Times Union*; they were the society editor, the women's columnist kind. A couple of them were on the copy desk. At the risk of sounding crude, they seemed like hard-bitten, cigarette-smoking old ladies, old maids, who probably had spent their entire life working in an environment that was not feminine or female, certainly. But they held their own and were sort of one of the boys. That was kind of the image.

Rose Sold is an interesting person. I would guess Rose is probably in her eighties. She covered a variety of news, general assignment kinds of things. Her husband, Earl Hoch, for many, many years covered courts. They were married when I came here in 1957. Rose always struck me as very feminine, very small, diminutive kind of person. Kind of a pretty, attractive person, as opposed to Betty Keiper with the heavy rouge, and Ruth Chamberlain with the gravely voice and the cigarette hanging out of her mouth who wrote all that drivel about society. Ruth did it with great style, and was beloved in the high society halls of Rochester; she knew everybody, and nobody moved without checking with Ruth. But she was like the iron-fisted bitch who just looked like something that came out of a movie. Those were the women.

Some reporters were beginning to show up and one of them, Sally Miles Watts [Sarah Watts], was a young female reporter in the early 1960s on the *Times Union*. She was very attractive, perhaps also by contrast to those crones who were around her—and I say that sort of with affection. Of course, I'm looking at all this through seventeen- or eighteen-year-old eyes. It struck me that Sally was quite flirtatious. Not with me, because she was five or six years older, but with several of the males, some of whom she wound up going out with. You could see all this sort of playing out. Ultimately she married one of them. I would say, though, that the women I've worked with for the most part just have been just outstanding people. I don't think that we who were here made a big deal out of that. Women here have pretty well held their own.

We have many more women who have come into the work environment in the news area in the last twenty-five years than perhaps the first ten or so that I was there. There were relatively few. But it has clearly swung the other way. With few exceptions, they're all as good as anybody I know and worked with, and have enjoyed working with. With one exception. I can think of some men I've worked with whom

I consider to be complete fools, just people that drive you nuts. I can only think of one woman that even I would grudgingly call a real bitch, who was just a nasty person. But people are people, so it doesn't make any difference, does it? I think women have enjoyed good working conditions here—Gannett has always been a leader in that. I think we practice what we preach around here.

(1994)

Upon reflection, I felt that my strategy of contrasting the views of male and female Gannett journalists was successful in that it brought issues to light and also illustrated two very different worldviews. During the interviews I sometimes found it challenging not to show emotion or to argue with the men who insisted that women loved working for Gannett. Of course, it was important that all of the journalists I interviewed felt comfortable to tell their own stories, so I learned not to argue with them. The following commentary suggested a very different story regarding the experiences of women journalists who worked for the Rochester, New York, *Democrat & Chronicle* and the *Times Union*. As you can see, this perspective differed significantly from most of the information provided by the male reporters.

Most of the men interviewed said that they thought the female newsworkers were happy working for the *Rochester Times Union* and the *Democrat & Chronicle*. Although a few men, like Flynn, suggest that Gannett had always been a leader in the hiring and treatment of female reporters, the women interviewed for this oral history project had somewhat different perceptions regarding their value to Gannett. Each woman mentions sometimes being given marginal assignments and occasionally being treated in a patronizing manner. *Times Union* feature writer Margaret Beck eventually became dismayed by the cynicism of both her editors and her male colleagues, and left journalism for a career in advertising. When she started work at the *Times Union* in 1952, Beck was the only reporter with an electric typewriter, which she thought might give her somewhat of an advantage. Unfortunately, her typewriter didn't seem to matter much to her male editors:

I think there was quite a bit of chauvinism, quite a bit. Kermit Hill, who had been the political reporter, dreamed up this story he wanted me to do. At Ontario Beach Park they still rented bathing suits; you could go and rent black wool tank suits. Somehow the idea came up that they should update their image, and he arranged an interview. I worked pretty hard on the story and one of the reporters came up to me and said, "It was a good story, who wrote the lead for you?" So there was that kind of attitude.

(1994, pp. 2–3)

Feature writer Sarah Watts, who later became editor of the *Times Union* weekend entertainment supplement, is described in these interviews by her male colleagues as attractive and flirtatious. Watts says that although some editors treated female reporters fairly, in general during the 1950s and 1960s women at Gannett were "second-class citizens":

Among the things that happened to me was great liberty under Howard Hosmer, and I was riding high on that for several years. And then the editors changed. He became managing editor, which was wonderful for him, but not for me because the new editor, John Dougherty, was a tough guy. I don't think he really liked women in the newsroom. I wanted to take classes offered to all reporters in speed writing that were being given at a public high school, tuition free. I asked if I could do that. He said, "No, because you're no doubt going to get married and have babies and leave us, and it won't be worth the one hundred dollar investment"—which I thought was terrible.

I looked around for things to do at the paper and I talked to a woman named Ruth B. Chamberlain. Why do we always remember their middle initials? Because the bylines were there every day. A wonderful woman who was a maiden lady, and a lady she was, who cared for her invalid sister, and ran the society page in the days when society pages were that. She had a little three-by-five [inch] file card index about everybody in Rochester, and whom they'd married, and so forth and so on. She was also a true trade unionist.

I asked her, "What are my chances around here?" She said, "If you're lucky and if I die, you could become society editor." The only other woman of any stature on the paper was Rose Sold, who had been there forever and had the church beat, hardly one I was coveting. There was a future for me opening up through a man named John C. Hadley who came into Rochester and was editing special sections, which included a weekly tabloid and then specials on fashion, on cars, even on the hot dog. I became his sole staff person, and it was an interesting job.

(1995, p. 6)

One other thing happened which again shows the status of women on that newspaper. When raises were handed out, I was offered a raise, but only got a modest, the lowest of the low, a five-dollar-a-week raise— two hundred and fifty dollars for the whole year. Because I had a husband who was working, he was supposed to provide for me. That's what I was told by the managing editor, a man named Vernon Croop.

(1995, p. 8)

The attitude toward women was just horrible and best explained, I think, by Gannett's treatment of a young woman named Pat Lemm who came to the paper when I was first there. A lovely woman, but without a lot of education and without much newspaper experience. Her father was the president of Edwards Department Store, the fourth largest department store in downtown Rochester, and she was given this job. But she was never trained. Nor was I trained. There was a lousy system. There was never any mentor for you. Bill Ringle kind of took me under his wing, and he was wonderful. I remember his helping me on a story about covering a gypsy funeral for one thing. But no one was there. There was no kind of training going on as there has been subsequently since those days in the fifties and sixties.

(1995, p. 20)

When I first arrived in 1956 at the *Times Union*, I went into what I thought was the rest room. I saw people coming and going. There were lockers there, but I never needed it because it was summer and I kept my purse in my desk. I just went in to use the bathroom. It was not until I was there several weeks and I heard this titter, did I realize that it was the men's room, and they were just trying to catch me there in the act. That was their idea of having fun with the women. I thought it was pretty childish but let them have their fun.

(1995, p. 22)

Jean Giambrone's experiences with Gannett were perhaps most telling regarding the role of women at Gannett during this era. Initially employed as a freelancer to write a women's athletics column while she was a student at the University of Rochester, Giambrone was hired on a full-time basis after her college graduation. For four years during World War II, Giambrone covered local news for the *Times Union*. After the war, Giambrone married and went back to writing a sports column on a part-time basis. She covered both women's and men's golf, bowling, soccer and other sports, and often wrote a variety of stories for the newspaper each day:

> Eventually, I covered everything that you can shake a fist at. I never covered a football game but I interviewed football players. You know what I'm saying? If they were stuck at the office, they'd say, "will you?" I'd go cover a basketball game or I'd go cover a soccer game—boy's, girls, high school, college, whatever. For my love of sports and my knowledge, etc. I would go cover those things. In my lifetime I've interviewed many athletes.
>
> (1994, p. 5)

Giambrone recounts with pride becoming the first woman allowed into the interview room of the Master's golf tournament:

> The first year I went, they wouldn't let me in. When I finally got in— some people talk about male chauvinism and all that stuff, they can talk all they want—I had nothing but thanks to the guys because they were the ones who got me in. The second year I went, they said, "What are you doing here?" I was the only woman; there were all men covering it, two to three hundred men at the Master's golf tournament.
>
> I looked at Will Grimsley, who in my book is one of the all-time great sportswriters. He was with AP [Associated Press] and I said, "I'll tell you what, I'm not here to write about Mrs. Arnold Palmer's clothes or something; I'm here to do what you do. I have a bigger assignment this year. I don't do this just for my paper—I'm doing it for the whole Gannett news service and I can't get in there to do interviews and I can't use the typewriters and I can't get at the Western Union machines at those times, and so I've got a problem." He said, "That's not fair; let me see what I can do about it."
>
> He spoke to a colleague and they went to a man who was retired and was a liaison between the press and the powers that be that run the tournament. At that time it was Clifford Roberts, and before that, Bobby Jones. They said to Clifford Roberts's secretary, "Give her press credentials; she needs to do what we do." She said, "Oh no, not until you speak to Mr. Roberts." They looked at me and said, "Come back in an hour," the guys did. I said, "Baloney, I've got to figure out a way to do this without having access to all this stuff." But, when I went back in an hour, the secretary was typing up my Class A press credentials.
>
> (1994, p. 5)

I couldn't get into the men's locker rooms from where they were getting great stories. I'd be the only woman there, and once or twice I had the men come out and say, "Want to listen to my tape?" But, for the most part I did my own work. I had terrific cooperation from the athletes themselves because once or twice I'd stop them short of the locker room and they understood my predicament, so they'd talk to me. There was one incident with Ken Venturi when a whole big mess of guys were standing around listening to the interview and they started interjecting their own questions. All of a sudden he looked up and said, "She can't go in the locker room; you can. Let her talk."

(1994, p. 11)

When the US Open was here, I think it was 1988, I just wanted to go back and visit. Because of the number of events I had covered for the US Golf Association I got a permanent pass; it's a pin with my name engraved on it and I can go into any of the things. I went and I said, "I don't want to run around the golf course, I want to go in the press room and see the people." I was amazed at the number of women in there. In the old days I was the only woman.

(1994, p. 6)

Giambrone considered herself lucky that she was at the right place at the right time to become the first woman to cover sports for Gannett in Rochester. However, after World War II, although she often worked more than forty hours a week for the remaining thirty-five years of her career with Gannett, she was considered a freelancer and she worked without employee benefits or retirement pay.

My strategy of letting each person tell his or her own story and comparing and contrasting individual perceptions during the writing process worked better than when I initially attempted to question male journalists' views on women reporters during the interview process. When I tried to use Jean Giambrone's experiences to illustrate challenges women faced in the Gannett newsrooms, the men I was interviewing began to shut down. They either became quiet, changed the topic or they suggested that Giambrone was not a "real" journalist but merely a "freelancer" or a part-time worker. As my goal for the oral history project was to gather the newsworkers' experiences, for them to tell their own stories, I knew that I had to earn and maintain their trust throughout the entire interview process. I felt it was important to tread lightly in controversial areas, and therefore my strategy was to bring up sensitive topics, casually and matter-of-factly, when the narrators were discussing related issues. In presenting a variety of experiences and opinions, a larger structure of feeling about working as a journalist for Gannett began to emerge from the interviews. The book project showcased the experiences of rank-and-file reporters who worked in Rochester, New York. Over the years, the feedback I have received from the men and women who were involved in the research project has been inspirational. Some of the narrators shared the book with family members and they found that it helped them to talk more openly about their journalistic careers.

Oral History Exercises

1. Conduct an open-ended oral history interview with an individual about his or her career. Plan for an hour-long in-person interview and be sure to record it. Before the interview, obtain some background about the person you plan to interview. To prepare for the interview, think about topic areas that you wish to explore but only craft one opening question. Remember, it is important to listen to the person speak and to ask additional questions based on the person's commentary.
2. Following the open-ended interview, transcribe the complete interview. After the transcription process is complete, go back and edit the interview.
3. Following the open-ended interview, complete an analysis of the interview process. Consider the behavior of the interviewee as well as your own behavior. What was your comfort level during the interview? How did non-verbal communication impact the interview process? How valuable was the information you obtained? It is helpful to compare your experiences during this interview with other, more structured interviews you have previously completed.

References

Anderson, Kathryn, and Jack, Dana C. (1998). Learning to listen: Interview techniques and analyses. In Robert Perks and Alistair Thomson (Eds.), *The oral history reader* (pp. 157–171). London: Routledge.

Beck, Margaret. (1994, August 5). Interview by Bonnie Brennen. Oral History of Gannett Newsworkers project.

Beck, Robert. (1994, August 5). Interview by Bonnie Brennen. Oral History of Gannett Newsworkers project.

Brandt, J. Donald. (1993). *A history of Gannett, 1960–1993*. Arlington, VA: Gannett.

Brennen, Bonnie. (2001). *For the record: An oral history of Rochester, New York, Newsworkers.* Bronx, NY: Fordham University Press.

Clune, Henry. (1947). *Main street beat.* New York: W. W. Norton.

Clune, Henry. (1994a, May 4). Interview by Bonnie Brennen. Oral History of Gannett Newsworkers project.

Clune, Henry. (1994b, June 6). Interview by Bonnie Brennen. Oral History of Gannett Newsworkers project.

Deutsch, Art. (1994, June 13). Interview by Bonnie Brennen. Oral History of Gannett Newsworkers project 13.

Fedler, Fred. (2000). *Lessons from the past: Journalists' lives and work, 1850–1950.* Prospect Heights, IL: Waveland.

Flynn, Thomas. (1994, November 4). Interview by Bonnie Brennen. Oral History of Gannett Newsworkers project.

Fradenburgh, Don. (1994, July 7). Interview by Bonnie Brennen. Oral History of Gannett Newsworkers project.

Frisch, Michael. (2016). Oral history in the digital age: Beyond the raw and the crooked. *Australian Historical Studies, 47*: 92–107.

General principles for oral history. (2010). *Oral history association.* Retrieved from www.oralhistory.org

Giambrone, Jean. (1994, July 6). Interview by Bonnie Brennen. Oral History of Gannett Newsworkers project.

Goodman, Jessica. (2016, July 15). Still sexy after all these years. *Entertainment Weekly, 1422*: 42–45.

Grele, Ronald J. (1991). *Envelopes of sound: The art of oral history* (2nd ed.). New York: Praeger.

Hardt, Hanno, and Brennen, Bonnie. (Eds.). (1995). *Newsworkers: Toward a history of the rank and file.* Minneapolis: University of Minnesota Press.

Hoffman, Alice. (1996). Reliability and validity in oral history. In David K. Dunaway and Willa K. Baum (Eds.), *Oral history: An interdisciplinary anthology* (pp. 87–93). Walnut Creek, CA: Sage.

Kaidy, Mitch. (1994, July 5). Interview by Bonnie Brennen. Oral History of Gannett Newsworkers project.

King, Floyd. (1994, June 23). Interview by Bonnie Brennen. Oral History of Gannett Newsworkers project.

Luckett, Charles. (1994, September 7). Interview by Bonnie Brennen. Oral History of Gannett Newsworkers project.

Markovitz, Adam. (2011, July 8/15). Casting the spell: An oral history. *Entertainment Weekly*: 36–47.

Matheson, Jennifer L. (2007). The voice transcription technique: Use of voice recognition software to transcribe digital interview data in qualitative research. *Qualitative Report, 12* (4): 547–560.

McCullough, David. (2008). *John Adams.* New York: Simon & Schuster.

Merrill, Arch. (1954). *Mr. and Mrs. Ezra R. Andrews: Our master builders.* Rochester, NY: Rochester Institute of Technology.

Morrissey, Charles T. (1998). On oral history interviewing. In Robert Perks and Alistair Thompson (Eds.), *The oral history reader* (pp. 107–113). London: Routledge.

Shopes, Linda. (2014). Insights and oversights: Reflections on the documentary tradition and the theoretical turn in oral history. *The Oral History Review, 41* (2): 257–268.

Terkel, Studs. (1967). *Division street: America.* New York: Pantheon.

Terkel, Studs. (1997). *My American century.* New York: The New Press.

Thompson, Paul. (1990). *The voice of the past: Oral history* (2nd ed.). Oxford: Oxford University Press.

Watts, Sarah. (1995, November 21). Interview by Bonnie Brennen. Oral History of Gannett Newsworkers project.

Williams, Raymond. (1977/1988). *Marxism and literature.* Oxford: Oxford University Press.

Yow, Valerie Raleigh. (2005). *Recording oral history: A guide for the humanities and social sciences* (2nd ed.). Walnut Creek, CA: AltaMira Press.

Zeigler, Michael. (1983, January 2). Frank E. Gannett. *Upstate Magazine*, pp. 14–26.

CHAPTER 7

Ethnography and Participant Observation

Any gaze is always filtered through the lenses of language, gender, social class, race and ethnicity. There are no objective observations, only observations socially situated in the worlds of the observer and the observed.
—Norman Denzin and Yvonna Lincoln (1998, p. 24)

Ethnography focuses on understanding what people believe and think, and how they live their daily lives. It is used to answer questions about people's beliefs, rituals, attitudes, actions, stories and behaviors, emphasizing what people actually do rather than what they say they do. Grounded in the concept of culture, ethnography was first associated with anthropology and involved long-term field research observing activities and behaviors and interacting with people from different cultures. Researchers originally lived and worked consistently with members of other cultures for many months or years.

More recently, ethnography has become a popular qualitative approach used by researchers in a variety of disciplines, including sociology, education, public policy, media studies and marketing to understand people's interests, practices and experiences. In the twenty-first century the realm of ethnography has expanded to consider many types of foreign and domestic cultures and interest groups, including organizational and online communities. Journalists and writers use ethnographic approaches to add greater depth of interpretation to their storytelling, and ethnography is currently used in business and industry as a strategy to assess consumers' actions, going beyond their self-reported activities and opinions.

Researchers suggest that the recent popularity of ethnography may be due to fundamental changes occurring in Western societies. Gobo (2011) sees Western cultures as being fixated on observation, and maintains that being observed and observing others are central aspects of our contemporary lives. For example, surveillance cameras document our public actions, we video many of our social interactions and activities, and we routinely post images and videos on YouTube, Instagram, Snapchat and Facebook. It is currently estimated that worldwide there are more than 1.6 billion active monthly users of Facebook and 400 million active users of Instagram (Chaffee, 2016).

Interestingly, when I completed the first edition of *Qualitative Research Methods for Media Studies*, it was then estimated that sixty hours of video were being uploaded to YouTube each minute (Grossman, 2012). Four years later, current estimates indicate that 300 hours of video are uploaded to YouTube each minute (Smith, 2016). In an era in which the public and private realms have become blurred, it makes sense that ethnography, with its emphasis on observing people's actions and behaviors, has become a widely used methodology.

As the field of ethnography has evolved, researchers have drawn on a variety of strategies, philosophies and theoretical positions, which have influenced the types of ethnographic research that have been produced. Some ethnographers continue to favor systematic observations in an attempt to uncover structures, patterns and relationships. Other researchers, particularly postmodern ethnographers, maintain that it is impossible to discover a final, fixed or authoritative meaning of people's actions, and in their work they stress the open-endedness and incompleteness of their observations, as well as their own role in the ethnographic process (Denzin and Lincoln, 1998). These days, even the term "ethnography" has become somewhat contentious: it has been called a synonym for all qualitative research, or described as a philosophical orientation, a methodology or a research tool. Some researchers insist that ethnography means the on-site study of foreign cultures over an extended period of time, while others suggest that ethnography may be done locally, within a researcher's culture, and that it need not take years to complete, as long as it helps us to understand a specific group, community or culture. In this chapter I use the term "ethnography" to describe the qualitative method of observing, talking to and interacting with people in their natural environments; that is, where they live, play and/or work. While researchers' definitions of ethnography may vary, observation is central to all understandings of this method.

Thick Description

Ethnography emphasizes listening, watching and interacting with people as they go about their lives. Researchers work to establish rapport and select informants so that they can observe, interview and participate in activities with members of a group, culture or organization in order to learn about the explicit and tacit realms of their experiences, routines and practices. The explicit aspects of culture are those that individuals are able to address and discuss with a researcher, while the tacit parts of a culture are those things that are outside people's consciousness or awareness (DeWalt and DeWalt, 2011). Establishing the relevant context for a researcher's observations is an integral aspect of ethnography. The contextual background may focus on key historical, political, economic or social aspects of the group or culture being observed, providing key information to give a researcher the relevant frames of reference for her or his observations.

Cultural anthropologist Clifford Geertz (1973) saw ethnography as a blending of observation and interpretation, which together provided the "thick description" of a culture or group. Within the interpretation process, researchers considered the relevant social context, which helped them to understand that their observations were representations of a group's cultural reality. Geertz used an example of the differences between a twitch and a wink to illustrate the importance of context in creating thick description. At first glance, a twitch and a wink may look exactly the same to an observer. However, a twitch is usually an involuntary action while a wink is considered a deliberate act of communication. A person who winks is drawing on a specific social code to attempt to communicate something in particular to someone else, on the sly. It is up to a researcher to understand the appropriate context and intention of the action in order to determine whether the facial movement is a twitch or a wink. As Geertz (1973) explained, the information that researchers collect is not objective data but is "really our own constructions of other people's constructions of what they and their compatriots are up to" (p. 9). Most of the information that a researcher collects about a group of people or an event, activity or custom requires additional contextual information before it can be fully comprehended.

Ethnography in Media Studies

The development of cultural studies, particularly its emphasis on the reception and consumption of texts, inspired the use of ethnography in communication and media studies. Researchers began to draw on ethnographic methods in an attempt to draw out broader contexts surrounding media usage, as well as to understand how people actually engaged with media. Researchers focused on the contexts for media consumption, the process of reception and the many experiences and practices of people as they used media (Morley and Silverstone, 1991). Drawing on Hall's (1980) model of encoding and decoding—which is discussed more fully in Chapter 8—researchers observed the routine usage of technologies and texts by audience members. In their audience-centered studies they focused on the role readers and viewers played in the production of meanings. These days, researchers often refer to the time when media studies began to emphasize the role of the audience as active participants as "the ethnographic turn" (Machin, 2002, p. 74). However, some media studies researchers doing ethnography suggest that because they often study aspects of their own culture, it is often challenging for them to obtain enough critical distance from their projects in order to make ordinary and everyday situations seem "strange" (Stokes, 2003, p. 139).

Contemporary ethnographic research projects in media studies often focus on work practices in communication industries and audience reception to popular cultural texts. The fieldwork is usually completed in a few months rather than over several years. Instead of living within a specific community, communication and media researchers often observe the work process at media outlets such as researching online investigative news agencies, broadcast news stations, news organizations, advertising agencies and public relations firms. For example, the ethnographic research project by Tracy Everbach (2006), "The Culture of a Women-Led Newspaper: An Ethnographic Study of the *Sarasota Herald-Tribune*," studied newsroom culture through participant observation and depth interviews. The researcher spent three weeks observing all aspects of the newsroom in one-week increments during a nineteen-month period and interviewed twenty-six reporters, editors, photographers and designers about newsroom policies and practices.

Digital Ethnography

Communication and media studies researchers also use new media to conduct ethnography online with special interest groups, professional organizations and virtual communities, a process known as digital ethnography. People with similar interests, values and beliefs create virtual communities in an effort to identify and bring together like-minded people to hang out, discuss issues and topics and coordinate activities. Often these online communities are based on popular culture interests, such as a favorite actor, musician or television show. People with particular political identifications, health problems, specific social values or similar religious beliefs often come together on the Web.

However, some virtual communities can go beyond discussing similar interests to activism and occasionally incitement. For example, Stormfront. org went online in 1995 as the first extremist hate-speech site posted to the Internet. Its creator, Don Black, is a white nationalist and former member of the Nazi party who was grand wizard of the Ku Klux Klan in the 1970s. Black created Stormfront to promote his ideas worldwide and to recruit new members to the KKK. Stormfront.org has been censored in Europe because of its racist, homophobic and anti-Semitic language and for content that has been judged to incite its readers to violence. In 2005, Stormfront had 30,000 members, but Bjork James, who has tracked the website for eleven years, reported that in 2016 there were 313,000 Stormfront members (Shapiro, 2016). Black maintained that Donald Trump's presidential campaign helped Stormfront to grow and prosper, and he claimed that one million unique visitors visited the website each month in 2016. After Trump called for banning all Muslims from entering the United States, Stormfront needed to upgrade their software and add new servers to manage the additional daily traffic (Shamsian and Banicki, 2015). Contemporary researchers study the conversations, stories, practices and rituals of online groups like Stormfront to understand how people communicate in virtual communities and to determine what constitutes activism and/or incitement.

One benefit of digital ethnography is that email messages, blog postings, online chats and other virtual communication can be stored, archived and searched by the researcher. Since media studies ethnographers working online are unable to observe the non-verbal social cues of their research participants, they focus on the context for the users' commentary as well as their writing style, site specific "lingo," shared memes, use of acronyms such as LOL (laugh out loud) and how participants use emoticons such as :-D to indicate their attitudes or emotions (Lindlof and Shatzer, 1998).

Digital ethnography challenges the belief in "dataism," which is the assumption that all answers may be found in big data. Attempting to move beyond "the one-dimensionality of data" (Lohmeier, 2014, p. 86) digital ethnographers augment online data and documents with field observations, interviews and other qualitative methods in an effort to understand the relevant context and the larger issues related to the use of digital media.

Participant Observation

In contemporary media studies, some researchers use the terms "ethnography" and "participant observation" interchangeably. Others define participant observation as fieldwork through which a researcher observes and interacts with others, or as ethnography done in one's own culture rather than in a foreign country (Machin, 2002). Whether you use the terms interchangeably or somehow distinguish participant observation from ethnography, qualitative researchers find participant observation integral to ethnography, and they often refer to it as ethnography's primary methodological tool. Researchers use participant observation to understand the language, practices and activities of a specific group, culture or institution. In participant observation, researchers go into the field to gain knowledge about activities, beliefs, values, relationships and interests so that they may learn more about how others make sense of their everyday lives. Participant observation is an open-ended and flexible research process that may be carried out by one researcher or by a research team.

Hoping to develop rapport with those being studied, researchers often spend extended periods of time in the community, watching and participating in daily activities, rituals and ceremonies and observing, describing and documenting their actions and experiences. Participant observers learn and use the local language or dialect, listen to conversations, ask questions, watch what happens and learn the basic rules, customs and procedures so that they can provide detailed descriptions of life at a particular time and place. Often, the closer the relationships that participant observers develop, the greater access they have to the social experiences of those being studied. Atkinson and Hammersley (1994) suggest that all social research should be seen as a type of participant observation because it is not possible to study aspects of our social world without actively engaging in it. From this perspective, participant observation is seen not as a specific research technique but instead as "a mode of being-in-the-world characteristic of researchers" (p. 249).

One of the most challenging aspects of participant observation is gaining access to a group, culture or organization. Some researchers use their personal and work contacts to begin the process while others opt for topics of study that they already have personal access to or knowledge about. It is helpful for participant observers to be outgoing, enthusiastic and friendly, and to enjoy interacting with others. Gaining access for participant observations of businesses and institutions often begins with researchers determining the organizational hierarchy and getting the approval of those in charge.

Of course, gaining access also requires members of the group being studied to communicate openly with researchers. And this is where social networking sites like Twitter, LinkedIn and Facebook can help researchers to get to know group members. It is important for participant observers to develop rapport with members of the group or organization so that the members will feel comfortable enough around them to act naturally and speak freely with them. Building rapport takes time and requires researchers to have good communication skills and to be open and truthful about their intentions. In order to build rapport with group members, sometimes it is necessary for researchers to illustrate their interest in, respect for and commitment to the community (DeWalt and DeWalt, 2011). When researchers and participants share the same goals for a research project, it is clear that rapport has been established.

Once researchers gain access and develop rapport, other challenges that they face in participant observation include deciding on a focus for their observations, learning how to document what they hear and see without overtly impacting group dynamics, separating their descriptions of events from their interpretations and negotiating the involvement required to build rapport without abandoning their role as a researcher (Berger, 1998). Researchers draw on their theoretical frameworks to help them craft their research questions and focus their observations.

It is helpful for researchers to be flexible, adaptable, resourceful and curious. While participant observers know that their background, sex, race or ethnicity may affect the way they are perceived, they must also understand that their clothing, hairstyles, speech habits and/or facial gestures may also influence people's response to them. Participant observers should be careful to avoid preconceived notions about a culture or group, and they should remain open to learning new observation strategies. Community members may be less likely to talk with researchers who appear rigid and inflexible about their research goals or who portray themselves as being judgmental or knowing too much about a group or organization.

The realm of participant observation is generally grouped into four major categories: complete observer, observer as participant, participant as observer and complete participant. The complete observer, sometimes referred to as a non-participant observer, is someone who observes from a distance and has no interaction with the people, group or community that is being observed. At first glance, it may be difficult to envision a researcher on-site who does not interact with participants in any way, because the presence of a researcher generally has an influence on a group of people and their environment. However, some researchers have done observations through one-way glass mirrors or by using binoculars to observe others at a distance. More recently, some researchers have chosen to record activities and events on video cameras that are strategically placed around the site. These non-participant observers watch and analyze the recordings off-site at a later date.

The description "observer as participant" applies to researchers who are on-site but who distance themselves from those being observed. Such researchers may talk with and interview people in an organization or community, but they do not actively participate in activities, rituals or events. Their field notes and observations emphasize what they have seen rather than what they have experienced, and they usually do not stay with members of the community because they find that their research role limits their interaction with those being studied.

The participant as observer, by contrast, is fully integrated into the culture being studied. This type of researcher spends considerable time in the community, participates in activities, and adopts specific interests, practices, rituals and procedures while taking extensive field notes about his or her observations and experiences. Considering full participation integral to the research process, the participant as observer strives to understand the meanings of actions within the community from an insider's position.

The complete participant has fully bonded with the organization, group or culture, adopting its members' values and beliefs, and may even abandon his or her research role. The complete participant usually lives in the community and no longer takes field notes or observes activities; instead, the researcher adopts the cultural values, interests and concerns of the group. Once researchers have become complete participants, they usually reject their analytical role as researchers and abandon the ethnographic project. While most researchers warn against becoming complete participants, Jorgensen (1989) suggests that if researchers can return to their research projects afterwards, they may get much richer information as a result of their direct access to and experience with the groups, organizations or cultures.

Participant Observation Through *Avatar*

The highest-grossing North American film ever made, *Avatar*, provides clear illustrations of the four different types of participant observation within its storyline. *Avatar*, the 2009 science fiction film written and directed by James Cameron, takes place during the mid-twenty-second century on Pandora, a moon in the Alpha Centauri star system. The ten-foot tall, blue-skinned Na'vi are the indigenous people of Pandora; they are a wise and insightful humanoid culture who live in harmony with nature. Pandora is more than four light years from Earth and its atmosphere is uninhabitable by humans, yet the RDA Corporation is on Pandora mining the precious mineral unobtanium because it is the most efficient superconductor in existence. Although the corporation's mining threatens the Na'vi culture, RDA can sell each kilo of unobtanium that it takes for $20 million. In an effort to learn more about the Na'vi culture, researchers created remotely controlled avatars, which are genetically engineered hybrid bodies that mix human and Na'vi DNA.

Jake Sully (played by Sam Worthington) is a paraplegic former Marine who is chosen by RDA management for a mission on Pandora. Sully's initial goal is to use his avatar to interact with the Na'vi, gathering information about them from the inside to help researchers find a diplomatic solution to the unobtanium problem. Once on Pandora, Sully's avatar is attacked, and a beautiful young warrior, the daughter of the Na'vi tribe leader Neytiri (Zoe Saldana), rescues him. Although Neytiri considers Sully stupid, she is directed to teach him about the Na'vi culture.

Now that I have provided some contextual material about the film *Avatar*, we can see that Sully's role on Pandora may initially be seen as that of a participant as observer. Through his avatar he learns about Na'vi customs, beliefs and behaviors. Neytiri teaches him their language and Sully actively participates in Na'vi rituals and activities. Yet, he learns about the Na'vi in an effort to gain useful information about them that may later be used by others to control them. Sully documents everything he sees, feels and learns in daily video logs that are shared with the researchers, RDA management and members of the security team in the human compound.

Sigourney Weaver plays Grace Augustine, who is an exobiologist and the head of the avatar program on Pandora. Grace mentors Sully and serves in the role of an observer as participant. Through her avatar she observes the Na'vi, studying them and learning about their culture mostly from a distance. While she speaks their language, her interactions with the indigenous people of Pandora are strictly professional. As a researcher she is interested in understanding the Na'vi culture, but she does not wish to participate in their rituals and/or activities or become a part of their culture.

Colonel Miles Quaritch (Stephen Lang) is the head of RDA's private security force, and he illustrates the role of a complete observer. He has no interaction with the Na'vi (apart from killing them) but often observes them on the video feeds provided by the surveillance cameras. Because the Na'vi have no knowledge that they are being watched, their actions are not influenced by his observations.

As Sully learns the ways of the Na'vi, he begins to become a member of the tribe. His military background helps the Na'vi warriors relate to him. Sully comments during one of his final video logs that everything has become backwards, that his time interacting with the Na'vi through his avatar is now his real life and that his time in the compound has become a dream. After Sully participates in a final ceremony to become a Na'vi man, he picks Neytiri as his mate and his allegiance shifts to the Na'vi tribe. At this point he may be seen to illustrate the complete participant role. Sully leads a successful Na'vi battle against the RDA, and all humans are deported from Pandora. At the end of the film, Sully abandons his human body for his avatar form and chooses a full-time existence as a Na'vi warrior. Thus, the *Avatar* example illustrates the four main ways in which participant observers interact with members of a culture, and details a process of learning about a group of people in an effort to understand their lives.

Field Notes

While many qualitative researchers consider the participant as observer the most effective category of participant observation, it is important to remember that the mere presence of a researcher changes the group dynamics and impacts the way people will react. At best, the group will become comfortable around the participant observer and will consider his or her presence natural and normal. However, even when an ethnographer is fully integrated into a community, the researcher is unable to know what community members are really thinking or how they will react when he or she is not there.

Systematic and purposeful observation helps researchers to understand the relationships, customs, rituals and sense-making practices within a community or group. Researchers observe as much as they can in order to gather impressions and information about the group being studied. However, it is important for these observations to be documented so that they can be analyzed and interpreted.

While it is helpful for participant observers to have excellent short-term memories, most researchers also keep detailed field notes throughout the observation process. Researchers include information regarding the locations of their observations, the dates and times that the observations take place and a description of the physical space where the observations are held in their field notes. They record information about the people they observe, including their ages, backgrounds, races and ethnicities, as well as commentary on their physical characteristics, style of dress and use of language. In their field notes, researchers describe the activities and rituals they observe and participate in, the rules and standards for activities and events, the type of technologies, tools and programs they use, the media they consume and the patterns of behavior between individuals in the group. They document the types of interactions between men and women, young and old, and people of different classes, religions, races and ethnicities. They also record the verbal comments that they hear, the relevant non-verbal communication they observe and their reactions to their own participation in events and activities, as well as their observations and reflections on the research process.

You may wonder whether it is necessary for researchers to write down everything that they see and hear. Participant observers usually keep a written record of all of their initial observations. As their observations progress, ethnographers' theoretical frameworks and research questions help them to shape their topics and interests and to put their observations into the relevant context. While it may seem impossible for researchers to document all of their observations, as they gain access to a group or community and become more comfortable with the observation process they begin to focus on activities, events and conversations that are new or different from their initial observations, and they tend to write less the longer they are with that community. They also become more at ease with the group, and community members become more comfortable with them.

Some participant observers jot down key words and phrases during their observations and later craft more detailed notes and descriptions. Others use audio and video recording devices during interviews and events to augment their field notes. Researchers also keep calendars and logs of events and activities they observe, as well as the names of people they speak with. It is important for ethnographers to be comfortable interviewing others as they will need to augment their observations by asking formal and informal questions about what they see and hear. Some ethnographers ask casual questions during their observations, while other researchers conduct formal interviews with group members. Additional detailed information about interviewing is provided in Chapters 3 and 6. Smart phones now make the process of taking field notes much more user-friendly. Voice memos record participant observers' audio notes on smart phones and they are easily saved in a variety of sharable formats. With permission, researchers can also take video and still images of group or community members on their phones.

Throughout their fieldwork, researchers also make mental notes about their observations that they find are particularly relevant to their research questions, a process known as inscription. While people tend to see things that they are trained to recognize as interesting or important to their culture, the inscription process encourages researchers to get outside of their comfort zone to observe things that are important to others (LeCompte and Schensul, 1999). Researchers' mental notes on their observations are later written down as field notes. Throughout the ethnographic process, researchers consult their field notes, rereading them, annotating them, reflecting on their observations, adding additional commentary and using them to provide preliminary analysis and interpretations.

It is important for new media researchers who do ethnography in virtual settings and online observation of social media, chat rooms, blogs and websites to also keep field notes. While many of these online interactions are recorded and archived electronically, field notes help media researchers to capture their own descriptions and perceptions of the interactions, and they also reinforce the research function for participant observers.

Reflexivity

Contemporary ethnographers think critically about their role in the research process, a concept known as reflexivity. Denzin and Lincoln (1998) found that at one level, reflexivity "is associated with self-critique and personal quest, playing on the subjective, the experiential, and the idea of empathy" (p. 395). However, reflexivity may also help researchers to consider the difficulty of understanding those being observed, particularly when their values, rituals and experiences are different than those of the researcher. An emphasis on reflexivity also challenges ethnographers to explain their theoretical positions and reminds them of the possibility that there may be alternative interpretations for their observations.

Reflexivity may also be used to showcase the collaborative nature of ethnography and to help researchers understand that, as outsiders, they may have only limited access to the lives of those being studied, which may impact the richness of their analysis and understanding. Researchers also use their field notes to think critically about their interpretations of their observations. In their field notes, ethnographers consider their role in the research process and their intentions for the research. Critically thinking about "the place from which they observe" (DeWalt and DeWalt, 2011, p. 93), researchers try to understand the relationships between themselves, those they observe and the stories they choose to tell about these interactions.

Analyzing and Interpreting Ethnographic Material

Ethnographers observe groups of people engaged in everyday activities. They record their interpretations of what they see and hear, and they analyze the documents and artifacts relevant to the group, culture or organization. For Geertz (1973), cultural interpretation is not a scientific method but, instead, a fluid process, with researchers "guessing at meanings, assessing the guesses, and drawing explanatory conclusions from the better guesses" (p. 20).

Through the analysis of their fieldwork, ethnographers use specific conceptual frameworks to uncover patterns, themes and experiences that they compare with other patterns, themes and experiences. Researchers analyze similarities and differences within events, rituals and interactions; they assess the omissions, gaps and/or absences in their observations, identify sequences and frequencies of commentary, activities and rituals. They discuss key observations, select relevant examples for further commentary and provide likely explanations for their observations. Some ethnographers use strategies from textual analysis to evaluate contextual information and transcriptions of their interviews, often comparing them with other documentary evidence that they obtain.

Ethnographers' interpretations are based on understanding the relevant social context for the activities, rituals and events they observe, as well as the tacit and explicit information they collect. They may revisit their research questions, discuss their observations with other researchers and reconsider key concepts and relevant theories to help them interpret their information. Through their interpretations, researchers create meanings from the materials they collect. After they have gathered their evidence and interpreted their findings, ethnographers create a written account of their interpretations to share with others. These stories are theoretically informed interpretations of the culture of a group, organization or community being studied. Ultimately, in ethnography it is important to remember that research is "always a matter of interpreting, indeed constructing, reality from a particular position" (Morley and Silverstone, 1991, p. 161).

Ethical Considerations

Informed consent is integral to all ethnographic research. As with other qualitative methodologies, it is crucial that no participant be harmed during the research process. Because participant observers usually spend considerable time watching and interacting with group members, it is easy for those being observed to forget that they are being watched and studied. Researchers should be up front about their intentions and should remind those being studied of their research goals. Because they spend a lot of time with members of a group or community, researchers often learn personal information about the lives of the people whom they observe. Some of this information is private and it could do potential harm to those involved if the information were disclosed. Therefore, it is imperative that all participants are able to willingly choose to participate in any ethnographic research projects, and they must be given the right to privacy throughout the research process.

The amount and type of interaction that researchers have with a group, organization or culture is a major ethical concern within ethnography. By definition, participant observation generally implies that researchers will become immersed in the culture and emotionally involved with those they observe. And yet, for participant observers to become successful researchers they must be able to step away from the community in order to craft field notes and think critically about what they have seen and heard. While ethnographers who develop relationships with group members have better access to the community, it is imperative that researchers be honest about their intentions.

In the field of media studies, ethnographic research is regularly done with online special interest groups and organizations. Given the ease of joining such groups, you may wonder whether it is acceptable to join a group and do research without getting explicit permission. It is important to remember that with qualitative research it is never acceptable for a researcher to deceive an individual or a group about her or his research intentions. Infiltrating any group, whether it is online or in person, without the members' specific permission is ethically wrong. It is deception if a researcher does not disclose, to any people who might be involved, her or his intentions about a research project. Researchers who join groups without disclosing their research intentions are using others and lying to them about their role in the group or organization. While it may seem expedient at the time, I would strongly urge all researchers not to do it.

An additional ethical issue postmodern ethnographers have raised regarding traditional ethnographic research is the role that the researcher plays in the observation process. Concerned that a participant observer may privilege the gaze of the researcher over that of those being observed, or may use the fieldwork merely to enhance his or her career, postmodern ethnographers attempt to dismantle the distinction between the observer and the observed in favor of a model of cooperative dialogue (Atkinson and Hammersley, 1994). Postmodern researchers maintain that when it is used ethically, ethnography may create opportunities that will enhance the quality of life for the people in the group, culture or organization.

Research Using Ethnography

Geertz (1973) suggested that researchers consider ethnographic reports to be fictional interpretations, not because they are false or inaccurate, but because they are interpretations made by a researcher. While Geertz raised an important point, other ethnographers currently maintain that it is not enough for researchers to consider ethnographic writings interpretive accounts. It is also important for them to address the theoretical perspectives framing the research as well as the literary devices and narrative conventions researchers use in constructing their reports.

The following research example, "The Relationship Between Organizational Leaders and Advertising Ethics: An Organizational Ethnography," by Erin Schauster, combined field work at an advertising agency with forty-five interviews to consider the relationship between organizational leadership and advertising ethics. Schauster's introduction and literature review situated advertising ethics within organizational culture and drew on Gidden's structuration theory as a framework from which to interpret ethics.

"The Relationship Between Organizational Leaders and Advertising Ethics: An Organizational Ethnography," by Erin Schauster

From *Journal of Media Ethics*, 30, 2015, 150–167

Ethical problems are faced within a unique organizational context, which is shaped in part by organizational leaders. Advertising ethics is defined as what is right or good in the conduct of the advertising function (Cunningham, 1999). However, the place where the advertising function takes place is afforded little attention in empirical research. A new approach to advertising ethics should consider the unique, and complex, organizational context where ethical problems are faced (Drumwright, 2007; Schauster, 2013). With the call for heightened ethical standards in advertising (Drumwright & Murphy; Snyder, 2009), it is important to study advertising ethics to better understand the relevant pressures of today and offer suggestions for tomorrow.

Organizational culture is shaped by leaders who are often the individuals first faced with solving organizational challenges (Schein, 1990, 2010). Understanding organizational members' perceptions of leadership provides a context-specific and valuable perspective for examining advertising ethics. Furthermore, structuration theory suggests that an environment both enables and constrains action (Giddens, 1984). Therefore, aspects of organizational culture such as leadership might act as both enablers and constraints to advertising ethical awareness.

The purpose of the study is to examine, through the lens of structuration theory, advertising practitioners' perceptions of advertising ethics and the relationship that leadership, as an aspect of organization culture, has with ethical awareness. Ethnography was conducted at a full-service advertising agency including observation, participation in organizational events, and one-on-one interviews. A total of 45 days were spent in the field as a participant observer and 45 in-depth interviews were conducted. A discussion is started regarding the complexity of advertising ethics as a process embedded within organizational culture and one sharing a relationship with culture by being both enabled and constrained by aspects of leadership.

Literature Review

Advertising Ethics

Advertising ethics is concerned with "what is right or good in the conduct of the advertising function. It is concerned with questions of what ought to be done, not just with what legally must be done" (Cunningham, 1999, p. 500; emphasis in original). The current study examines advertising ethics from the practitioners' perspectives (e.g., Drumwright and Murphy, 2004, 2009). Developing ethical messages and managing ethical relationships with clients are perceived problems (Rotzoll and Christians, 1980), as are treating clients fairly, creating honest ads, treating employees fairly, and treating other agencies fairly (Hunt and Chonko, 1987).

Reasonable persons will disagree on what constitutes an ethical problem (Cunningham, 1999). Therefore, ethics serve as the tools to evaluate problems and guide normative decision making, which suggests how one ought to act (Patterson and Wilkins, 2008). The TARES test has been applied to advertising to evaluate the extent to which persuasive messages are truthful, authentic, respectful, equitable, and socially responsible (Baker and Martinson, 2001; Lee and Nguyen, 2013). To guide normative decision making during ethical dilemmas, Bush, Harris, and Bush (1997) propose a normative model, which sets guidelines for decision making as well as compares and contrasts a service provider's morals with the client's morals. These ethical tools are grounded in moral theory, such as virtue theory. For example, how one ought to act might be determined by moral virtues, or duty to act (Hill, 2006). Baker (2008) proposes that virtuous role models in advertising with humility, honesty, transparency, respect, care, authenticity, equity, and social responsibility navigate dilemmas and guide other practitioners during decision making. Neill and Drumwright (2012) find that public relations (PR) professionals serve as ethical role models. These professionals act as organizational conscience, which is when the professional's role is broadened to provide ethics counsel and to include a "duty to the public interest" (p. 224). The authors further define organizational conscience as a professional who raises concerns when organizational actions pose ethical consequences both to and outside of the organization.

Inherent in normative action is an ability to identify principles of moral quality, evaluate those qualities, and act in a seemingly right way. Assigning a moral quality, whether good or bad, is the reflection of an individual making a moral judgment (Blasi, 1994). From the perspective of the advertising practitioner, there is confusion on determining what is right or good in the advertising function. Moral myopia, or moral blindness, is an inability to ascertain moral qualities. In advertising, moral myopia is the inability of advertising practitioners to identify an advertising-related problem as ethical or to express the problem in terms of morality (Drumwright and Murphy, 2004). Instead, problems in advertising have been expressed in terms of intelligence and autonomy, such as when a practitioner suggests ethics are unnecessary because the consumer is smart (Drumwright and Murphy, 2004). Davis (1994) finds that the law guides advertising practitioners in decision making more so than ethics. Moral myopia, including interpreting problems as legal questions, buffers the moral qualities inherent within ethical problems. On the other hand, there are practitioners who are able to identify ethical problems and express these problems in terms of rightness and wrongness (Drumwright and Murphy, 2004). These practitioners discuss ethical issues openly with clients and with one another. To understand perception of ethics, the current study asks,

RQ1: What are advertising practitioners' perceptions of advertising ethics?

Organizational Culture and Organizational Leaders

Organizational culture tells us what it means to be an organization and to engage in the act of organizing, and tells us about the members involved. An organization is "a dynamic system of organizational members, influenced by external stakeholders, who communicate within and across organizational structures in a purposeful and ordered way to achieve a superordinate goal" (Keyton, 2005, p. 10). The full-service advertising agency has the goal of providing clients with creative and business services including the "planning, preparing and placing [of] advertisements" (O'Guinn, Allen, and Semenik, 1998, p. 39; 2009, p. 55). Acts of organizing involve relationships between members internal and external to an advertising agency. Members internal to the agency include those working in account service, creative, media and research departments, and external members include an agency's clients as well as vendors hired by an agency such as printers, photographers, and so forth.

Organizational culture defines an "agency's style, sense of values, ethical principles, atmosphere, and standing in the business community, as well as the (stated or unstated) norms of behavior that an agency expects of its employees" (Jones, 1999, p. 135). Organizational culture is deeply held (Keyton, 2005; Schein, 1990, 1992, 2010) and shared (Alvesson, 2002). Therefore, organizational culture serves as a frame of reference (Alvesson, 2002) that allows members to make sense of their environment and their experiences and to share these experiences, feelings, and thoughts with others (Gabriel, 2000). Socialization is the process for teaching new members of a group the correct way to think and feel. Furthermore, socialization is what Gabriel (1999) describes as the connection between the individual and an organization. New members of an advertising agency are taught a philosophy of advertising, for example, and as a result, the correct way to solve clients' advertising problems. A leader might share with a new employee the story of how the agency landed its first client. The story describes late nights and long weekends until the pitch was made and the client account was won. Paired with a philosophy of "hard work pays off," the new employee becomes socialized into a culture and expectation of "we work until the job gets done." This learning process begins with organizational leaders.

Schein (2010) argues that the beliefs, values, and assumptions of leadership, or the founder(s) of an organization, play a crucial role in sourcing organizational culture. Specifically, the original visions of an advertising agency's founder can drive the agency's culture (Thorson and Duffy, 2011). New employees also learn from other interpersonal relationships, such as from coworkers, and from noninterpersonal encounters, such as observations and written documents (Feldman, 1976; Ostroff and Kozlowski, 1992). Furthermore, Keyton (2005) suggests that members of an organization are more likely to behave in accordance with organizational values when those values are known.

Based upon the divided versus consensus view of organizational culture, Keyton (2005) suggests that not all members agree or that not all values, goals, and so forth are shared. In relation to ethics, for example, within a small advertising agency run by a Catholic chief executive officer (CEO), practitioners were able to articulate clear operative values at work within their agency. These values were "strongly shaped" by their CEO who translated his personal moral values into the agency's philosophy of advertising, by not only serving the clients' needs but also by advancing the moral values of the agency (Krueger, 1998, p. 12). However, an employee expressed a level of discomfort with the moral-laden convictions of the CEO and found that the CEO's morals conflicted with the agency's duty: to create ads that sell products.

Leaders influence organizational culture (Schein, 2010). Therefore, it is important to understand perceptions of organizational leadership as part of an organizational approach to advertising ethics. Therefore, the current study asks,

RQ2: What are advertising practitioners' perceptions of organizational leadership?

Structuration

Structuration theory is concerned with the dynamic relationships of human agents influenced by and influencing their environments. Furthermore, structuration theory is concerned with dualities, including the duality between agent and structure (Giddens, 1984). The human agent, with agency to act, is both enabled and constrained by the rules and resources of her environment. Rules and resources comprise structure, which the agent both produces and reproduces as a result of taking action. Structure serves as both "medium and outcome of the practices they recursively organize" (Giddens, 1984, p. 25). Within this duality, an agent creates the environment in which she acts, and the structures of that environment recreate her.

Human action is a social process. People do not act in isolation but in relationship with and to one another. The presence and co-presence of social actors is essential to the existence of social systems and organization, which "only exist in and through the continuity of social practices" as sustained by encounters (Giddens, 1984, p. 83). During daily activities, "individuals encounter each other in situated contexts of interaction—interaction with others who are physically copresent" (Giddens, 1984, p. 64). Giddens builds upon Goffman (1963) to explain encounters and co-presence. Encounters are understood as situated interaction with others who are physically co-present, as well as mediated forms of encounters that allow for some of the "intimacies" of co-presence (Giddens, 1984, p. 68).

Human action is also a reflection of conscious knowledge. Giddens (1984) contends that human agents are knowledgeable and conscious and, as a result, reflexive. According to Giddens, "structure has no existence independent of the knowledge that agents have about what they do in their day-to-day activity" (1984, p. 26). If you asked an agent, she could describe her actions and the expected actions of others. Furthermore, agency to act implies power by assuming the agent has the capability to act, regardless of intentions, and the capability to act differently at any point in time. However, this does not assume that an agent *will* act differently and as a result unintended consequences or contradictions can emerge. Canary (2010) defines contradiction as an oppositional tension within social contexts. For example, in-home daycare providers offered childcare services to working families as a means to stay home with their own children (Butler and Modaff, 2008). However, according to the study's findings, these providers reported feelings of tension, due to both stress and lack of appreciation from parents that affected both their parental and marital relationships, which were the unintended consequences of their own organizing structures and policies. Unintended consequences, such as those experienced by in-home daycare provides, are another means of interpreting rules and resources as enabling and constraining structure.

Structuration theory provides a perspective for interpreting ethics as medium and outcome, enabling and constraining, and situated within an organizational context. If ethics are situated, this suggests that a person's knowledge of ethics is derived from and embedded within organizational culture. Ethics serve in a duality with structure; as we draw upon ethics to guide professional activity, we constitute and reproduce the structures of organizational culture. To examine the relationship between advertising ethics and organizational culture, specifically aspects of organizational leadership, this study asks,

RQ3: What is the relationship, if any, between organizational leadership and advertising ethics?

The next section described the process for this ethnographic study. Schauster served as a participant observer, augmenting a forty-five-day observation process with an analysis of organizational artifacts and interviews with forty-five agency employees. The researcher took field notes throughout the fieldwork process, which produced 175 single-spaced pages of information. Her research strategy supported a triangulation of the research evidence, which helped to provide validity for the study. All but one of her interviews were conducted in person, resulting in 43 hours and 21 minutes of interview recordings. An interview guide is provided as an appendix. The researcher analyzed her field notes and interviews, identifying themes and interpreting meanings from the information. Please note the strategy Schauster used to insure the confidentiality of the company and all of its employees.

Method

This study is part of a larger research project that used ethnography. The fieldwork of ethnography allows the researcher to understand other people's social reality by experiencing their environment firsthand (Van Maanen, 1988). Methods of the current study include observation, one-on-one interviews, and the collection of organizational artifacts. These methods have been applied to examine advertising ethics (e.g., Alvesson, 1994; Drumwright and Murphy, 2004; Krueger, 1998) and organizational culture of advertising agencies (e.g., Rosen, 1985, 1988). Ethnography also refers to the written representation of the social reality of others. Findings for the current study represent a combination of realist and impressionist tales (Van Maanen, 1988), which bring together the agency members' perceptions, the researcher's interpretation, and the context. Together, these various perspectives, from observation, participation, and members' perceptions of both self and others, allow for the triangulation of data, which Johnson (1997) suggests promotes qualitative research validity.

AdCompany

Fieldwork was conducted at a full-service advertising agency. AdCompany[1] was selected for its services offered, number of employees, location, and willingness to participate. AdCompany began in 1996 when two seasoned advertising executives decided to "break from the corporate agency,"[2] which exists as part of their mantra still today. AdCompany has grown from two founders to more than 125 employees at its largest. In 2006, the privately held agency sold to a media holding company but retained its name and two founders, its CEO and chief creative officer (CCO). AdCompany is located in a major metropolitan city of the United States.

Participants and Confidentiality

The agency employed approximately 70–75 people at the time of the study.[3] Confidentiality was granted to the agency to protect the identity of the organization as well as to each individual participant, which helped establish trust during fieldwork. The agency also required a signature on a nondisclosure agreement (NDA). Treatment of participants, data collection, and data storage were in accord with Institutional Review Board regulations.

Fieldwork and Interviews

A total of 45 days, spanning five months and 332 hours, were spent in the field. The time spent was to gain a "critical threshold of interpretive competence" (Lindlof and Taylor, 2002, p. 129). Fieldwork was spent 1) working on personal tasks, 2) working on agency tasks, 3) attending impromptu events, 4) attending events by invitation, and 5) conducting interviews. Access to meetings and other events were requested and provided on a per event basis. Jottings, a shorthand version of fieldnotes, were taken during meetings and during observation from a workspace such as the desk provided, and were typed, handwritten, or audio recorded. Jottings were then typed into comprehensive fieldnotes resulting in 175 single-spaced pages.[4]

A total of 45 interviews were conducted with agency employees.[5] Forty-four interviews were conducted face-to-face, and one interview was conducted over the phone. All but one interview were audio recorded. Interviews totaled 43 hours and 21 minutes with an average length of 58 minutes. An interview guide was used,[6] which is a more flexible and informal option to an interview schedule (Lindlof and Taylor, 2002). Furthermore, the interview guide allowed agency members to define concepts, such as advertising ethics, in his/her own terms. Interview transcriptions totaled 464 single-spaced pages.[7]

Analysis

As an ethnography, analysis began in the field (Bruyn, 1963). Open coding, the line-by-line analysis of fieldnotes, was performed after all comprehensive fieldnotes were taken (Emerson, Fretz, and Shaw, 1995). During analysis in the field and during open coding, memos were written on fieldnotes and interview transcriptions. Memos were used to identify themes. Focused coding followed, which included a focused reading of the identified themes that had been reduced and organized during open coding and memos. During focused coding, findings began to emerge and were written into draft form. Thereafter, active writing ensued. Writing is considered active because as one writes, within and upon leaving the field, a researcher is still analyzing, interpreting, and developing a thesis (Emerson, Fretz, and Shaw, 1995).

The following section presented two key themes on relationships between the advertising agency and issues of ethics: constrained awareness of advertising ethics and enabled awareness of advertising ethics.

Findings

The current study examines the relationship between and perceptions of organizational leadership and advertising ethics. Findings suggest that some members have a constrained view of ethics, while others perceive advertising ethics as what is right and good, both guiding and explaining ethical awareness and action at AdCompany. These findings suggest two overarching themes: constrained awareness of advertising ethics and enabled awareness of advertising ethics.[8]

AdCompany members learn the organizational values of open communication, honesty, and collaboration from leaders, including from founders CEO and CCO. Leaders set an example of open communication by sharing sensitive, financial news with employees during monthly meetings, for example. By working alongside and with others in the agency, including with newly hired employees, leaders enact the value of collaboration. And by leading with honesty and maintaining a consistency of action, AdCompany's employees learn what virtuous characteristics leaders possess. When faced with an ethical decision, employees reference AdCompany's espoused organizational values and leaders' virtuous character, which several members perceive as a shared ethic.

Concurrently, leaders suggested there were no ethical intentions when founding AdCompany. The organizational intentions of AdCompany were to create award-winning advertising and place a value on creativity. While organizational values such as open communication and collaboration are shared, several members do not assign moral qualities to these values nor recognize what an ethical problem or decision might be. Therefore, ethical awareness is simultaneously constrained at AdCompany. These findings suggest a dynamic relationship between organizational leadership and ethics. Organizational leadership is represented by members' perceptions of leaders' characteristics and the organizational values they espouse. Furthermore, organizational values derive, in part, from the leaders' intentions for founding the agency. The findings suggest that the values and organizational intentions simultaneously constrain ethical awareness for some while enabling ethical awareness for others.

Leadership of AdCompany

Leaders of AdCompany are perceived as, first and foremost, CEO and CCO who are both respected and admired by others. AdCompany employees holding an executive or director title are also perceived as leaders, as are individuals without a title but who depict certain characteristics. Characteristics of leaders include being hands-on, communicative, and virtuous.

Three members hold a "chief" title: CEO, CCO, and the chief financial officer (CFO). CEO and CCO were mentioned most often as the leaders (n = 30). Furthermore, a majority of members expressed having great respect for the CEO and CCO (n = 26). Positive adjectives used to describe these leaders were "great" (8, 15, 20, 27, 31, 38), "good" (23, 46), "nice" (8, 24), "lovable" (20), "strong" (17, 44), "passionate" (17), hardworking (17, 34), and smart (2, 17, 41). In addition to the three "chief" positions, 11 employees hold an executive or director's title at AdCompany. Anyone holding an executive, director, and/or chief title is considered a "director" at AdCompany, and those individuals attend weekly directors' meetings. Directors shared their philosophies of leadership. The first is leading by setting examples (n = 5). It was suggested that a leader would never ask an employee to complete a task him/ herself would not complete (30). The second philosophy of leadership is best summarized as supportive leadership. Leaders of the agency are there to provide direction to their employees (25, 37). However, not all directors are seen as leaders. It was suggested that some directors have simply been promoted to a director based upon years of service at the agency or the title was negotiated during the hiring process.

Even without director status, an individual might be perceived as a leader based upon certain characteristics. Leaders are characterized as being hands-on, communicative as well as having integrity. Everyone is expected to contribute equally to the agency workload, leaders included (n = 28). While most leaders are responsible for supervising anywhere from one to several employees, no one just supervises; "everybody also does hands-on work" (29). Hands-on leadership is not the same as micromanaging. Neither the employees nor leaders support or believe a micromanagement style exists at AdCompany (14, 15, 24, 26, 35, 37, 45). Instead, collaboration was suggested as evidence of the hands-on working style, which was described as leaders and employees working together. For example, CEO and CCO work with others, such as on new business projects, and it is understood that they will make time for employees (1, 6, 7, 19, 23, 26). Through collaboration, employees learn from leaders (4, 17, 31, 33, 36, 40, 41, 44), and collaboration results in an environment of trust and support (1, 2, 3, 19, 32, 37, 38, 43, 44, 45). By contrast, several members presented perceived weaknesses of hands-on leadership (n = 16). Weaknesses include a lack of direction. When leaders are hands-on and responsible for their own work tasks, members suggested, neglect of employees' growth and development results (10, 25, 27, 31). In addition, during the time of the study, AdCompany was facing an organizational challenge of growth and decline, according to members (n = 24), which included gaining new business, maintaining client accounts and adapting to the loss of a financially-substantial client account. The challenging time was referred to as one of "survival" (18), and it was suggested that when vision for the agency was needed, it was lacking from leaders (22, 28, 31, 37).

Communication is a perceived characteristic of leadership at AdCompany (n = 19). Leaders are good communicators (31) who keep members of the agency informed, such as during monthly agency meetings (41). Leaders are open, which means that they share both good and bad news with members of the agency (8, 10), such as new business opportunities and the loss of client accounts. Leaders are seen as honest (13, 14, 33). And as part of communicative leadership, leaders encourage dialogue among their employees (16). While most members suggested leaders have good communication skills, others suggested that leaders' communication is deficient at times (3, 16, 33, 40), which suggests a divided view.

Members described their leaders in terms of virtuous character. For example, leaders of AdCompany have integrity (n = 8). Several aspects supporting the characteristic of integrity include leaders who do the right thing, have respect for others, and hold true to the convictions of the agency.

CEO and CCO established organizational values when they founded AdCompany, which are still espoused and maintained today (n = 13). AdCompany leaders live the values of equality, integrity, and open communication, according to members (9, 29). As one member pointed out, "It's hard to talk about culture, the agency, without talking about the founders. They created it." (30). For example, integrity has "trickled" down from CEO and CCO. "It's a pretty high integrity shop, I think. I think that definitely trickles down from [CEO] and [CCO]." (24) Furthermore, the integrity of the shop is maintained by hiring like-minded people (6, 13, 14, 15, 43, 44, 46). Members believe that the leaders do a good job hiring the right people at AdCompany (4, 8, 17, 34, 38). By setting an example, establishing and espousing values, and hiring like-minded people, leaders maintain AdCompany's organizational culture. The relationship culture has on advertising ethics follows.

Constrained Awareness of Advertising Ethics

Several members stated that there are no ethics at AdCompany, which suggests lack of ethical awareness and a limited ethical vernacular (n = 20). In part, this perception was based upon the "straightforward" nature of the work. Furthermore, AdCompany does not work on client accounts that would be considered unethical, and it is not the agency's job to be ethical. For others, there is a void of ethics due to an abundance of virtue. A description for each supporting theme follows.

Several members indicated that the agency and work done at the agency such as analytics and direct mail was "straightforward" (22, 23, 33, 38). A member explained, "You're either leveraging the numbers correctly or you're not, and if you're not, you're going to be caught fairly quickly" (22). Therefore, for AdCompany, the straightforward nature of the work suggests there is a right course of action and a punishable, wrong action. Having clear delineation between the two prevents unethical behavior. The straightforward nature of the work relates to services offered at AdCompany as well as client accounts serviced. Members indicated that they do not run into ethical challenges because they do not work on client accounts they oppose (33, 36, 43) or to which they have "moral objection" (20), such as a tobacco account.

AdCompany is hired by a client to create ads that sell products, not concern itself with ethics. Therefore, for some members, ethics does not factor into the creative process. When asked what ethical challenges they face, members could not pinpoint an ethical challenge in an AdCompany-specific scenario (42, 44, 46) but suggested what challenges the advertising industry might face (14). In response to describing the ethical challenges at AdCompany, one respondent answered, "And honestly, [Interviewer], I don't know how that comes in to play. How would ethics in what I do here at the office really impact what we do?" (24). Consequently, moral qualities are not ascribed to client accounts, agency services, challenges faced, and so forth.

For several members, there are no ethics in lieu of an abundance of virtue (16, 30, 43, 44, 45, 46). Members viewed themselves and AdCompany's leaders as people of integrity. However, for these members, virtuous character is not perceived as evidence of ethics. Instead, ethical awareness was reduced to challenges and acts that were only considered unethical, which suggests a limited understanding of and vernacular for advertising ethics. Instead of presenting virtuous character as evidence of ethics, members suggested that because AdCompany does not engage in unethical acts, that there are "no ethics" at the agency.

Moral Myopia: Ethical Awareness Constrained by Organizational Intentions

As suggested by several members, AdCompany does not face ethical challenges. AdCompany does not work on client accounts that would be considered unethical, as one example; therefore, there are "no ethics" at AdCompany. These perceptions imply that ethical awareness is constrained, and this lack of awareness presents an opportunity for new members to become socialized into a morally myopic culture.

The founders of the agency, and current leaders, influence these myopic views. Before founding AdCompany, CEO and CCO worked together at a large, full-service advertising agency. During the first few months on their own, they honored a non-compete agreement[9] with their previous employer, which limited their ability to acquire new business. Several months later, they won a large client account, growing from 2 to 20 employees. Business "took off" by the next year's end. Early on, AdCompany occupied a small building with limited resources. One employee brought her/his own card table and that was her/his workspace. Years later, AdCompany employed upward of 100 employees during its peak only to experience layoffs starting around 2006, when the agency was sold to a media holding company, and which continued up until the time of the study. At the start of the study, there were about 75 employees who occupied three floors of the building. After a few months, the agency lost several employees, who either quit or were laid off, and merged office space from three to two floors. However, several members identified as the "core" group of people, including the founders, still remained (16).

Ethics was not an impetus for starting the agency. When asked, "How would one create an agency that encourages or supports ethical decision making?" a founder replied, "My gut answer is, you can't . . . No one will hire you just because you're ethical." Ethics cannot be the reason for starting an advertising agency because it is not a reason for clients to hire an agency. The purpose of starting an agency is not to be ethical; you start an agency, s/he explained, to create good ads and to work with reputable clients. At AdCompany, hard work is both valued and expected.

To illustrate this point, a founder explained that AdCompany previously serviced a dry cleaner account. The client wanted to be perceived as environmentally friendly. Well, the founder explained, that is the client trying to be ethical, but dry cleaning products are the worst thing for the environment. The agency's job is to sell the client's product. It does not matter what the product is or is not, ethical or unethical. Whether the client or the commercial message is right or wrong need not come into question. AdCompany has one bottom line, the founder explained, which is to create good ads. Today, several members share organizational values such as open communication and collaboration, but perceive these values sans ethics. The values, instead, relate to business practices of hard work and creative work for reputable clients.

These findings suggest moral myopia, ethical awareness constrained by organizational culture. Members believe in values of creativity and maintaining client relationships. What these values enable is the recreation of the agency's bottom line: to service client accounts by producing creative ads. However, what they simultaneously constrain, is an ethical awareness for the client, or for the client's product or service as right or wrong. Five members interviewed and one observed (n = 6) referenced a client or product as unethical. Of these members, two justified servicing what might be perceived as an unethical client account. For example, a member suggested that the agency is not known to be "arrogant"; therefore, AdCompany does not condemn client accounts. The agency instead evaluates a client based upon the ability to create good advertising.

During the time of the study, a new client account was prospected and pitched. A member suggested that the product was harmful and unethical, and, while s/he was excited to work on the account because it offered creative opportunities, s/he was afraid of having to turn the work opportunity down if the account was won. However, during several observations of meetings regarding the new account, neither leaders nor employees broached the subject of ethics. Instead the potential account was discussed in terms of new business, strategy, objectives, an opportunity to "impress the client" (F 19), and as "cool" (F 23). This example further suggests that what is good for the agency is upholding creativity and advertising expertise, which, contingent upon a successful new business pitch, the agency is hired to provide.

Awareness of Advertising Ethics

Compared with the perception that there are "no ethics" at AdCompany, other members suggested that organizational values are the reasons why the agency is ethical (n = 25). Organizational values perceived as ethical included i) communication, ii) fair treatment of others, iii) trust, iv) virtuous character, v) honesty versus deception, vi) acceptable use of time, vii) respect, vii) work ethic, viii) longevity as loyalty, and ix) leadership.

Open communication (i) is the process and expectation of sharing honest thoughts with one another internally, as well as externally with clients and vendors. Leaders expect their employees to be open and honest (4). To support their employees in this process, leaders are accessible (37). CEO and CCO teach open communication by sharing some of their mistakes with new employees (13). Employees come to learn that if they do not agree with something personally, such as a project, campaign, or morally questionable client, they can go straight to the leaders to voice concern (38). Conversely, one member shared that the founders do not know of her/his moral objections to client accounts. Whether s/he was uncomfortable or fearful of sharing this information was unclear. This does, however, suggest a divided view of open communication.

What makes the agency ethical is its fair treatment of others (ii). For example, agency executives do not steal each other's ideas, which creatives are known to do at other agencies (38). Furthermore, AdCompany is not a sweatshop (24), executives do not cuss each other out (37), and creatives do not make demands of account executives, which also happens at other agencies (37). As a result of how employees, clients, and vendors are treated, trust develops. Trust (iii) allows the agency to maintain relationships with its clients and vendors (14, 24, 29, 38, 44). Trust is established over time, and as a result of trust, AdCompany maintains long client and vendor relationships, as well as long-term employment. However, breaching trust has consequences. For example, if employees shared confidential information, their employment would be terminated (21).

Members of AdCompany are people of virtuous character (iv). Virtues possessed include integrity, equality, honesty, and respect. Integrity has to do with consistency of action (13), respect shown to others (14), honoring commitments (13), and one's reputation (14). Members believe CEO and CCO have integrity. Equality relates to the fair treatment of clients, no matter the project or size (e.g., billings) (9), as well as fair and equal treatment for all employees (13). According to a leader, if one employee asks for a raise and another does not but does the same work and as good of a job as the person who asked for the raise, then s/he too will get a raise.

Acts of honesty (v) constitute AdCompany's ethic. Honesty in advertising is important (13, 25, 33, 44), and, more specifically, honesty plays a role in building relationships with clients and vendors (13, 29). By comparison, and suggesting a divided view, message honesty is debatable. A leader suggested the following scenario. Your client has a 100-calorie candy bar on the market. Your client's competitor introduces a 100-calorie product in addition to its already popular 200-calorie product. By comparison, the competitor calls its new 100-calorie product "low-fat." Since your client also has a 100-calorie bar, can you start "promoting it as a low-fat candy? Is that unethical?" Advertising is based on perception, versus reality, which allows for ambiguity and deception. Furthermore, the participant's response suggests that deception is inherent in the competitive nature of advertising, thus suggesting deception is justifiable.

Several members applied moral qualities to decision making related to the acceptable use of agency time (vi), respect for others' time (vii), and to having a work ethic (vii). Members voiced concern for the work they were doing in regard to not liking their work (27), not having enough work (F 45), and by suggesting that certain tasks were inappropriate (F 5, F 6, F 8). For example, during a time of layoffs, an executive was not comfortable with spending time, and the agency's money, on entering award shows with $1,000 entry fees. Use of agency time also related to respect for others' time. The agency has a flexible schedule that allows employees to work from home and/or during a shortened workweek. While taking advantage of this flexibility, members acknowledged that their need for time off and others' need for work to be done are respected, as well as balanced (17, 37, F 31). This balance, along with hard work, is part of a "blue collar" work ethic valued at the agency (24).

Establishing trust and respecting clients and vendors lead to long client-agency relationships. Telling the truth (22) and avoiding "flying by the seat of your pants" (24) are important to developing client relationships and building trust, which come after years of working together (29). Members perceive the longevity of relationships as a sign of loyalty (viii), another organizational value ascribed with moral qualities. Finally, leaders (ix) support the agency's perceived ethic by setting examples, being open and honest, having integrity, and hiring likeminded people.

Ethical Awareness: Enabled by Virtuous Character

Some members of AdCompany determine right from wrong by being open and honest with one another. A member suggested that when you are open and honest, you always know what the right thing to do is. These members ascribe moral qualities to the organizational values and actions guided by values. Therefore, leaders who espouse organizational values of open communication, as well as act transparently and honestly, enable ethical action by setting an example for others.

Furthermore, leaders believe that being ethical begins with character (13, 14, 15), and the character of those you hire is equally important (13, 14). The founders of AdCompany were the first members faced with solving the agency's challenges, and as a result, determining what was most important. Values include doing the best work, but also having integrity. Integrity is consistency in action and upholding shared values of open communication, honesty, respect, and equality for others. Integrity and honesty, as two examples, depict the leaders as persons of virtuous character. Members agreed, which was depicted time and again by the respect shown toward the CEO and CCO. Since founding the agency, leaders have set the example of hard work. In addition, loyalty is depicted by members' long-term employment, including the leaders' commitment to the agency even after the holding company buyout. The CEO is regarded as the hardest working person at AdCompany, because s/he does not have to work but enjoys the work. By continuing to hire people that are of similar virtue, the leaders continue to reproduce a culture of virtuous character.

The final section of the research provided additional analysis and interpretation of the ethnographic study, placing the results into a larger context and drawing on Giddens' understanding of structure to help understand the relationship between organizational culture and ethics. Schauster ended her study with recommendations for how advertising agencies might incorporate advertising ethics more fully into their companies, and she also provided suggestions for future studies.

Discussion

The current study seeks to understand the relationship between organizational leadership and advertising ethics. Leaders play an important role in the socialization process according to Schein (1990, 1992, 2010). If the leaders of an advertising agency state and believe that ethics have no place in starting an agency and, thereafter, ethics are not part of the organizational discourse, then employees have an opportunity to become socialized into this belief system. At AdCompany, leaders are characterized as hands-on workers, as well as mentors. Directors at AdCompany enact a philosophy of leadership by example reinforced by organizational values. According to their shared philosophy of leadership, a leader would never ask an employee to complete a task s/he herself would not complete (30). Organizational values are espoused during events such as the monthly agency meetings and new-hire breakfasts. The founders instituted both the leadership philosophy and organizational values. However, examples must be set for ethics as well. At AdCompany, ethical values and moral qualities are not espoused by leaders, nor explicitly articulated in shared organizational values, philosophies of leadership, and so forth.

Suggesting that all members will be socialized into the same belief system is a limited view of culture, in general, and of ethics specifically. The idea that culture is composed of both a consensus and divided view supports the opportunity for alternative meaning (Keyton, 2005). The current findings support the divided view of culture as well as a divided view of ethics. At AdCompany, members and leaders disagreed at times. For example, some members disagreed with a founder, suggesting that certain products are inherently evil and, therefore, that they would have objections to servicing certain client accounts. Others suggested honesty in client and vendor relationships was important and upheld, but message honesty was open to interpretation.

While moral myopia is representative of several members' beliefs about AdCompany's culture, ethical awareness simultaneously exists. Members suggested ways in which the agency is ethical. For example, by working alongside and learning from leaders possessing virtuous character, members know what action is right versus wrong when faced with a client- or vendor-related problem. Members, and the founders, believe they are people of character and hire like-minded individuals who can uphold the organizational values of collaboration, open communication, and integrity. These characteristics, virtues, values espoused and enacted, and hiring process together enable ethical awareness.

The current study extends our understanding of advertising ethics in several ways. First, defining advertising ethics mandates the acknowledgment of an organizational context. For example, an advertising executive's ethical response to a problem is enabled and constrained by organizational culture, which is influenced by leaders, characteristics of leadership, and values instituted, shared, and espoused. Therefore, defining advertising ethics should go beyond what was previously defined as what is right or good (e.g., Cunningham, 1999). The current findings suggest that advertising ethics is awareness of ethical problems, which includes an ability to ascertain moral qualities, and subsequent ethical decision making, which are influenced by and in a relationship with organizational culture. This revised definition should be considered during future advertising ethics research.

Second, Drumwright and Murphy (2004) found similar perspectives of moral myopia among agency practitioners. However, the authors classified ethical perceptions, from myopia to ethical awareness, as a bifurcation. Through an organizational perspective and consideration of the divided view of culture (Keyton, 2005), the current study suggests a continuum better represents the shared and divided perspectives of advertising ethics, which exist simultaneously. On one end of the continuum, members' ethical awareness is constrained and influenced, in part, by the intentions for starting the agency, which makes no mention of ethics. Simultaneously, acute ethical awareness exists. While the discourse of ethically aware members was primarily one of virtue and character, the shared perspective suggests ways in which AdCompany engages in normative decision making. These members prescribed moral qualities to organizational values and characteristics of leadership. Through virtuous character of honesty, integrity, and respect for others, AdCompany is quite ethical. Within a single organization a value such as honesty is shared, but alternate perceptions of this value suggest that ethical awareness falls along a continuum. Members' responses ranged from an inability to perceive ethics, an ability to ascertain ethics but not apply ethics to AdCompany, to an ability to perceive what is ethical including what is virtuous in advertising. There are, therefore, varying degrees of myopia on one end, which extend along a continuum into an awareness of ethics and virtuous character on the other end.

Third, amorality is a means to understand the organizational and ethical intentions for starting an advertising agency. Amorality should not to be confused with moral nihilism, which is the view that there are no moral facts. Nihilism states that nothing is right or wrong (Dreier, 2006). Nor is amorality to be confused with immorality, which acknowledges that moral facts or rightness exist but explains behavior done in opposition. The amoralist, by comparison, believes that right and wrong exist but does not care about morality (Shafer-Landau, 2010). To suggest that the founders of AdCompany do not care about morality would be an overstatement. By virtuous character, self-reported and observed by others, and the deliberate effort to hire like-minded individuals, the founders are morally invested characters. Instead, amorality, in the context of examining advertising ethics from an organizational approach, suggests that morality, as a priority, is not the impetus for starting an agency. The proposition that organizations operate amorally, or more specifically intend amorality, does not implicate unethical or immoral behavior. AdCompany members purported perceptions reflecting an acute ethical awareness and behavior. Therefore, amorality, morality, and immorality can co-exist and are not mutually exclusive. Amorality can exist alongside ethical awareness and ethical decision making as the current findings suggest.

Finally, advertising ethics is in a dynamic relationship with organizational culture. Giddens's (1984) structure refers to the rules and resources that both enable and constrain human action. Neither structure nor action receives primacy; instead, they serve in a duality to explain the production and reproduction of a social system. The duality Giddens proposes is supported by the current findings, which suggest that leadership serves as a rule and resource for ethical awareness. Two founders of AdCompany had clear intentions. They wanted to create great advertising while working for good clients. Through their hands-on leadership, collaboration with employees, and examples set, leaders socialized new members into AdCompany's culture. This socialization contributes to the reproduction of the agency's culture with an emphasis on creativity and client relationships, versus an emphasis on ethics. However, other members are simultaneously ethically aware. By collaborating with leaders of virtuous character, ethical awareness is enabled. Leaders, specifically the CEO and CCO, believe in open communication, honesty, and respect for others. Many of AdCompany's members perceive these aspects of leadership as the very reason AdCompany is ethical.

These findings, while rich in detail and description, pertain specifically to AdCompany. While generalizations can be made over time, as more organizational studies are conducted, the findings presented here should not be taken out of context. Nevertheless, three managerial implications should be addressed. First, organizational intentions, including ethical intentions, influence the culture of an advertising agency. Advertising ethics is important for the industry to uphold, which arguably begins at an organizational level. Therefore, ethical intentions such as ethical values or codes of conduct are necessary for leaders to establish when founding an advertising agency. Second, if moral myopia is an inability to ascertain moral qualities, to circumvent moral myopia leaders should espouse and clearly qualify organizational intentions and values as moral. Third, leaders can embrace their role as ethical role models (Baker, 2008). It is important to recognize the role of socialization in this recommendation. Professionals learn from one another, and, more importantly, new employees look to leaders for direction and guidance. Leaders can sustain ethical values by first introducing them, such as during an interview or employee initiation, and then by reinforcing ethical values during regularly scheduled agency-wide meetings. Furthermore, by clearly identifying these individuals as ethical mentors rather than simply as directors or agency leaders, employees will know whom to consult during an ethical dilemma.

Future Research

An organizational approach to understanding advertising ethics constitutes a new and important stream of research. Future studies might compare the organizational cultures of 1) an agency that explicitly espouses an ethical code of conduct with either A) an agency that does not explicitly espouse an ethical code or B) an agency that explicitly refutes ethics. Future studies might also narrow focus from general aspects of organizational culture (e.g., leadership) to more specific rules and resources (e.g., virtues such as honesty and integrity) that both enable and constrain ethical awareness and behavior. Identifying an agency as ethical or amoral upfront allows emphasis on specific rules and resources. In addition, moral exemplars in advertising should be identified. Empirical research can recognize leadership characteristics, such as virtues both self-reported and ascribed by others, and ways in which leaders espouse and enact ethical values. Finally, ethical codes of conduct could be examined from a structuration perspective 1) as a resource to action, 2) regarding how the codes enable and/or constrain ethical awareness, and 3) regarding what unintended consequences arise from action or inaction.

Notes

1 For confidentiality, the agency will be referred to as "AdCompany" or "the agency." Titles and participant ID numbers will identify members except when sensitive data is presented, in which case participants will be referred to as "member."
2 The mantra has been altered to protect confidentiality.
3 AdCompany made a few hires, several layoffs, and two employees quit during fieldwork.
4 Field notes were formatted Times New Roman, 12 pt., 1-inch margins, and single-spaced.

5　Each interview was assigned a unique participation number, which will appear within the findings.

6　See Appendix for the interview guide.

7　All interviews were transcribed by the researcher and were formatted as Times New Roman, 12 pt., 1-inch margins, single-spaced.

8　Findings are supported by exemplar quotes pulled from members' responses during interviews and from the field. Paraphrased responses and quotes are identified by participant ID number (e.g., 1) and by field notes according to the day (e.g., FN 1).

9　A noncompete agreement is a contract between an employer and employee that states, upon termination, conditions and timeframes for working within the industry and with competing organizations.

Appendix

Interview Guide for AdCompany's Employees

1. To start, can you talk about what you do for the agency? How long you've worked here, your role and what that role entails?
2. What values do people share at the agency? Does everyone agree on these values?
3. What are the agency's goals?
4. Does the agency have a mission or vision?
5. How would you describe the leadership at the agency? Who are the leaders?
6. What are some of the tough decisions or challenges you face in your job? How do you solve these challenges?
7. What are some of the ethical challenges that come to mind? Do you face those ethical challenges here at the agency?

Interview Guide for AdCompany's Leaders

1. What advice would you give someone starting an agency?
2. Can you talk about your philosophy of leadership? If you have one and what it is?
3. What are the agency's values?
4. What are the agency's goals?
5. What are some of the tough decisions you make? How do you make these decisions?
6. How can a leader create or support an agency that encourages and supports ethical decision making? Can you define ethics?

Participant Observation Exercises

1. Pick a research topic that you are interested in exploring. Explain how participant observation might be used to study this topic. Discuss the advantages and disadvantages of using participant observation as your research method.
2. With a partner, observe an event for one hour. Both of you should write down everything that you see and hear. Then compare your observations with those of your partner. How similar were each of your observations? Where did they differ? Did each of you see the

same things? If you saw different things, why do you think your observations differed?

3. Observe an event or an activity for at least one hour. Try to blend in and do not interact with others or take any notes. Following your observation, write down what you think you observed. Then try to critique your observations and attempt to understand why you think you saw what you saw.

References

Alvesson, Mats. (1994). Talking in organizations: Managing identity and impressions in an advertising agency. *Organization Studies*, 15 (4): 535–563.

Alvesson, Mats. (2002). *Understanding organizational culture*. Thousand Oaks, CA: Sage.

Atkinson, Paul, and Hammersley, Martyn. (1994). Ethnography and participant observation. In Norman K. Denzin and Yvonna S. Lincoln (Eds.), *Handbook of qualitative research* (pp. 248–261). London: Sage.

Baker, Sherry. (2008). The model of the principled advocate and the pathological partisan: A virtue ethics construct of opposing archetypes of public relations and advertising practitioners. *Journal of Mass Media Ethics*, 23 (3): 235–253.

Baker, Sherry, and Martinson, David L. (2001). The TARES test: Five principles of ethical persuasion. *Journal of Mass Media Ethics*, 16 (2&3): 148–175.

Berger, Arthur Asa. (1998). *Media research techniques* (2nd ed.). Thousand Oaks, CA: Sage.

Blasi, Augusto. (1994). Moral identity: Its role in moral functioning. In Bill Puka (Ed.), *Fundamental research in moral development* (pp. 168–179). New York, NY: Garland.

Bruyn, Severyn T. (1963). The methodology of participant observation. *Human Organization*, 22 (3): 224–235.

Bush, Victoria, Harris, Sharon, and Bush, Alan. (1997). Establishing ethical boundaries for service providers: A narrative approach. *The Journal of Services Marketing*, 11 (4): 265–277.

Butler, Jennifer A., and Modaff, Daniel P. (2008). When work is home: Agency, structure, and contradictions. *Management Communication Quarterly*, 22 (2): 232–257.

Canary, Heather. (2010). Constructing policy knowledge: Contradictions, communication, and knowledge frames. *Communication Monographs*, 77 (2): 181–206.

Chaffey, Dave. (2016, August 8). Global social media research summary 2016. *Smart Insights*. Retrieved from www.smartinsights.com/social-media-marketing-social-media-strategy/new-global-social-media-research/

Cunningham, Peggy H. (1999). Ethics of advertising: Oxymoron or good business practice? In John Philip Jones (Ed.), *The advertising business* (pp. 499–515). Thousand Oaks, CA: Sage.

Davis, Joel J. (1994). Ethics in advertising decision making: Implications for reducing incidence of deceptive advertising. *Journal of Consumer Affairs*, 28 (2): 380–403.

Denzin, Norman K., and Lincoln, Yvonna S. (1998). Introduction: Entering the field of qualitative research. In Norman K. Denzin and Yvonna S. Lincoln (Eds.), *The landscape of qualitative research: Theories and issues* (pp. 1–34). Thousand Oaks, CA: Sage.

DeWalt, Kathleen M., and DeWalt, Billie R. (2011). *Participant observation: A guide for fieldworkers* (2nd ed.). Lanham, MD: AltaMira Press.

Dreier, James. (2006). Moral relativism and moral nihilism. In David Copp (Ed.), *The Oxford handbook of ethical theory* (pp. 240–264). New York, NY: Oxford University Press.

Drumwright, Minette E. (2007). Advertising ethics: A multi-level theory approach. In Gerald J. Tellis and Tim Ambler (Eds.), *The Sage handbook of advertising* (pp. 398–416). London, England: Sage.

Drumwright, Minette E., and Murphy, Patrick E. (2004). How advertising practitioners view ethics: Moral muteness, moral myopia, and moral imagination. *Journal of Advertising*, 33 (2): 7–24.

Drumwright, Minette E., and Murphy, Patrick E. (2009). The current state of advertising ethics: Industry and academic perspectives. *Journal of Advertising, 38* (1): 83–107.

Emerson, Robert M., Fretz, Rachel I., and Shaw, Linda L. (1995). *Writing ethnographic fieldnotes.* Chicago, IL: University of Chicago Press.

Everbach, Tracy. (2006). The culture of a women-led newspaper: an ethnographic study of the *Sarasota Herald-Tribune. Journalism and Mass Communication Quarterly, 86* (3): 477–493.

Feldman, Daniel Charles. (1976). A contingency theory of socialization. *Administrative Science Quarterly, 21* (3): 443–452.

Gabriel, Yiannis. (1999). *Organizations in depth: The psychoanalysis of culture.* London, England: Sage.

Gabriel, Yiannis. (2000). *Storytelling in organizations: Facts, fictions, and fantasies.* Oxford, England: Oxford University Press.

Geertz, Clifford. (1973). *The interpretation of cultures: Selected essays.* New York: Basic Books.

Giddens, Anthony. (1984). *The constitution of society: Outline of the theory of structuration.* Berkeley, CA: University of California Press.

Gobo, Giampietro. (2011). Ethnography. In David Silverman (Ed.), *Qualitative research: Issues of theory, method and practice* (3rd ed., pp. 15–34). Los Angeles: Sage.

Goffman, Erving. (1963). *Behavior in public places.* New York, NY: Free Press.

Grossman, Lev. (2012, January 30). The beast with a billion eyes. *Time,* pp. 38–43.

Hall, Stuart. (1980). Encoding/decoding. In Stuart Hall, Dorothy Hobson, Andrew Lowe, and Paul Willis (Eds.), *Culture, media, language: Working papers in cultural studies, 1972–79* (pp. 128–138). London: Hutchinson.

Hill, Thomas E, Jr. (2006). Kantian normative ethics. In David Copp (Ed.), *The Oxford handbook of ethical theory* (pp. 480–514). New York, NY: Oxford University Press.

Hunt, Shelby D., and Chonko, Lawrence B. (1987). Ethical problems of advertising agency executives. *Journal of Advertising, 16* (4): 16–24.

Johnson, R. Burke. (1997). Examining the validity structure of qualitative research. *Education, 118* (2): 282–292.

Jones, John Philip. (1999). The culture of an advertising agency. In John Philip Jones (Ed.), *The advertising business* (pp. 133–152). Thousand Oaks, CA: Sage.

Jorgensen, Danny L. (1989). *Participant observation: A methodology for human studies.* Newbury Park, CA: Sage.

Keyton, Joann. (2005). *Communication & organizational culture: A key to understanding work experiences.* Thousand Oaks, CA: Sage.

Krueger, David. (1998). Ethics and values in advertising: Two case studies. *Business and Society Review, 99* (1): 53–65.

LeCompte, Margaret D., and Schensul, Jean J. (1999). *Analyzing and interpreting ethnographic data.* Walnut Creek, CA: AltaMira Press.

Lee, Seow Ting, and Nguyen, Hoang Lien. (2013). Explicating the moral responsibility of the advertiser: TARES as an ethical model for fast food advertising. *Journal of Mass Media Ethics, 28* (4): 225–240.

Lindlof, Thomas R., and Shatzer, Milton J. (1998). Media ethnography in virtual space: Strategies, limits, and possibilities. *Journal of Broadcasting and Electronic Media, 42* (2): 170–189.

Lindlof, Thomas R., and Taylor, Brian C. (2002). *Qualitative communication research methods* (2nd ed.). Thousand Oaks, CA: Sage.

Lohmeier, Christine. (2014). The researcher and the never-ending field: Reconsidering big data and digital ethnography. *Big Data? Qualitative Approaches to Digital Research Studies in Qualitative Methodology, 13*: 75–89.

Machin, David. (2002). *Ethnographic research for media studies.* London: Arnold.

Morley, David, and Silverstone, Roger. (1991). Media audiences: Communication and context: Ethnographic perspectives on the media audience. In Klaus Bruhn Jensen and Nicholas W. Jankowski (Eds.), *A handbook of qualitative methodologies for mass communication research* (pp. 149–162). London: Routledge.

Neill, Marlene S., and Drumwright, Minette E. (2012). PR professionals as organizational conscience. *Journal of Mass Media Ethics, 27* (4): 220–234.

O'Guinn, Thomas, Allen, Chris, and Semenik, Richard J. (1998). *Advertising.* Cincinnati, OH: South-Western College Publishing.

O'Guinn, Thomas, Allen, Chris, and Semenik, Richard J. (2009). *Advertising and integrated brand promotion* (5th ed.). Mason, OH: South-Western Cengage Learning.

Ostroff, Cheri, and Kozlowski, Steve W. J. (1992). Organizational socialization as a learning process: The role of information acquisition. *Personnel Psychology, 45* (4): 849–874.

Patterson, Philip, and Wilkins, Lee. (2008). *Media ethics: Issues and cases* (6th ed.). Boston, MA: McGraw-Hill.

Rosen, Michael. (1985). Breakfast at Spiro's: Dramaturgy and dominance. *Journal of Management, 11* (2): 31–48.

Rosen, Michael. (1988). You asked for it: Christmas at the bosses' expense. *Journal of Management Studies, 25* (5): 463–480.

Rotzoll, Kim B., and Christians, Clifford G. (1980). Advertising agency practitioners' perceptions of ethical decisions. *Journalism Quarterly, 57* (3): 425–431.

Schauster, Erin. (2013). Putting problems into context: An organizational approach to advertising ethics. In Minette E. Drumwright (Ed.), *Ethical issues in communication professions: New agendas in communication* (pp. 131–152). New York, NY: Routledge, Taylor & Francis.

Schauster, Erin. (2015). The relationship between organizational leaders and advertising ethics: An organizational ethnography. *Journal of Media Ethics, 30*: 150–167.

Schein, Edgar H. (1990). Organizational culture. *American Psychologist, 45* (2): 109–119.

Schein, Edgar H. (1992). *Organizational culture and leadership* (2nd ed.). San Francisco, CA: Jossey-Bass.

Schein, Edgar H. (2010). *Organizational culture and leadership* (4th ed.). San Francisco, CA: Jossey-Bass.

Shafer-Landau, Russ. (2010). *The fundamentals of ethics.* New York, NY: Oxford University Press.

Shamsian, Jacob, and Banicki, Adam. (2015, December 14). The founder of a white nationalist website says Donald Trump is helping his cause. *Business Insider.* Retrieved from www.businessinsider.com/trump-helping-white-supremacist-website-2015-12

Shapiro, Ari. (2016, July 5). Trumps words and tweets spur interest in white supremacist groups. *NPR: All Things Considered.* Retrieved from www.npr.org/2016/07/05/484832465/trumps-words-and-tweets-spur-interest-in-white-supremacist-groups

Smith, Craig. (2016, August 16). By the numbers: 135 Amazing YouTube statistics. *Expanded Ramblings.* Retrieved from expandedramblings.com/index.php/youtube-statistics/

Snyder, Wally. (2009). *Advertising ethics: Wally Snyder's rallying cry for the industry.* Retrieved from http://rjionline.org/news/advertising-ethics-wally-snyders-rallying-cry

Stokes, Jane. (2003). *How to do media and cultural studies.* London: Sage.

Thorson, Esther, and Duffy, Margaret. (2011). *Advertising age: The principles of marketing communication at work.* Mason, OH: South-Western Cengage.

Van Maanen, John. (1988). *Tales of the field: On writing ethnography.* Chicago, IL: The University of Chicago Press.

CHAPTER 8

Textual Analysis

Humanity is a mess and it takes the immensity of a coiled and supple lan-
guage to do it justice.

—Pat Conroy (2010, pp. 87–88)

Textual analysis is all about language, what it represents and how we use it
to make sense of our lives. Language is a basic element of our human interactions, and it is through language that the meanings of our social realities
are constructed. As cultural theorist Raymond Williams, who was one of
the founders of British Cultural Studies, explained:

> No expression, that is to say—no account, description, depiction,
> portrait—is "natural" or "straightforward." These are at most
> socially relative terms. Language is not a pure medium through
> which the reality of a life or the reality of an event or an expe-
> rience or the reality of a society can "flow." It is a socially shared
> and reciprocal activity, already embedded in active relationships,
> within which every move is an activation of what is already shared
> and reciprocal or may become so.
>
> (1977, p. 166)

For Williams, language does much more than describe our lives: it actually helps us to create our social realities. *The Power of Words* is a short film

that nicely illustrates Williams's understanding of language as an active and shared experience. Available on YouTube and Facebook, *The Power of Words* and its sequel, *The Power of Words* 2, have been viewed more than 25 million times. Created by the UK online content specialists Purplefeather, the film opens with a blind man sitting on a piece of cardboard in a public area; he has an empty can and a handwritten sign that reads, "I'm blind please help." People are enjoying the sunny day and as they walk by him, a few toss the man a coin or two. A young woman walks past the man and his sign but quickly returns to him. As he feels her trendy leather shoes, she grabs his sign, writes something on it and leaves. Many people begin to throw the man coins and his can quickly fills up. After a while, the woman returns and the man asks her, "What did you do to my sign?" She replies, "I wrote the same but different words." A little overwhelmed, he thanks the young woman and we finally see what she wrote on his sign: "It's a beautiful day and I can't see it." The film ends with the words "Change your words, change the world."

What Is a Text?

Understanding the concept of a "text" is a key aspect of the method of textual analysis. In qualitative research we use the term text to describe more than a printed document, textbook or a written cell phone message. In textual analysis we see texts as cultural artifacts, material documentary evidence that is used to make sense out of our lives. Cultural theorist Stuart Hall (1975) defined texts as "literary and visual constructs, employing symbolic means, shaped by rules, conventions and traditions intrinsic to the use of language in its widest sense" (p. 17). In other words, texts are things that we use to make meaning. Books, films, newspapers, photographs, magazines, websites, video blogs, games, television programs, podcasts, advertisements, fashions and popular music are all examples of the types of texts that qualitative researchers interpret in an effort to understand some of the many relationships between media, culture and society. From this perspective, texts are thought to provide traces of a socially constructed reality, which may be understood by considering the words, concepts, ideas, themes and issues that reside in texts as they are considered within a particular cultural context (Atkinson and Coffey, 2011).

When we do textual analysis, we evaluate the many meanings found in texts and we try to understand how written, visual and spoken language helps us to create our social realities. Rather than only judging the strengths, weaknesses, accuracy or inaccuracy of texts, qualitative researchers look at the social practices, representations, assumptions and stories about our lives that are revealed in those texts. Qualitative researchers do not study texts to predict or control how individuals will react to messages but instead to understand how people use texts to make sense of their lives. Researchers consider texts rich with interpretation and meaning that may be assessed through many different types of qualitative analysis. For example, contemporary studies of *Star Trek* illustrate how texts may be used to help people understand major changes in their lives. Researchers have completed several different types of textual analyses based on this television show/movie franchise and they suggest that the socially progressive role of technology depicted over the years on *Star Trek* has provided millions of people with a conceptual framework that has helped them to understand NASA's space exploration program (McKee, 2003).

The Development of Textual Analysis

In media studies the development of textual analysis is linked to the publication of "The Challenge of Qualitative Content Analysis" by German sociologist and critical theorist Siegfried Kracauer. Kracauer (1952–1953) questioned the use of quantitative content analysis in communication research, disputing the reliability and objectivity of a method that broke things down into separate pieces and parts and then counted them. For Kracauer, quantitative content analysis focused entirely on describing the surface content of texts, a strategy that resulted in incomplete and often "inaccurate analysis" (p. 632). For example, content analysis considered repetition an important measure of value, insisting that the more times a word, concept or idea was coded in a document, the greater significance there was to the evidence. In contrast, for Kracauer, repetition was less important than a consideration of texts in their entirety as a complete entity. He explained that analysis was an act of interpretation that considered both the surface meanings and the underlying intentions of a text. Kracauer maintained that the goal of textual analysis (which he initially called qualitative content analysis) was to bring out the entire range of potential meanings in texts.

One way in which the differences between qualitative textual analysis and quantitative content analysis may be illustrated is for us to consider how each method might address a specific research project. In the United States, Black Friday is the day following Thanksgiving Day. A very busy shopping day, it is generally considered the beginning of the Christmas season. If we consider the coverage of Black Friday published on daily urban news sites throughout the United States, we will be able to see key differences between textual analysis and content analysis.

If we were to use quantitative content analysis, we could sample urban news sites and count the number of articles appearing that focused on Black Friday. We could count the number of references to Black Friday in each of the articles that appeared. Apparently, several years ago my local newspaper, the *Milwaukee Journal Sentinel*, actually did such a study and found that in 2010 there were 350 references to Black Friday in the twenty daily newspapers with large circulations that its investigators studied (Romell, 2011, p. 7A). For a content analysis we could count how many times a particular word or phrase was used, count the number of images that accompanied the news articles or even count the number of sources used in each article. We could measure the length of the articles, measure the size of the images or even measure the size of the headlines accompanying the news articles. Another strategy might be to code each article as being a positive, negative or neutral story about Black Friday. We could even code each image accompanying the articles as illustrating a positive, negative or neutral depiction of Black Friday.

In contrast, if we were to use a qualitative textual analysis for our research on Black Friday we could look at the historical context for the development of the holiday, or we might consider whether Black Friday is merely a marketing or media slogan or if it has become a significant aspect of American culture. We could consider how online shopping may be impacting Black Friday and we might assess whether Black Friday is being used by online retailers and marketers. We could look at the themes that emerge in the news articles on Black Friday, the content and structure of the articles; or we might consider the language used to describe Black Friday. We could consider the relationship between the images and the articles, the placement of the stories, and how sources are used in the articles. We could also consider the absences in each of the articles and how they might help to frame the stories in a particular way.

As you can see from the Black Friday example, a qualitative textual analysis would look at the news coverage in its entirety and would attempt to make connections between Black Friday and larger issues in contemporary American society. In contrast, a quantitative content analysis would focus on counting or measuring specific parts of the coverage, which would require us to break each news article into a series of ratings, categories and components that we would have previously determined. For Kracauer, these categories, components and ratings are actually qualitative considerations that researchers make to simplify their work. Yet, Kracauer maintained that breaking a text into pieces and parts, rather than considering it as a whole, resulted in research of lower quality because there was less depth to the analysis.

The Influence of Semiotics

The first qualitative textual analyses were often based on literary analysis. Researchers rejected the idea of sampling a limited number of materials and chose to immerse themselves in all of the available texts. After a "preliminary long soak" (Hall, 1975, p. 15) in all of the materials, during which they began to identify categories and select examples for more thorough analysis, qualitative researchers then used a deep reading or exegesis to interpret the range of meanings within the texts. In the early textual analyses, specific patterns, themes and categories of analysis were not predetermined but emerged from the researchers' immersion in the material and deep reading of the texts. During the 1960s, textual analysis became influenced by semiotics and the concept of exegesis began to give way to a more systematic approach, one that emphasized "fundamental narrative structures" (Larsen, 1991, p. 127).

Semiotics is the study of signs that exist in our social lives. Signs are drawings, photographs, paintings, words, acts, sounds, objects and gestures; that is, a sign is anything that represents or stands in for something else. While semiotics is a general term that includes a variety of different methodological tools and theoretical perspectives, it provides insights for analyzing texts within culturally specific social practices. According to the creator of the field of linguistics, Ferdinand de Saussure, each sign is made up of two elements: a signifier and a signified.

A signifier portrays the physical letters, shapes or sounds, or other physical aspects of something. For example, the letters R, O, S, E represent the signifier for the word *rose*. The signified is the idea characterized by the word, shape or sound. In the case of a rose, the signified could be described as a fragrant flower with thorns. The relationship between the signifier and the signified creates a sign, which is evaluated from conventions or codes that have been previously agreed upon in a culture. The understanding of codes is based on factual information as well as the contextual knowledge of living in a particular culture at a specific place and time.

In semiotics, the associations between the signifier and the signified are considered arbitrary; that is, there is no definitive reason why the letters that constitute a word must refer to that specific word. For example, there is no specific or natural reason why the concept of a rose should be represented by a particular word or sound made up of the letters R, O, S, E. However, it is through the codes, ideas and conventions of a culture that the specific meanings of a signifier and a signified become systematized and fixed (Strinati, 1995).

Researchers who draw on semiotics not only study the definitional meaning or the denotation of signs but also consider the representative or connotative meanings.

> Semiotics invites us to examine texts not just for their obvious content, for what they have to say. It also gets us to think about representation; that is, about how texts show us events, objects, people, ideas, emotions and everything else that can be signified.
> (Gripsrud, 2006, pp. 39–40)

Overall, semiotics may be seen as a type of textual analysis that helps us to interpret codes and signs in order to understand how aspects of a text work with our own cultural knowledge to make meaning in our lives.

Currently, there are many different types of textual analyses being done by researchers in communication and media studies. For many qualitative researchers, "textual analysis" is the preferred term to describe the broader category of qualitative content analysis. However, some communication researchers prefer the term "discourse analysis" because of its emphasis on words in texts and talk (Peräkylä, 2008). The use of the term discourse analysis reminds researchers that it is through our use of language that our reality is socially constructed. Some contemporary researchers continue to follow Kracauer and prefer to immerse themselves in the texts and let the themes of analysis slowly emerge. The research example, "Historical Continuities in News Coverage of the Baltimore 2015 Riots and the 1965 Watts Riots," found at the end of this chapter, is an example of this type of textual analysis. Other researchers prefer to use specific procedures and predetermined categories of analysis, such as ideological analysis, genre analysis, semiotics or rhetorical analysis.

Theory and Interpretation

As I have previously discussed, a researcher's philosophical orientation and choice of theoretical framework is an integral part of all qualitative research. No matter what type of textual analysis they might undertake, most qualitative researchers also focus on the theoretical underpinnings of the text, because they see theory as central to the process of interpretation (Denzin and Lincoln, 1998). In textual analysis, researchers' theoretical perspectives can inform the type of textual analysis they use, as well as the types of questions that they ask. Using the musical drama television series *Empire* as an example, we can consider how the choice of a theoretical framework influences the types of questions that we ask and how we might focus our textual analysis of the music series.

A good place to begin is with some contextual information about *Empire*. The award-winning television series, created by Lee Daniels and Danny Strong, debuted on January 7, 2015. *Empire* is a family drama that focuses on a hip-hop entertainment company and the family who owns and runs it. Terrence Howard stars as Lucious Lyon, CEO of Empire Entertainment, and Taraji P. Henson portrays Cookie Lyon, ex-con matriarch of the family. The television series addresses contemporary social issues such as police brutality, mental illness, homophobia and race relations.

Currently broadcast internationally, each episode of *Empire* features original songs produced by hip-hop artist Timothy "Timbaland" Mosley. Columbia Records creates soundtracks of the *Empire* music that are released on iTunes following each episode. Well-known recording artists, including Mariah Carey, Alicia Keys and Mary J. Blige, have appeared on the show, and two of the main characters are professional musicians. Rapper Bryshere Gray plays Hakeem Lyon, and Jussie Smollett, who stars as Jamal Lyon, is a singer-songwriter. The original songs featured on *Empire* have consistently been on the iTunes weekly Top 100 (Kennedy, 2015).

Now if we were to use political economy as a theoretical framework for our textual analysis of *Empire*, we would want to focus on the economic aspects of the music industry as well as issues of ownership and control as they relate to the production of the television series. We could consider the commercial success of the songs, the money made from iTunes downloads, the promotion of the guest artists, as well as their increased earnings as a result of the released songs. We could address ownership issues in the popular music industry, the exclusion of recording artists who may lack broad-based appeal and pressures that may be placed on *Empire* to remain commercially successful.

British cultural studies would guide us to not only consider the social, political and economic context for the television series but also to address Daniels and Strong's authority and intention in creating *Empire*, as well as the way audience members interpret or decode the episodes. Because British cultural studies rejects the notion of a passive audience that uniformly accepts the intended meaning of a text, as researchers we might consider the many ways audience members make meaning from the television series. We could address the way dominant ideas of contemporary culture (also known as the ideology) are showcased in the series. An emphasis on the stereotypes, visual imagery, use of language and popular culture references in *Empire* might also help us to understand specific cultural relationships in contemporary society.

If we were to use social feminism as our theoretical framework, we would look at how women are represented on the television show. We could consider whether the gender relations depicted in *Empire* perpetuate sexist stereotypes or whether they are used to empower women. We might address the economics of using female sexuality to enhance commercial success and we could also evaluate any depictions of women in stereotypical male roles. We might consider how these roles may help women to resist the power of men to dominate and oppress them—a concept known as patriarchy. As you can see from this example, differing theoretical perspectives provide researchers with guidance, offering a conceptual framework to help guide their textual analyses. Theoretical frameworks do not actually analyze texts; they are used to suggest key issues and questions for researchers to address in their research.

Encoding and Decoding

Researchers using textual analysis often focus on the production of texts. They consider the author's intention as well as his or her specific rationale for the creation of a text. Understanding the importance of context to the interpretation process, researchers seek out insights regarding the historical, cultural and economic relationships that exist between a text and a specific society at a particular place in time. When we research the relevant context for a textual analysis, it is important to consider the concept of intertextuality, which is the way one text actually refers to other texts. It is actually possible for us to analyze a text in terms of the relationships it has with other texts, and therefore it is important for researchers to consider how the elements of a text may refer to other texts. For example, if we go back to the *Empire* example and we wanted to do a textual analysis of the television show, we would also want to consider the reviews of *Empire*, the news and entertainment coverage of the series, blog posts, relevant tweets, fan sites and other audience responses as well as considering related television shows. By looking at the intertextuality among these texts we would gain greater insight into the meanings of *Empire*.

Qualitative researchers also go beyond the production of texts to consider how meaning moves from the author or creator of a text to the readers and audience members who encounter the text. While all texts are produced for particular reasons at a specific place and time, a text's meaning may change once others evaluate it. Before Stuart Hall developed his encoding/

decoding model of communication, researchers emphasized a sender/message/receiver approach to the communication process. The sender/message/receiver model focused on the construction of messages, maintaining that once a message was sent, then as long as there was no interference on the line, all people would understand the message as intended.

However, Hall (1980) explained that when a text is created, its author/producer constructs or encodes a specific intended meaning into each text. This intended or dominant meaning is what the text's creator hopes we will all understand and take away from the text. Yet, Hall maintained that people actually interpret or decode texts in a variety of different ways. Some people will decode a text as the author intended, understanding the dominant code reproduced by the author. Others will take a negotiated position, understanding the intended meaning but also considering their own experiences and decoding the text while taking both views into consideration. Still others will take an oppositional view, rejecting the intended meaning and constructing a completely different interpretation of the message.

Political commercials that support a specific presidential candidate provide a good example to illustrate the ways viewers decode messages. The dominant encoded meaning that is constructed in this type of commercial urges viewers to support the featured candidate. Some viewers will see these commercials and agree with the positions outlined in the ads, and they may even vote for that presidential candidate. Other viewers will understand the intention of the commercials and they may add their own experiences or knowledge about the candidate to the broadcast advertisements. They may or may not agree with the intended meaning of the commercials, but they may consider the political commercials before making their voting decisions. However, other viewers will take the information in the commercials and turn it around, as evidence to support another candidate. These viewers will completely reject the intended meaning of the advertisements, refusing to accept the dominant position, and will instead construct an oppositional reading of the political commercials. Given that texts may be decoded in a variety of different ways, Hall suggested that it is important for researchers to go beyond analyzing the intended meaning that is produced in texts to explore the ways texts are understood by readers and audience members.

Ideological Analysis

Ideology has been a central concept in textual analysis throughout the development of the methodology. Ideology may be understood as the dominant ideas of an individual, group, class or society, the way meanings are socially produced, or even as the false ideas upon which a social, political or economic system is based. Kracauer (1952–1953) maintained that texts represented dominant ideological positions within a culture at a specific historical place and time. He suggested that many of these dominant ideologies appeared to us as common sense—things that we logically did, rationally decided and morally believed were right. Our beliefs as well as our resulting actions were thought to be based on ideas that were used to create and maintain a particular worldview that was culturally specific and quite changeable. As Graeme Turner (1997), a key researcher in Australian cultural and media studies explained, from this perspective all societies are based on "sets of unspoken, unwritten assumptions about the way the world works." There is no need for these ideological values and/or assumptions to be written down in one place "because they are inscribed into virtually every aspect of one's life in that culture" (p. 327).

The common tradition of giving one's fiancée a diamond engagement ring provides us with an example of how ideology works. I would suggest that many people consider giving a diamond engagement ring a romantic gesture and an appropriate custom, and most people assume that diamond engagement rings have a long and interesting history. Given that about 80 percent of American brides actually receive diamond engagement rings (O'Rourke, 2007), we can consider the custom part of the dominant American ideology. While the history of betrothal rings dates back to the thirteenth century, it might surprise you to learn that the popularity of diamond engagement rings actually began in the 1930s, when De Beers started a public advertising campaign to combat its declining sales of diamonds. In 1947, female copywriter Frances Gerety came up with the slogan, "A Diamond Is Forever," which De Beers combined with an image of young, attractive honeymooning newlyweds in a new advertising campaign (O'Rourke, 2007). The advertising campaign was a hit, and diamond engagement ring sales rose dramatically. Between 1939 and 1979, De Beers' wholesale diamond sales soared from 23 million to 2.1 billion (Friedman, 2015). The custom of giving a diamond engagement ring quickly became part of the dominant ideology. In this case, external advertising forces subtly reshaped the public consciousness as it related to engagement customs, probably without people realizing it.

Interestingly, in the 1960s, De Beers began to market diamond rings in Japan, advertising them as examples of "modern western values." When their campaign began in 1967, less than five percent of Japanese women were given a diamond engagement ring. By 1981, De Beers had built a billion dollar diamond industry in Japan and 60 percent of Japanese women received a diamond engagement ring (Friedman, 2015). Overall, the De Beers advertising campaign is an example of how economic relations can shape the cultural realm of a society, which in turn begins to influence people's consciousness and ideological beliefs (Berger, 2000).

Early textual analyses were based on the view that a singular dominant ideology existed, through which a group maintained its power and legitimacy, and that it was a researcher's goal to uncover that ideology. As the field developed, some qualitative researchers, particularly those from a constructivist philosophical orientation, began to insist that while texts "function ideologically" (Larsen, 1991, p. 129) because they illustrate societal principles and values, they do not provide a single ideological vision but instead offer multiple versions of our socially constructed reality.

In contemporary media research, while some qualitative researchers identify multiple ideological positions in texts, others focus on understanding how dominant ideological power relations within race, class, age, gender and ethnicity are encoded in texts. Maintaining that texts help to construct our knowledge, values and beliefs and work to reinforce our commonsense understandings, these researchers examine the political, economic and/or ideological perspectives that shape texts. The research example at the end of this chapter is an example of this type of research, specifically as it relates to issues of race and class. In other words, these researchers understand that power can operate within the realm of ideas, and so they see texts as sources of power (Gillespie and Toynbee, 2006).

Clearly, ideology is a complex concept: it stabilizes and supports the status quo, reinforces the dominant beliefs of those with power in society, produces our socially constructed meanings and acts as "social cement and social control" (Cormack, 1995, p. 20). Researchers who focus on dominant ideological power relations analyze texts to understand how ideology works within a society's culture. Initially, researchers who undertook ideological analysis drew on literary methods of analysis, immersing themselves in the material and intuitively analyzing the texts.

Currently, most researchers doing ideological analyses draw on specific categories and guidelines to help frame their work. In his book *Ideology*, Mike Cormack (1995) outlined a specific method of analysis for an ideological critique, based on a British cultural studies framework, which assessed five main areas of emphasis: content, structure, absence, style and mode of address. Cormack suggested that evaluating the content of a text, including the opinions, beliefs, values and other judgments, the vocabulary used, the stereotypes and characterizations of people, and the conflicts, resolutions and other actions within the text, helped us to understand how a specific social reality is constructed. The structure—in particular, the opening and closing aspects of a text—are also important to assess. The opening of a text not only sets an agenda but also frames how the issues, concerns and information will be handled. The closing often attempts to answer questions and solve any problems addressed in the text. Cormack explained that a text's structure and its emphasis on binary oppositions, such as good and evil, may be used to guide readers or audience members toward a specific ideological view by limiting the ways a text may be interpreted.

For Cormack (1995), an emphasis on absence, the "elements which might have been expected to be in the text but which are missing from it" (p. 31), is crucial to understanding how ideology influences a text. You may wonder how it is possible to assess something that is not there. While at first glance this may seem to be a difficult undertaking, we actually expect to see certain things, and those expectations are based on customs, conventions and experiences. For example, if you watched a broadcast news story about a major snowstorm, you would expect to see images of the storm: pictures of people digging out, playing in the snow, building snowmen, or even images of road closings, accidents, salt piles or plow trucks. If the broadcast included no images of the storm, you would be surprised and might wonder what had happened. Therefore, considering those aspects that are absent, unsaid, missing or avoided allows us to consider how a specific ideological argument may have been constructed.

A focus on style assesses aspects of the text apart from the actual language, including the use of color, design, fashion or genre, and the mode of address considers the way each text talks to us. Does it speak to the audience directly or does the text use a strategy of indirect address? When taken together, the five areas of analysis outlined by Cormack may help us to understand the role of ideology in constructing a specific view of reality in a text that readers and viewers are encouraged to share.

Genre Analysis

Earlier in this chapter I mentioned how one text often refers to other texts, which is a process known as intertextuality. In media studies we often try to make sense of one text by considering it in relation to other, similar kinds of texts. We call these different types of texts "genres." News, documentary, sports, romantic comedies, drama, reality television, science fiction and cartoons are all different types of genres that help audience members, media producers and critics to communicate with each other. Genres also help us to distinguish, evaluate and make sense of various types of media.

Within each genre there are narrative and aesthetic conventions that reproduce and reinforce a system of beliefs about our social reality. The rules and conventions of different genres also help researchers to assess how audience members may evaluate any given text. For example, when we think about gangster films we expect to see movies that take place in gritty urban environments, with Italian restaurants, violence, betrayals, police stakeouts and chase scenes. People like to go to genre films to watch the types of films that they know they like and to see how each element that is central to the genre has been reinvented or reinterpreted by the filmmaker (Stokes, 2003). Genres help us to categorize cultural texts by types and conventions, yet genre products should not be dismissed as merely standardized commodities. While genre texts include the repetition of central elements, they also include speculation and uncertainty. Genres work because we enjoy the predictability of the genre, and we also take pleasure from the differences, enjoying the surprises and trying to guess what might come next. As Alan McKee (2003) explained, "[W]hy would someone go down into a cellar by themselves in a horror film? Because it's a horror film" (p. 97). We all have certain expectations when we read the news, watch a new science fiction television show or take in the latest action film at our neighborhood movie theater.

For instance, viewers familiar with the animated television show *South Park* did not worry that one of the characters, Kenny, was killed almost every week during the first five seasons of the program. They were familiar with the rules and conventions of cartoons, and understood that Kenny's death was a running gag, allowing another character to remark each time, "Oh, my God—they killed Kenny!" Viewers felt assured that Kenny would return alive during the next episode of *South Park*. However, when Charlie Harper died on the situation comedy *Two and a Half Men*, viewers realized that his death was authentic and that the character would not return to the show. Characters rarely die in situation comedies, but when they do, it is for real. In addition, the actor Charlie Sheen had been fired from his role as Charlie Harper following public disagreements with management and after a series of derogatory comments that Sheen had made about the series' creator. This context helped viewers to make sense of Charlie Harper's death on a metro platform in Paris.

In genre analysis, researchers consider other texts in the same genre, the wider social context for the text along with how the text may speak to other similar texts. Stories, issues and concerns raised by the text are explored. Researchers who study genre focus on broad patterns within specific texts. They are particularly interested in changes that occur in different genres and they assess what those changes may say about social and political issues in society. "Popular genres can be seen as revealing underlying preoccupations and conflicts in a social order. Studying genre may reveal how the media offer mythical solutions to these preoccupations" (Branston, 2006, p. 45).

Some genres, such as news and documentary, are considered to have a high modality because they are considered strongly connected to reality. These genres are expected to provide accurate information that we may draw on for guidance about our lives. In contrast, other genres, such as cartoons and science fiction, have low modalities, and the expectations that these genres will provide us with usable information are lower.

Rhetorical Analysis

As I have mentioned throughout this chapter, there are many different types and techniques of textual analysis that we can use to analyze media texts. Rhetorical analysis looks at how speakers and writers use words to influence readers and audience members. The use of rhetorical analysis is particularly appropriate when one is assessing aspects of advertising and public relations, or when persuasion is an integral part of a media text. Aristotle's three modes of persuasion—ethos, pathos and logos—are considered central to a rhetorical analysis. Ethos is concerned with the character, credibility and confidence of a writer or speaker; pathos involves rousing readers' and audience members' emotions through the use of description and word usage; and logos focuses on appeals to the reasoning skills of audience members and readers, specifically considering how arguments are framed in the text through the use of statistics and facts (Berger, 2000).

Researchers using a rhetorical analysis consider the relationships between a text, its author or producer, the intended audience and the relevant context for the production and reception of that text. In their work, researchers use a variety of rhetorical devices to understand the persuasive aspects of texts. As with semiotics, they consider the metaphoric language used to reinforce an argument, comparing elements using analogy and association. They assess verbal appeals, including the use of sarcasm and irony, the offering of expert advice, problem solving and playing on people's anxieties and fears. For example, advertising campaigns for deodorants often target individuals' fear of rejection, loneliness and their desire for approval to persuade them to buy their products.

Rhetorical analysis also considers catchy slogans, melodies and jingles that can get caught in our heads and are nearly impossible to forget. McDonald's "You deserve a break today"; "I wish I was an Oscar Meyer Wiener"; and Coca-Cola's "It's the Real Thing" are three of AdAge.com's top ten advertising jingles of the twentieth century. Advertising jingles are hard to forget; just writing about the Oscar Meyer Wiener made me start humming the jingle. Researchers using rhetorical analysis as a method may also focus on images and other visual aspects of a text, assessing how colors, typefaces and other typographical elements help sell a product or service to the public. For example, a researcher using a rhetorical analysis to analyze an advertising campaign could consider the people used in the advertisements, specifically assessing the age, gender, ethnicity, physical characteristics and expressions of the models. They could also evaluate the models' hairstyles, fashions, expressions and interactions within the ads (Berger, 1998). As in the use of semiotics, and other types of textual analysis, researchers find that assessing rhetorical concepts and appeals provides them with a variety of ways to understand how texts create meaning and help to shape individuals' socially constructed realities.

In this chapter I have described several different types of textual analyses, including semiotics, rhetorical analysis, genre analysis and ideological analysis. They are only a few of the many different types of textual analysis that qualitative researchers use. However, it is important to remember that as researchers work to understand the full range of meanings that exist within texts, textual analysis continues to evolve as a qualitative methodology. For me, the choice to use a specific type of textual analysis, with predetermined categories of analysis, or to instead allow categories to emerge after immersing myself in the material, is less important than making sure to go beyond surface representations to focus on the deeper meanings of the texts.

Using New Technologies in Textual Analysis

Computer assisted qualitative data analysis software (CAQDAS) has been available since the 1990s, and some researchers regularly use it to manage their research projects. For example, the native Mac application, Atlas.ti, consolidates large numbers of documents, keeps track of a researcher's notes, annotations and memos, codes texts and evaluates and analyzes images, videos and audio files. MAXQDA 12, which operates on both Macs and PCs, has no limits on the size of text documents, the number of texts used, or the number of variables, text groups or codes that a researcher may incorporate. MAXQDA 12 can search for key terms within all documents, and the program can code or label different types of texts, including PDFs and images. It can produce data about all of a researcher's codes and the relations between the codes; it can write memos about the coded material and can call up all of the coded or labeled texts of one kind.

However, some qualitative researchers remain skeptical about the use of CAQDAS. Their concerns are often based on the view that computing technology assumes a positivist worldview, which insists on a singular knowable and findable reality. This is a view that is in opposition to the notion of a socially constructed reality, which frames much of qualitative research. These qualitative researchers maintain that the use of CAQDAS limits the depth of textual analysis, resulting "in the loss of shades of meaning and interpretation" (Rodik and Primorac, 2015, p. 2). Other qualitative researchers are not ruling out the use of CAQDAS, but they distinguish between using computer-assisted data analysis and incorporating data management tools to help organize the large amount of material that they work with. These researchers differentiate between the conceptual foundations of qualitative analysis and the mechanical aspects of keeping track of information. They use programs like Atlas.ti and MAXQDA 12 to consolidate information and to keep track of images, audio and video files, but they prefer to do their own labeling, coding, evaluating and analyzing of research materials for their textual analyses.

Ethical Considerations

Given that there is no one correct way to analyze a text and that researchers bring their own interpretive strategies to their work, you may be wondering about the value of textual analysis as a qualitative methodology. Textual analysis, like other qualitative methodologies, does not provide researchers with knowledge that can be replicated or generalized within a wider population. Instead, researchers use textual analysis to try to understand how people use texts to make sense of their lives. While no two textual analyses produce the same interpretation, researchers draw on the relevant social, historical, political and/or economic context as well as their own knowledge of the text's place within the broader culture in order to understand the most likely sense-making strategies. While there is not one "true" interpretation of a text, it is not a free-for-all, and there are certainly interpretations that are more reasonable than others. It is important for researchers to understand that "[w]ays of making sense of the world aren't completely arbitrary; they don't change from moment to moment. They're not infinite, and they're not completely individual" (McKee, 2003, p. 18).

Qualitative researchers draw on the relevant context for their textual analysis to specifically understand how each text fits into the dominant worldview of a culture. It is from an emphasis on the cultural context that researchers construct their most likely interpretations of the relationships between a text and the larger society. While researchers base their analyses on theoretical and/or conceptual frameworks, it is important for them to stay open to discovering unknown possibilities that may differ from what they thought they might find.

For example, in a previous textual analysis that I did on the press coverage of Thanksgiving from 1905–2005 (Brennen, 2008), I originally wanted to look at how the practice of journalism had changed over the past century. I was interested in understanding how journalistic values and news conventions might have changed and how newspapers represented and interpreted social, political and economic change through their coverage of routine news stories. Initially I was not interested in religious changes in society or in researching the role of advertising in newspapers. However, from my textual analysis of the newspaper coverage, issues of advertising and news, and the role of religion, emerged as central themes of the coverage. Had I ignored these themes because they were not of interest to me, I would have considered my research to be ethically suspect because I would have attempted to manipulate the evidence to support my interests and concerns. While interpretation is a subjective endeavor, it is important for qualitative researchers to let the evidence guide their interpretations rather than attempting to make the evidence fit with their preconceived opinions and beliefs.

Research Using Textual Analysis

The following research example grew out of an invitation to research news media coverage of the 2015 Baltimore riots. What initially struck me when reading the news reports was the language and the tone used by news organizations to describe poverty, unemployment, police brutality and other sociological "causes" for the riots. It seemed to me that these issues had been addressed in the press for many years, and I wondered how the new coverage might have differed or compared over the years. My questions regarding press coverage of riots resulted in a critical literary textual analysis that evaluated the news reports of the 1965 Watts riots and the 2015 Baltimore riots in five daily urban newspapers published in the United States. The first section of this research project discussed the use of British cultural studies as a theoretical perspective—specifically, how Stuart Hall's work on media's conceptual frameworks about race should be considered within specific historical and social contexts. In this section I also described the approach I used to textually analyze the 214 news reports on the Watts Riots and the 352 news articles on the Baltimore riots.

"Historical Continuities in News Coverage of the Baltimore 2015 Riots and the 1965 Watts Riots," by Bonnie Brennen

Chapter in *Race, News, and the City: Uncovering Baltimore*, Linda Steiner and Silvio Waisbord, eds. Forthcoming, Routledge, 2017.

On December 2, 1965, the California Governor's Commission on the Los Angeles Riots released its report, *Violence in the City—An End or a Beginning?* The eight-member, blue-ribbon commission, headed by former CIA director John A. McCone, determined that police brutality, substandard schools, poor living conditions and overcrowding, high rates of unemployment and a lack of public transportation were the fundamental causes for the Watts riots, the largest urban uprising of the Civil Rights era.

The committee recommended increased communication between the police and the community, a new system for handling citizen complaints, new education programs emphasizing literacy and language skills, preschool education beginning at age three, jobs training and employment bringing together the black community, employers, government and organized labor. In addition, the committee urged the state to upgrade health-care services, create better public transportation services, and build additional low-income housing (*Violence in the City*, 1965). Unfortunately, most of the commission's recommendations were never adopted. Fifty years after the Watts riots, similar issues of racism, segregation and economic disparity were once again debated as key issues in the 2015 Baltimore riots.

The critical cultural analysis offered here compares legacy newspaper coverage of the 1965 Watts riots and the 2015 Baltimore riots. Using cultural materialist theorizing, this research considers media texts to be cultural artifacts as well as explicit forms of communication. Media texts create meanings, thereby providing historically based insights about social, economic and/or political realms of society (Williams, 1981). News reports provide examples of the prevailing ideology of a culture at a particular place and time and so analyzing them can help to understand how standards, values and perceptions of race and class have been framed on urban daily newspapers during the past fifty years.

A variety of the media's conceptual frameworks construct, represent, understand and interpret issues of race. Insisting that issues of race must be addressed within specific social and historical contexts, Stuart Hall (1981) described how these frames also produce, reproduce and transform ideological positions. Language is crucial to the production of meaning (Hall, 1997). For Hall (1986), people construct their understandings of the world through language; ideology is created and reinforced through language. All media texts may be seen to present racist and/or stereotypical representations that serve to protect the power of dominant or elite groups in society. Hall distinguished two types of racism found in media texts: overt racism and inferential racism. Overt racism, usually considered the purview of extremist groups, refers to explicitly racist views that are frequently framed around biological differences. This type of racism is rarely found in mainstream news coverage. Yet Hall continued to see in contemporary news coverage a more subtle type of racism that is based on popular understandings of race. Hall (1981) defines inferential racism as:

> representations of events and situations related to race, whether "factual" or "fictional," which have racist premises and propositions

inscribed in them as a set of unquestioned assumptions. These enable racist statements to be formulated without ever bringing into awareness the racist predicates on which the statements are grounded.

(p. 36)

Guided by Hall's distinction between overt racism and inferential racism, this research analyzed news coverage of the Watts riots and the Baltimore riots in five legacy newspapers: the *Los Angeles Times*, *The New York Times*, the *Washington Post*, the *Chicago Tribune* and the *Atlanta Journal Constitution*. (In 1982 the *Atlanta Journal* and the *Atlanta Constitution* merged to form the *Atlanta Journal Constitution*.) These geographically diverse newspapers are large circulation urban dailies available in the 1960s and still published today. They represent excellence in journalism as indicated by quality rankings ("These are the best," 2012; "Top 100 Newspapers," 2016).

The reportage was assessed using critical literary methods, which are appropriate in analyzing texts' ideological frames as well as in unearthing dominant attitudes on race (Brennen, 2013). I focused on the use of language and tone of the articles, the recurrence of specific topics, themes and frames. I also looked for news reports that represented exceptions to the dominant or major patterns as well as elements of the coverage that one would expect to see included but that were missing from the reportage. Overall, I analyzed 214 news reports on Watts Riots published from August 13–20, 1965 and 352 news articles published about the Baltimore riots in the same five newspapers, from April 19–29, 2015.

Please note how the next two sections provided key historical context for the Watts riots and how key systemic issues such as police brutality, segregation in housing and schools and racial inequality not only framed the Watts riots but continued to be societal issues fifty years later.

The Back Story

In 1965, Los Angeles was the third largest city in the United States, with a population of approximately 2.5 million people. About 16 percent of the population was African American. The national unemployment rate was 5.7 percent but the rate of unemployment for African Americans was 16 percent. At the time of the riots, in the South Central area of Los Angeles, 34 percent of adults were unemployed (Hillinger and Jones, 1965, p. 3). Only one out of 22 Los Angeles hospitals admitted African American patients. Black entertainers and businessmen were banned from staying in "white" hotels and clubs. African

American women were forbidden from trying on hats in downtown department stores. Black teachers were not allowed to teach at public junior or senior high schools in Los Angeles. ("In L.A.," 1992)

In the 1960s, four percent of the Los Angeles Police Department (LAPD) was black and the LAPD had a reputation among African Americans and its police officers for brutalizing black suspects. Yet, according to a special report by *The Los Angeles Times* published in 1992, white residents of Los Angeles were "blithely unaware" of racial inequality and police brutality both because neither of the local newspapers covered such issues and these issues were not a part of the daily lives of white L.A. White locals saw Los Angeles as drive-ins, orange groves and Disneyland while many people living in other states bought into the myth of Los Angeles as "a glamorous Oz, populated by movie stars and beach boys, jet planes and convertibles" ("In L.A.," 1992, p. T5).

Poverty and discrimination produced de facto segregation, keeping most African American families in South-Central Los Angeles ghettos. Several suburbs in the Los Angeles area restricted non-whites and Jews from buying or renting housing. For example, Highland Park, a suburb, known as a cultural and artistic center of Los Angeles, posted signs that said, "No Negroes or Orientals desired." As increasingly more African Americans moved to Los Angeles, the Board of Education readjusted zoning lines to keep African American students in overcrowded black schools. The Watts-Willowbrook part of South-Central Los Angeles, where the riots occurred, was an area "of low family income, substandard housing and substandard education" ("Scene of Rioting," 1965, p. 3).

In 1963, a coalition of civil rights activists in Los Angeles requested that the L.A. Board of Education address problems resulting from overcrowding and underfunding but the board did not respond. In November 1964, shortly after the federal Civil Rights Act was enacted into law, California voters "overwhelmingly approved" Proposition 14, a Constitutional Amendment that voided all fair housing laws in the state. Proposition 14, which violated the new Civil Rights Act, and was later found unconstitutional by the courts, was endorsed by the *Los Angeles Times*. ("In L.A.," 1992, p. T5)

The Precipitating Moment

On August 11, 1965 Marquette Frye was stopped for reckless driving and speeding by California Highway Patrolman Lee Minikus, who also administered a sobriety test. Local citizens gathered, harsh words were exchanged and Minikus radioed for backup. Meanwhile, Frye's brother, a passenger in the car, walked to their house nearby, and returned with their mother. Angry when Minikus arrested not only Frye but also his mother, observers began to throw bottles and rocks. Thus began a six-day conflict, during which thousands of African Americans in

South-Central Los Angeles rioted. They burned down buildings, looted stores, and clashed with police, "unleashing in one fierce, frightening explosion decades of pent-up anger and frustration" ("The Word," 1992, p. T6). Reacting to years of broken promises, inequality, neglect and abuse, and to a lack of respect by political leaders, police and the justice system, the Watts rioters represented an urban climate of disillusionment and despair. By the end of the riots, 31 people were killed by police and three others also died; 1,032 individuals had been injured and 3,952 rioters were arrested, including 500 young people under 18. Two hundred buildings were destroyed and an additional 400 buildings were looted and burned, resulting in hundreds of millions of dollars of damage. In its evaluation of the Watts riots, the Governor's commission determined that of the approximately 430,000 African Americans living in South Central Los Angeles at the time of the riots, "only" two percent of them participated in the violence (*Violence in the City*, 1965)

Local white residents and political leaders, including Governor Edmund G. Brown, insisted that they were shocked by the Watts riots; they maintained that there was no racial injustice in Los Angeles. However, civil rights leaders, black activists, and local African Americans pointed out that they had challenged the racial injustice in Los Angeles for decades. Dr. Martin Luther King Jr. called the surprise of public officials over the Watt's Riots "dishonest." King suggested that while Northern political leaders praised the courage of African Americans in the South, when questions were brought up about racial inequality in their communities their "rejection was firm and unequivocal" (quoted in Theoharis, 2015).

During the 1950s and 1960s, civil rights groups in Los Angeles had protested against police brutality, housing and school segregation as well as racial inequality. Nonetheless, according to political science professor Jeanne Theoharis (2015), news outlets framed the civil rights movement as a righteous Southern issue. In contrast, these same kinds of activities in the North and the West were framed as "episodic, disorderly disturbances" rather than as a focused movement. Theoharis suggests that fifty years after Watts, legacy media outlets still frame demonstrations in places like Ferguson and Baltimore as surprising and as individual law enforcement and/or policy problems that break from the norm. Journalists do not investigate the systemic problems, she notes, and they ignore groups who have been addressing these issues.

In the following two sections I addressed key themes that emerged from the coverage of the Watts riots in the five newspapers and the word choice and tone of the coverage. While there were differences in the coverage, with *The Washington Post* and *The New York Times* offering more in-depth and balanced reportage, inferential and explicit racism was a fundamental component of the news coverage in all five newspapers.

Themes of the Watts Coverage

As the local newspaper of record, the *Los Angeles Times'* coverage of the Watts riots was comprehensive and multi-faceted. Each day, reports addressed the carnage: the costs of the riots, the buildings burned and businesses looted, officials injured, as well as the number of rioters arrested, injured and killed. Journalists detailed the work of the LAPD and the National Guard, and their efforts to re-establish law and order, no matter how much force it took. The coverage addressed legal strategies for processing and prosecuting those arrested in the riots, efforts to feed people in Watts after their grocery stores were looted and burned out, speculation about insurance coverage for business people who lost property in the riots, first person reaction pieces as well as cleanup efforts following the riots and the establishment of a riot inquiry panel after the end of the conflict. Of the 87 articles written about the Watts riots published the *Los Angeles Times* during the eight-day period, 83 articles were written by *Times* staff members. The vast majority of the *Los Angeles Times* coverage framed the riots as "largely spontaneous outbursts of mob violence" by a group of lawless hoodlums (McCurdy and Berman, 1965, p. 3).

The *Los Angeles Times* reportage drew extensively on Police Chief William H. Parker and Mayor Samuel W. Yorty to help understand the riots. Like Governor Edmund G. Brown they insisted that race relations had always been good in Los Angeles. News stories quoted Mayor Yorty referring to race relations as "exemplary" (Baker, 1965, p. 16) while Police Chief Parker insisted that he would not negotiate with the rioters because they were thugs without leaders. Mayor Yorty called civil rights leaders' charges that police brutality and the riots were connected a "big lie" "shouted by Communists, dupes and demagogues." Mayor Yorty complained of a "worldwide subversive campaign to stigmatize all police as brutal" (Baker, 1965, p. 3) and warned that allegations of police brutality could not justify the rioters' acts.

While the *Los Angeles Times* coverage was comprehensive and in depth and attempted to strive for some balance in its coverage, The *Chicago Tribune* seemed to make no attempt at neutrality in its reportage. Its 17 news reports from a variety of wire services, including the Chicago Tribune Press Service, framed the riots as mob violence by out-of-control, marauding bands of rioters. In addition to reporting on the looting, burning and destruction of property, the *Chicago Tribune* coverage also focused on white people who had been injured and the restraint used by the police in dealing with the rioters.

Several *Tribune* articles focused on the alcohol consumption of the rioters, informing readers that looters took liquor and "smashed the necks of whisky bottles on the curb, then swilled down the contents, and staggered drunkenly thru the streets" (Korman, 1965, p. 2). Attribution for these charges was missing from the *Chicago Tribune* news reports. For example, a front-page news article reported that the police and guardsmen managed to take control of Watts the previous night, yet the article commented that "most of the residents in the district last night were out looting and pillaging in other districts" (Korman, 1965). This incendiary statement was not attributed and no other newspaper confirmed the charge.

The vast majority of the 35 articles that ran in the *Atlanta Journal* about the Watts Riots were a mix of AP and UPI wire service accounts, along with articles from the Chicago Daily News Service and the New York Times News Service. The wire service reports, however, provided a much wider variety of perspectives on the riots than did the other newspapers. While some of the articles focused on the riots as mob violence, other addressed larger systemic issues of police brutality, high unemployment and limited educational opportunities. Some of the articles referred to the police as peace officers, yet other articles addressed police brutality as the cause of the riots, aggravating "the disease of poverty and despair" ("Righter sees," 1965, p. 5). Nevertheless, other articles in the *Atlanta Journal*, such as an AP story from Rome, Georgia, used Watts as an example of why white people needed to organize to protect themselves from African Americans. The un-bylined AP writer interviewed Calvin Craig, grand dragon of the Georgia Ku Klux Klan, who warned that race riots would come to the South and said that President Lyndon Johnson and Dr. King "must share the blame" for the Watts riots because "you cannot legislate society to integrate the people" ("Craig says," 1965, p. 32).

Given the framing of the Watts riots as leaderless mob violence on the *Los Angeles Times*, the *Chicago Tribune* and the *Atlanta Journal*, it is not surprising that most of the news stories used official business, legal and political sources and white observers who witnessed the riots. The vast majority of the news articles included no testimony from participants in the riots or local civil rights leaders. The coverage included some quotes from African Americans who were critical of the rioters; one news article detailed the "heroism" of African Americans who saved "white victims" while putting their own lives at risk. News articles featuring Dr. Martin Luther King Jr. focused on the fact that he decried the violence; they quoted but downplayed his belief that "economic deprivation, social isolation, inadequate housing and general despair" were responsible for the Watts riots. However, one *Los Angeles Times* news report included commentary from Watts residents who witnessed police attacks on citizens during the riots. One local mother was quoted saying: "My husband and I saw 10 cops beating one man. My husband told the officers, 'You've got him handcuffed.' One of the officers answered, 'Get out of here, nigger. Get out of here, all you niggers!'" (Hillinger and Jones, 1965, p. 24). Other Watts locals witnessed police officers beating rioters with clubs and shooting at them with shotguns. Interestingly, neither the commentary by Dr. King nor the African American residents seemed to influence the news reportage: the majority of the coverage continued to frame the Watts riots as mob violence.

Comparing *The New York Times* and *The Washington Post's* coverage to the three other newspapers makes clear why both newspapers enjoyed a reputation for excellence during this era. The Watts riots coverage in *The Washington Post* included a mixture of 34 news articles written by *Post* reporters, wire service reports and bylined stories from *Los Angeles Times* reporters. The *Post* ran the *Los Angeles Times* news stories prominently on page one, providing updates on the status of the riots and offering the latest statistics on those killed along with estimates of property damage and destruction. The news stories written by *Washington Post* staff members included analysis and interpretation of the riots and addressed police brutality, racism, illiteracy and economic deprivation. The wire service articles the *Post* chose to run also addressed larger systemic issues; along with the *Washington Post* news articles, these balanced the *Los Angeles Times* news reports, providing a point, counter-point on key riot-related issues.

Similarly, *The New York Times* coverage was neutral, balanced and measured. Most of the 41 news articles were credited to stringers with the tagline "Special to the New York Times." The news reports mixed updates on the progress of the riots with analysis of the larger issues related to civil rights, community issues, poverty, and violence. The *Times* included reports of the work of relief agencies and compared the problems in Watts with those in urban Eastern slums. While news reports appearing in other newspapers distanced Watts geographically and emotionally from white residents living in other parts of Los Angeles, *The New York Times* reported the riot-based fears of white people who lived in the greater Los Angeles area. According to that article, one parent said his son had joined "an adolescent vigilante band organized to fight marauding Negroes" (Bart, 1965, p. 1); other white citizens considered what they might do if African Americans attacked their neighborhoods. *The New York Times* was the only newspaper to report a meeting between Governor Brown and 50 prominent African Americans regarding police brutality as the precipitating cause of the Watts riots. The article quoted local African American leaders criticizing Los Angeles newspapers, television and radio stations for never investigating their complaints of police misconduct. (Turner, 1965)

All five newspapers addressed President Johnson's response to the Watts riots, emphasizing the President's condemnation of the violence. Yet, only *The*

New York Times emphasized that President Johnson also wanted to try to solve the causes of the violence so that everyone would "have an equal chance to share in the blessings of our society." This *New York Times* report made clear that the President understood the systemic issues related to the Watts riots and planned to address those concerns. Perhaps some of the other newspapers did not feel that including these aspects of the President's comments was necessary given that they had framed the riots as mob violence.

All five newspapers addressed the international response to the riots, including by carrying an AP news report on the Communist reaction. This article noted that Chinese and the Soviet Union news agencies had reported that the riots resulted from racial discrimination in housing, employment and education, as well as police violence ("Reds Call L.A.," 1965, p. A) While the AP framed the response as Communist propaganda, a report in *The Washington Post* on Cuba's reaction to the Watts riots used a Cuban source as an authentic source of news. The *Post* reported that Cuba had denounced the killing of African American demonstrators in Los Angeles and had said, "The deliberate murder of Negroes in Los Angeles constitutes genocide, a deed which deserves the unreserved condemnation of all humanity" ("Total support," 1965, p. A9).

Of particular note, the *Atlanta Journal, New York Times* and the *Washington Post* included a news article from the Chicago Daily News Service, which reported that earlier in 1965 Los Angeles Mayor Yorty had refused to cooperate with a secret federal government program that was established to try to prevent summer race riots (McCartney, 1965). Notably, however, although the *Los Angeles Times* extensively covered the riots, it did not address this issue.

The Language of the Watts Riots Coverage

The language used in the news reports was telling: many pejorative terms that may be seen as inferentially racist were used without attribution, and were presented as statements of fact. Early on some terms were attributed to an official; but subsequent articles used the terms as if they could be assumed to be accurate and truthful identifiers.

News reports in all five of the newspapers compared the riots with a guerilla war—like fighting the Viet Cong—and the language used to describe the police and National Guard actions often read like war coverage. For example, a front page *Los Angeles Times* news article, on August 14, reported: "Helmeted, shotgun-carrying police formed skirmish lines and cleared various intersections of mobs. They frequently exchanged gunfire with snipers" (Berman, 1965a, p. 12). Readers were informed that the National Guard was brought in to address "a virtual civilian insurrection" (Hartt, 1965, p. 15) and that the initial 2,000 troops "reported in with helmets, field packs, bayonets, gas masks and weapons.

The cavalry units are armed with M-14 rifles, the infantry with M-1s" (Hartt, 1965, p. 1). Another page one article directly compared Watts to the Vietnam War, adding that the death toll from the riots "exceeded last week's U.S. losses in Vietnam and more than all losses in racial disturbances in the nation last year" (Berman, 1965b, p. C).

Rioters were consistently referred to as "hate-filled Negroes," "uncivilized savages," "arsonists," "snipers" and "guerrilla bands" "running wild," "burning," "looting," "screaming for vengeance" and "directing their hatred at police and Caucasians." In addition, they were referred to as "seething," "brutal" and "insane," "Negro mobs," "hard-core hoodlums," "looters," "firebugs," "terrorists," and "marauding bands." Rioters were "hellbent on death and destruction" ("Riots unreal," 1965, p. 3). In a first-person page one account that was picked up by other newspapers, a *Los Angeles Times* advertising salesman noted: "The rioters were burning their city now, as the insane sometimes mutilate themselves" (Richardson, 1965, p. 1).

The *Chicago Tribune* termed the Watts riots "the most vicious racial uprising in Los Angeles' history," and its news coverage called the riots "chaotic," "dangerous," "terrifying," "an armed insurrection," "a scene of wild frenzy with men, women and children chanting, 'Burn, burn, burn.'" *Atlanta Journal* reporters referred to the riots as "a Negro insurrection," "destructive savagery," and "a Negro revolution." The *Los Angeles Times* considered the riots "examples of anarchy" and termed them "shameful," "senseless," and "appalling." In an often repeated quote, Police Chief William H. Parker explained the riots as outbursts of Negro mob violence caused because these "people have lost all respect for the law" (McCurdy and Berman, 1965, p. 3).

While much of the coverage offered up by the *Los Angeles Times, Atlanta Journal* and the *Chicago Tribune* was sensational and while the descriptions of the Watts riots and the rioters may be seen as inferentially racist, a first person account by a white *Los Angeles Times* reporter pushed the line towards direct racism. In a story that was re-published in three other newspapers, Philip Fradkin, a reporter who was injured in the riots and who shared in a Pulitzer Prize the *Los Angeles Times* won for its local spot news reporting on the Watts riots, mentioned that three local ministers asked him if he planned to mention charges of police brutality in his article. As if to answer the ministers' question, his account included the following statement: "No officer I talked to, overheard or questioned referred to the residents of the area as 'niggers' or made derogatory comments" (Fradkin, 1965, p. 24). In addition, one of the few news articles written by an *Atlanta Journal* journalist included an explicit racist description of the rioters by the governor of Georgia; the governor was quoted as saying that the Watts riots demonstrated that the "organized disobedience of masses stirs up the primitive instinct" (quoted in Pou, 1965, p. 2).

The word choice and tone of the reportage was decidedly different in the *Washington Post* and the *New York Times* than in the other three newspapers. The language in the coverage was factual, neutral, and free of racist slurs or inferences. Information from official sources was augmented with commentary from both African American and white civil rights activists, witnesses and observers. A front-page first person account by *Washington Post* staff writer William J. Raspberry (1965) included quotes from local residents. Raspberry also identified a bookshop owner by name but not race although later in the article, Raspberry noted that the man's store had "the familiar 'Negro Owned' sign on it" (A1). This approach was a much more subtle way of identifying the bookstore owner's race than the conventional description of name followed by the word Negro used by the other newspapers. Here Raspberry addressed local community members' hatred and resentment of the police. Comparing this anger with the positive response Watts residents had for National Guardsmen, Raspberry noted: "People talk easily, once they're sure you're not a cop. And each one who talks has a story of police brutality to tell you. It's hard not to believe them" (A1).

Apart from a lack of reporting on the larger issues and how they set the scene for the riots, the most glaring omission regarding the Watts riots news was that none of the five newspapers reported anything about the 31 rioters who were killed by police. The newspapers did include information about the two police officers and one fire fighter who lost their lives in the conflict. But the rioters who were killed were never identified or discussed.

I found the response to the Watts Riots coverage particularly interesting. Not only were there recommendations for the news media to report racial issues responsibly and to provide accurate representations about race relations in the United States, but researchers found that negative media coverage has had a lasting impact on the public's perception of African Americans.

Response to the Watts Riots Coverage

The international response to the Watts riots focused on racial discrimination, police brutality, unemployment and illiteracy as systemic causes for the riots—as did the California Governor's Commission on the Los Angeles riots. The commission's report noted that its members were "depressed and stunned" by "the dull, devastating spiral of failure" (*Violence in the City*, 1965, p. 5) within South Central Los Angeles that was due to de facto segregation, willful discrimination in employment, illiteracy and police brutality. The commission commented on evidence of a "deep and long standing schism" (*Violence in the City*, 1965, p. 27) between the Los Angeles Police Department and the African American community. It observed that its research on seven riots occurring in Northern cities during 1964 showed that all of the riots began with an incident involving the police.

After studying the press's reporting of "inflammatory incidences" during the Watts riots, the commission urged news media to report issues responsibly, to address both positive and negative information about African American communities, and to be careful not to inflame racially charged situations. While reporting about dramatic incidents is easy, the commission insisted, "the highest traditions of a free press involve responsibility as well as drama" (*Violence in the City*, 1965, p. 84).

The recommendations of the Governor's commission were not an isolated rebuke of the mainstream press. In response to the 1967 urban riots, President Lyndon B. Johnson assembled the National Advisory Commission on Civil Disorders, chaired by Illinois Governor Otto Kerner. The resulting 1968 *Report of the National Advisory Commission on Civil Disorders*, known as the Kerner Report, indicted white society for isolating and neglecting African Americans and insisted that it was the responsibility of the news media to provide an accurate account of race relations in the U.S.

In addition, researchers who have analyzed the 1965 news media coverage of the Watts riots maintained that press coverage not only inflamed the racial tension but that it has had a lasting impact on the public's perception of African Americans and has been used to justify the repression, inaction, and inattention of African Americans. Matei and Ball-Rokeach (2005) found that news portrayals of Watts as the "problematic zone" (p. 319) of Los Angeles led to a persistent collective memory of Watts as the "Fear Epicenter" of the region. They determined that the news media framing has had significant economic and social consequences that continue to impact racial and ethnic issues in Los Angeles.

Johnson, Sears, and McConahay (1971) found that following the conflict, the majority of African Americans living in South-Central Los Angeles saw the Watts riots as "a violent protest against white mistreatment and neglect" (p. 699); in contrast, white citizens, mainstream news media, and public officials viewed the riots as "a threat to public safety" rather than a serious issue that needed to be addressed. In their content analysis of L.A. newspapers from 1892–1968, Johnson, Sears, and McConahay (1971) found a consistent pattern of "black invisibility" in the coverage, with little attention given to minority issues of racial segregation related to housing, employment, education and social life. Echoing the recommendations of the Governor's committee, Johnson, Sears and

McConahay found that the post-Watts riots news coverage, like the pre-riot coverage, was focused on the needs and interests of whites, often to the exclusion of African Americans. The researchers suggested that if the mainstream press included more coverage of African American issues and concerns, the coverage could overcome black invisibility and improve race relations.

In the next section the research addressed the precipitating event for the Baltimore riots—the murder of Freddie Gray while he was in police custody. While I was familiar with the story of Gray's arrest and death, I had not realized the level of poverty in the Sandtown-Winchester area of West Baltimore.

Background for the Baltimore Riots

Some 50 years later, according to police, an officer "made eye contact" with Freddie Gray, who lived in a West Baltimore neighborhood known for its drug activity ("Friends: Man's death," 2015). Gray was apprehended after he ran: police officers "pinned him to the ground and dragged him to the back of a police wagon" (Schwartzman, 2015) and charged him with possessing a switchblade. While in police custody, Gray's spinal cord was 80 percent severed and his neck was broken; he died one week later on April 19. Shortly after his arrest, local community members began peaceful protests. Following Gray's funeral the protests turned violent. Overall the protests led to 202 arrests, 144 vehicle fires, 15 building fires and 15 police officers injured (Eichensehr and Popper, 2015). In September 2015, the city of Baltimore reached a $6.4 million settlement with Gray's family.

The Sandtown-Winchester neighborhood where Gray lived was known for extreme poverty, the region's highest rates of domestic violence, and high unemployment. In April 2015, more than 50 percent of the residents were unemployed, poverty rates were double the city's average, and 25 percent of the buildings were vacant (Lopez, 2015). In the wake of Gray's death, Michael Fletcher (2015), a national economics reporter described Baltimore, where he has lived for more than 30 years, as "a combustible mix of poverty, crime, and hopelessness, uncomfortably juxtaposed against rich history, friendly people, venerable institutions and pockets of old-money influence."

Please note how the news themes and use of language in the coverage of the Baltimore riots were strikingly similar to the coverage of the Watts riots. Despite government commissions and research recommendations, it shocked me to realize that not much had changed.

News Themes of the Baltimore Conflict

The news coverage of the Baltimore riots combined detailed information about the conflict, with reactions from community leaders, politicians and government officials. Presidential candidates, celebrities and sports figures also weighed in about the conflict. While none of the newspapers reporting about the Watts riots mentioned local citizens who were killed by police, the Baltimore coverage described, debated and psychoanalyzed the life of Freddie Gray; reporters interviewed family members and friends and connected his death with the deaths of other young black men like Trayvon Martin in Sanford, Florida and Michael Brown in Ferguson, Missouri. Some articles even discussed why Freddie Gray's story did not trend on Twitter. All five newspapers offered multiple news reports that attempted to understand the violence in Baltimore, with the common theme being that Gray's death illustrated an "ongoing national discussion about policing tactics in minority communities" ("Mayor reed," 2015)

Although the local newspaper of record, the *Baltimore Sun*, was not a part of this study, its news reports, particularly the breaking news coverage of the conflict, figured prominently in much of the coverage of the Baltimore riots in the *Chicago Tribune*, the *Atlanta Journal Constitution* and the *Los Angeles Times*. Two thirds of the 96 articles published in the *Chicago Tribune* were bylined news reports from the *Baltimore Sun*. About a third of the 61 *Los Angeles Times* and the 15 *Atlanta Journal Constitution* reports were from the *Baltimore Sun*. While *The New York Times'* 103 articles relied extensively on AP and Reuters wire service reports, all of *Washington Post's* 77 articles on Baltimore were written by its own staff reporters. The majority of the daily news updates on the number of injuries, arrests and damages relied on the *Baltimore Sun* and wire service reports, although articles written by the newspapers' own staff reporters provided important context and commentary.

One common newspaper strategy was to compare the Baltimore protests with other violent conflicts. For example, the *Chicago Tribune* and the *Los Angeles Times* compared the Baltimore riots with the 1992 riots in Los Angeles following the Rodney King beating, which resulted in the deaths of 53 people, 2000 injuries, 11,000 arrests and $1 billion in damages. These accounts noted that in both cases the "controversial use of police force on a man of color was the plunger on a powder keg decades in the making" (Lopez, 2015). Similarly, the *Washington Post* and the *Los Angeles Times* coverage included comparisons with the April 1968 Baltimore riots following the assassination of Dr. King, during which six people were killed, 700 injured, 5,800 people were arrested and 1,000 businesses were damaged or burned. Noting that the same issues of poverty, racism and discrimination still exist today as they did in 1968, the reporter quoted Assistant Professor of History Elizabeth Nix: "There's still a lot of people who don't feel like their voices are heard and that they're cut off from the economic and social life of Baltimore" (Wheeler, 2015).

A focus of Baltimore coverage was police brutality and the "broken relationship" (Stolberg, 2015, p. A1) between African American residents and the police as a fundamental cause for the conflict. Noting that years of wrongful-death lawsuits led Baltimore's Mayor, Stephanie Rawlings-Blake to ask the Justice Department to review the problem, a *The New York Times* analysis of Justice Department data indicated that Baltimore police had killed more people than police officers in other similar sized cities. According to the *Baltimore Sun*, between 2011 and 2014 local taxpayers paid $5.7 million in judgments and settlements on "102 lawsuits alleging police misconduct" (quoted in Stolberg, 2015, p. A1).

Upbeat reports about local children handing out water to the police and articles sometimes compared the Baltimore of the HBO drama "The Wire" to the actual city. The fact that an Orioles game was postponed due to the riots and that a subsequent Orioles game was played without fans merited multiple news articles in all five newspapers. All five newspapers covered the destruction of the local CVS, and a Baltimore mother who dragged her son away so he would not throw rocks at the police. Journalists often combined official governmental, legislative and police sources with eyewitness accounts from local citizens and commentary from protesters and civil rights leaders.

The language of the Baltimore coverage was primarily careful, courteous and politically correct. Overt racism was absent and reporters were cautious not to use inflamed rhetoric in describing events. Early coverage referred to the conflict as a protest because the demonstrations were peaceful. However, instances of inferential racism emerged in the coverage both before and after the conflict became violent. During the early protests, Baltimore police union president Gene Ryan compared the protesters to a "lynch mob" because they insisted that the officers involved in Gray's death be immediately jailed. Following Ryan's comments the community became outraged, and Twitter users called his comments "racially insensitive and inappropriate" ("Developments on Baltimore," 2015). The *Chicago Tribune* quoted the Gray family attorney William Murphy calling for "an immediate apology and a retraction." Murphy pointed out that African Americans have been the ones lynched in the United States:

> The president of the police union called the peaceful protests and the anger at the death of a man to severe and unfathomable injuries while

in police custody a lynch mob? It doesn't get more insensitive or insult-
ing than that. These remarks illustrate why black people and the police
don't get along.

(quoted in Campbell and George, 2015)

Once the protests turned violent, news reports began to refer to the conflict as
a riot. Each of the newspapers quoted Baltimore's mayor referring to the rioters
as "thugs." In response to Rawlings' comment, *The Washington Post* addressed
the etymology of the term thug and explained how "thug" has always been used
"to paint people as lawless, violent, corrupt" (Ohlheiser, 2015).

In the final section, I drew on Martin Luther King's speech following
the Watts riots to highlight how Stuart Hall's understanding of inferential
racism continued to exist in media coverage fifty years after the 1965 Watt's
riots. The research project ended with a discussion of the *Orlando Sentinel*'s
coverage of the Pulse nightclub massacre as an example of how journalists
can go beyond stereotypes and generalities by adding the necessary context
to their coverage of conflict and crisis.

Looking Forward

Although he preached non-violence as the "most potent weapon" in African
Americans' struggle for equality, in his speech "The Other America," Martin
Luther King, Jr. (1968) described a riot as "the language of the unheard." King
explained that the U.S. had failed to hear that the lives of African Americans had
worsened over the past decade. He decried the "intolerable conditions" of poverty, unemployment, substandard housing and inadequate education that millions of African Americans still faced and he noted that the American public
had not heard "that the promises of freedom and justice" had not been met.
King maintained that the U.S. was still a racist country where whites were seen
to embody purity, dignity and knowledge while blacks were considered ignorant,
unclean and inferior.

Almost 50 years after King's speech, the focus on violent conflict rather
than reporting on the systemic issues facing many urban African Americans
may be seen as evidence of the continuation of inferential racism that Stuart
Hall described. As President Barack Obama noted in response to the Baltimore
conflict, the entire country needs to do some "soul searching" regarding this
ongoing social crisis. While he decried the violence, the President criticized
news media and some politicians "for failing to address the chronic problems

of men, women, and children who live in poverty and find their opportunities limited because of poor schools or long stints in prison" (quoted in Mufson and Eilperin, 2015). President Obama urged the press to regularly report on issues of social and economic inequality, poverty and violence and to pay attention to impoverished communities apart from when a CVS is destroyed or another young black man is killed while in police custody.

While this analysis showed much greater diversity in the topics and issues during the Baltimore riots compared with the reportage of the Watts riots, the issue of the Baltimore riots isn't just the story of Baltimore. It is also the story of the continued exclusion, invisibility, brutality and segregation of African Americans in the United States. Systemic issues including police brutality, poverty, unequal opportunities, unemployment, de facto segregation in schooling and housing continue to be ignored by mainstream news organizations, politicians and business leaders except during a riot or some other type of violent protest. During the last 50 years, the academic research as well as a variety of government and commission reports have zeroed in on systemic issues as causes of civil unrest. But while news media continue to cover the conflicts, they neither address the systemic issues nor follow up on the aftermath of these violent conflicts. That is, both the Watts riots and the Baltimore riots illustrate that ongoing complex, societal issues and concerns are rarely covered unless a conflict erupts.

In our postmodern era, many people are skeptical about truth claims, see all information as opinion, do not distinguish between news, public relations and spin and filter their news consumption to support their individual beliefs and interests. It is also a time when journalism is "disintegrating" because advertisers and commercial interests no longer see it as a smart investment. (McChesney, 2014, p. 231) Once hugely profitable, corporate-owned monopoly newspapers were unprepared for the rise of expanded media outlets and the Internet. They responded to the resulting economic crisis by shuttering newspapers and slashing newsroom staff and editorial spending. Between 2006 and 2009, legacy newspapers cut editorial spending by more than 25 percent and by 2011 newsrooms employed 25 percent fewer reporters than they had in 2006 (Lebovic, 2016, p. 230). This economic crisis is sometimes being used to explain weak reporting—but great journalism is still being done.

While journalists know how to report conflicts, crises and events, they also need to understand the context for conflicts and to put events into a broader perspective. For example, the *Orlando Sentinel* reporting of the Pulse nightclub massacre is an excellent example of how news media should cover violent, catastrophic issues and occurrences. As the news broke Sunday morning June 12, 2016, *Orlando Sentinel* reporters began to investigate all aspects of attacks. Although newsroom personnel had been cut from 350 to about 100, throughout the day *Orlando Sentinel* staff ran 30 videos and 40 news stories online about the shooting and they published an eight-page print section on the violent attack.

However, the *Sentinel*'s actions on June 13 especially stand out as a model for what contemporary journalism can provide. Rather than focusing on the gruesome details of the numbers of people dead and injured, or providing graphic images of the crime scene, Monday's print edition of the *Orlando Sentinel* lead with a message of unity in a front page editorial that was accompanied by an image of two individuals hugging at a candlelight vigil. Headlined, "Our Community Will Heal," the editorial insisted that the people of Orlando could not let "Sunday's heinous act of brutality and cowardice define our community." The editorial reassured those injured in the attack that they were not alone now and would not be alone in the future; it encouraged the community to "define itself by our unequivocal response. United" (quoted in Hare, 2016). Subsequent coverage has focused on systemic issues of homophobia, racism and terrorism as well as the stories of the victims and the impact of the attack on the families of Orlando.

While the First Amendment is a fundamental principle in the U.S., freedom of the news involves more than the right of news outlets to publish and to speak one's opinions without censorship; it also involves the publication of accurate and relevant information that people need in order to fulfill their role as citizens in a democracy (Lebovic, 2016). Today, more than ever it is important for news media to showcase its role as a public good in democratic society. A regular, continued and sustained emphasis on the cultural, ethical, political and economic issues facing citizens in the U.S. is an important way to illustrate the ongoing relevance and value of an independent, vibrant and vigorous free press.

Textual Analysis Exercises

1. Pick a national news story and compare the coverage in three different news venues. Consider the following questions for your analysis: How are sources used in the news stories? What is the focus of each of the articles? How are images used in the coverage? How do the headlines relate to the news story? Is the coverage similar? What (if any) differences in the coverage did you find?

2. Pick an international online news story and compare the coverage on news websites from three different countries. Consider the following questions for your analysis: How are the news stories framed? How are sources used? What themes emerge from the coverage? Is the coverage similar? What (if any) differences in the coverage did you find? If there are differences, why do you think that the story was covered differently?

3. Conduct an ideological analysis of a print advertisement using a specific theoretical orientation to help frame your analysis. Remember to use Cormack's categories of content, structure, absence, style and mode of address to guide your analysis.

References

Atkinson, Paul, and Coffey, Amanda. (2011). Analysing documentary realities. In David Silverman (Ed.), *Qualitative research: Issues of theory, method and practice* (3rd ed., pp. 56–75). Los Angeles, CA: Sage.

Baker, Erwin. (1965, August 18). Yorty hits brutality charges as 'Big Lie.' *Los Angeles Times*, pp. 3, 16.

Bart, Peter. (1965, August 17). Los Angeles Whites voice racial fears. *The New York Times*, pp. 1, 16.

Berger, Arthur Asa. (1998). *Media research techniques* (2nd ed.). Thousand Oaks, CA: Sage.

Berger, Arthur Asa. (2000). *Media and communication research methods: An introduction to qualitative and quantitative approaches.* Thousand Oaks, CA: Sage.

Berman, Art. (1965a, August 14). Eight men slain: Guard moves in. *Los Angeles Times*, pp. 1, 12.

Berman, Art. (1965b, August 15). Negro riots rage on; death toll 25. *Los Angeles Times*, pp. 1, C.

Branston, Gill. (2006). Understanding genre. In Marie Gillespie and Jason Toynbee (Eds.), *Analysing media texts* (pp. 43–78). Maidenhead, UK: Open University Press.

Brennen, Bonnie. (2008). From religiosity to consumerism: press coverage of Thanksgiving, 1905–2005. *Journalism Studies, 9* (1): 21–37.

Brennen, Bonnie. (2013). *Qualitative research methods for media studies.* New York: Routledge.

Campbell, Colin, and George, Justin. (2015, April 22). Baltimore police union President likens protests to 'Lynch Mob.' *Chicago Tribune*. Retrieved from www.chicagotribune.com/bs-md-ci-fop-news-conference-20150422-story-html

Conroy, Pat. (2010). *My reading life.* New York: Doubleday.

Cormack, Mike. (1995). *Ideology.* Ann Arbor: University of Michigan Press.

Craig says White people must organize. (1965, August 16). *Atlanta Journal*, p. 32.

Denzin, Norman K., and Lincoln, Yvonna S. (Eds.). (1998). *The landscape of qualitative research: Theories and issues.* Thousand Oaks, CA: Sage.

Developments on Baltimore Man Fatally Injured in Custody. (2015, April 22). *The New York Times*. Retrieved from www.nytimes.com/aponline/2015/04/22/us/ap-us-suspect-dies-baltimore-things-to-know.html

Eichensehr, Morgan, and Popper, Daniel. (2015, April 28). How the media covered the Baltimore riots. *American Journalism Review*. Retrieved from http://ajr.org/2015/04/28/how-the-media-covered-baltimore-riots/

Fletcher, Michael A. (2015, April 28). What you really need to know about Baltimore, from a reporter who's lived there for over 30 years. *Washington Post*. Retrieved from www.washingtonpost.com/news/wonk/wp/2015/04/28/what-you-really-need-to-know-about-Baltimore

Fradkin, Philip. (1965, August 13). Reporter tells violence, fear during rioting. *Los Angeles Times*, pp. 3, 24.

Friedman, Uri. (2015, February 13). How an ad campaign invented the diamond engagement ring. *The Atlantic*. Retrieved from www.theatlantic.com/international/archive/2015/02/how-an-ad-campaign-invented-the-diamond-engagement-ring/385376/

Friends: Man's death after arrest reveals Baltimore dynamics. (2015, April 22). *The New York Times*. Retrieved from www.nytimes.com/aponline/2015/04/22/us/ap-us-suspect-dies-baltimore.html

Gillespie, Marie, and Toynbee, Jason. (Eds.). (2006). *Analysing media texts*. Maidenhead, UK: Open University Press.

Gripsrud, Jostein. (2006). Semiotics: Signs, codes and cultures. In Marie Gillespie and Jason Toynbee (Eds.), *Analysing media texts* (pp. 9–41). Maidenhead, UK: Open University Press.

Hall, Stuart. (1975). Introduction. In Anthony C. H. Smith with Elizabeth Immirzi and Trevor Blackwell (Eds.), *Paper voices: The popular press and social change, 1935–1965* (pp. 11–24). London: Chatto & Windus.

Hall, Stuart. (1980). Encoding/decoding. In Stuart Hall, Dorothy Hobson, Andrew Lowe, and Paul Willis (Eds.), *Culture, media, language: Working papers in Cultural Studies, 1972–79* (pp. 128–138). London: Hutchinson.

Hall, Stuart. (1981). The Whites of their eyes: Racist ideologies and the media. In George Bridges and Rosalind Brant (Eds.), *Silver linings: Some strategies for the eighties* (pp. 28–52). London, UK: Lawrence and Wishart.

Hall, Stuart. (1986). The problem of ideology—Marxism without guarantees. *Journal of Communication Inquiry*, 10 (2): 28–44.

Hall, Stuart. (1997). The work of representation. In Stuart Hall (Ed.), *Representation: Cultural representations and signifying practices* (pp. 13–74). London, UK: Sage Publications.

Hare, Kristen. (2016, June 13). *Monday's Orlando Sentinel leads with a front-page editorial*. Retrieved from www.poynter.org/2016/mondays-orlando-sentinel-leads-with-a-front-page-editorial/416366/

Hartt, Julian. (1965, August 14). Guard force from 40th Armored. *Los Angeles Times*, pp. 1, 15.

Hillinger, Charles, and Jones, Jack. (1965, August 13). Residents put blame on police for uproar. *Los Angeles Times*, pp. 3, 24.

In L.A., you don't know where the lines are. (1992, May 11). *Understanding the riots: The path to fury: Part 1 Los Angeles Times Special Report*, pp. T4, T5.

Johnson, Paula B., Sears, David O., and McConahay, John. (1971). Black invisibility, the press and the Los Angeles riot. *American Journal of Sociology*, 76 (4): 698–721.

King, Martin Luther Jr. (1968, March 14). "The other America," Speech. Grosse Point High School. Retrieved from www.gphistorical.org/mlk/mlkspeech/

Kennedy, Gerrick. (2015, March 11). 'Empire' aims to climb music charts as well as TV rankings. *Los Angeles Times*. Retrieved from www.latimes.com/entertainment/music/la-et-ms-empire-music-timberland-jim-beanz-20150311-story.html

Korman, Seymour. (1965, August 14). Troops are Told to use Gas and Bayonets. *Chicago Tribune*, pp. 1, 2.

Kracauer, Siegfried. (1952–1953). The challenge of qualitative content analysis. *Public Opinion Quarterly*, 16 (4): 631–642.

Larsen, Peter. (1991). Media contents: Textual analysis of fictional media content. In Klaus Bruhn Jensen and Nicholas W. Jankowski (Eds.), *A handbook of qualitative methodologies for mass communication research* (pp. 121–134). London: Routledge.

Lebovic, Sam. (2016). *Free speech & unfree news: The paradox of press freedom in America*. Cambridge: Harvard University Press.

Lopez, Steve. (2015, April 28). Baltimore riots and the long shadow of 1992 Los Angeles. *Chicago Tribune*. Retrieved from www.chicagotribune.com/news/nationworld/la-me-1n-lopez-baltimore-los-angeles-riots

Matei, Sorin Adam, and Ball-Rokeach, Sandra. (2005). Watts, the 1965 riots, and the communicative construction of the fear epicenter of Los Angeles. *Communication Monographs*, 72 (3): 301–323.

Mayor Reed weighs in on Baltimore protests; defends rawlings-blake. (2015, April 28). *Atlanta Journal Constitution*. Retrieved from www.ajc.com/news/news/local-govt-politics/mayor-reed-weighs-in-on-baltimore-protests

McCartney, James. (1965, August 17). Riot city mayors shunned plan talk. *Atlanta Journal*, p. 7.

McChesney, Robert W. (2014). *Blowing the roof off the twenty-first century*. New York: Monthly Review Press.

McCurdy, Jack, and Berman, Art. (1965, August 13). New rioting: Stores looted, cars destroyed. *Los Angeles Times*, pp. 1, 3.

McKee, Alan. (2003). *Textual analysis: A beginner's guide*. London: Sage.

Mufson, Steven, and Eilperin, Juliet. (2015, April 28). Obama urges country to do 'Soul Searching' in wake of Baltimore riots. *The Washington Post*. Retrieved from www.washingtonpost.com/news/postpolitics/wp/2015/04/28/baltimore-riots-bring-

Ohlheiser, Abby. (2015, April 28). The changing context of who gets called a 'Thug' in America. *The Washington Post*. Retrieved from htts://www.washingtonpost.com/news/morning-mix/wp/2015/04/28/the-changing-context-of-who-gets-called-a-thug

O'Rourke, Meghan. (2007, June 11). Diamonds are a girl's worst friend: The trouble with engagement rings. *Slate*. Retrieved from www.slate.com/articles/news_and_politics/weddings/2007/06/diamonds_are_a_girls_worst_friend.html

Peräkylä, Anssi. (2008). Analyzing talk and text. In Norman K. Denzin and Yvonna S. Lincoln (Eds.), *Collecting and interpreting qualitative materials* (pp. 351–374). Thousand Oaks, CA: Sage.

Pou, Charles. (1965, August 18). Sanders again rips mass disobedience. *Atlanta Journal*, p. 2.

Raspberry, William J. (1965, August 17). Stillness descends on battered streets. *The Washington Post*, pp. A1, A5.

Reds call L.A. rioting evidence of race bias. (1965, August 15). *Los Angeles Times*, p. A.

Richardson, Robert. (1965, August 15). 'Burn, Baby, Burn' slogan used as firebugs put area to torch. *Los Angeles Times*, p. 1.

Righter sees error in troop use. (1965, August 17). *Atlanta Journal*, p. 5.

Riots unreal to most in Los Angeles. (1965, August 15). *Chicago Tribune*, p. 3.

Rodik, Petra, and Primorac, Jaka. (2015). To use or not to use: Computer-assisted qualitative data analysis software usage among early-career sociologists in Croatia. *Forum: Qualitative Social Research*, 16 (1): 1–20.

Rodricks, Dan. (2015, April 20). Eyes wide open to problems experienced by Black men. *Chicago Tribune*. Retrieved from www.chicagotribune.com/news/nationworld/bs-md-rodricks-0421-20150420-column

Romell, Rick. (2011, November 25). Why "Black Friday"? How popular term has troubled roots in Philadelphia. *Milwaukee Journal Sentinel*, pp. 1A, 7A.

Scene of rioting is substandard district. (1965, August 14). *Los Angeles Times*, p. 1.

Schwartzman, Paul. (2015, April 27). At Gray's funeral, outrage over way in which he died. *Washington Post*. Retrieved from http://www,washingtonpost.com/local/mourners-gather-in-baltimore-after-clashes-

Stokes, Jane. (2003). *How to do media and cultural studies*. London: Sage.

Stolberg, Sheryl Gay. (2015, April 24). Baltimore's 'Broken Relationship' with police. *The New York Times*, pp. A1, A12.

Strinati, Dominic. (1995). *An introduction to theories of popular culture*. London: Routledge.

Theoharis, Jeanne. (2015, August 11). 50 years later, we still haven't learned from Watts. *The New York Times*. Retrieved from http://nyti.ms/1lBhDfF

These are the best English newspapers in the world. (2012). Retrieved from www.onlinecollegecourses.com/2012/12/17/the-best-english-newspapers/

Top 100 newspapers in the U.S. by circulation. (2016). Retrieved from www.infoplease.com/ipea/A0004420.html

Total support offered to rioters by Cuba. (1965, August 18). *The Washington Post*, p. A9.

Turner, Graeme. (1997). Media texts and messages. In Stuart D. Cunningham and Graeme Turner (Eds.), *The media in Australia: Industries, texts, audiences* (pp. 293–347). St. Leonards, NSW: Allen & Unwin.

Turner, Wallace. (1965, August 16). *The New York Times*, p. 16.

Violence in the city—an end or a beginning: A report by the Governor's commission on the Los Angeles riots. (1965, December 2). Distributed by College Book Store, Los Angeles.

Wheeler, Timothy B. (2015, April 28). City rioting evokes memories of 1968 unrest. *Los Angeles Times*. Retrieved from www.latimes.com/bs-md-riots-1968-20150428-story.html

Williams, Raymond. (1977). *Marxism and literature*. London: Oxford University Press.

Williams, Raymond. (1981). *Politics and Letters: Interviews with New Left Review*. London: Verso.

The word in the streets: 'Burn, Baby, Burn.' (1992, May 11). *Understanding the riots: The path to fury. Part 1: Los Angeles Times special report*, pp. T6, T7.

Acknowledgments

"Good Journalism: On the Evaluation Criteria of Some Interested and Experienced Actors." By Risto Kunelius. From *Journalism Studies*, Vol. 7, No. 5, 2006. 671–690. Copyright © 2006 Taylor & Francis. Reprinted by permission of the publisher, www.tandfonline.com.

"US Teenagers' Perceptions and Awareness of Digital Technology: A Focus Group Approach." By Heather L. Hundley and Leonard Shyles. From *New Media & Society*, Vol. 12, No. 3, May 2010. 417–433. Reprinted by permission of SAGE.

"Radio Utopia: Promoting public interest in a 1940s radio documentary." By Matthew C. Ehrlich. From *Journalism Studies*, Vol. 9, No. 6, 2006. 859–873. Copyright © 2006 Taylor & Francis. Reprinted by permission of the publisher, www.tandfonline.com.

Excerpts from *For the Record: An Oral History of Rochester, New York Newsworkers*. By Bonnie Brennen. Copyright © 2001 Fordham University Press. Reprinted by permission.

"The Culture of a Women-Led Newspaper: An Ethnographic Study of the Sarasota Herald-Tribune." By Tracy Everbach. From *Journalism & Mass Communication Quarterly*, Vol. 83, No. 3, September 2006. 477–493. Copyright © 2006 AEJMC. Reprinted by permission.

"Religiosity to Consumerism: Press Coverage of Thanksgiving, 1905–2005." By Bonnie Brennen. From *Journalism Studies*, Vol. 9, No. 1, 2008. 21–37. Copyright © 2008 Taylor & Francis. Reprinted by permission of the publisher, www.tandfonline.com.

Index